Educational Adequacy and the Courts

A Reference Handbook

CONTEMPORARY EDUCATION ISSUES

Educational Adequacy and the Courts

● A REFERENCE HANDBOOK

Elaine M. Walker

A B C ● C L I O

Santa Barbara, California • Denver, Colorado • Oxford, England

Library of Congress Cataloging-in-Publication Data

Walker, Elaine M.
Educational adequacy and the courts : a reference handbook / Elaine M. Walker.
    p.   cm.
  Includes bibliographical references and index.
  ISBN 1-85109-535-7 (hardcover : alk. paper); ISBN 1-85109-540-3 (eBook)
1. Educational equalization—Law and legislation—United States.
2. Educational accountability—Law and legislation—United States.
3. Education—Finance—Law and legislation—United States.
4. Education and state—United States. I. Title.

  KF4155.W35 2005
  344.73'07—dc22

                                                                    2004030709

08   07   06   05   04   10   9   8   7   6   5   4   3   2   1

This book is also available on the World Wide Web as an eBook. Visit abc-clio.com for details.

ABC-CLIO, Inc.
130 Cremona Drive, P.O. Box 1911
Santa Barbara, California 93116-1911

This book is printed on acid-free paper ∞.
Manufactured in the United States of America

For My Mother, Alice Sutherland;
Daughters, Jody and Ashleigh;
Siblings, Marcia, Grace, Ian, and Eldom;
Nephews, Kalonji and Jared;
And to the memory of my father, Norman W.

•❖ Contents

Series Editor's Preface

The Contemporary Education Issues series is dedicated to providing readers with an up-to-date exploration of the central issues in education today. Books in the series will examine such controversial topics as home schooling, charter schools, privatization of public schools, Native American education, African American education, literacy, curriculum development, and many others. The series is national in scope and is intended to encourage research by anyone interested in the field.

Contemporary education can be conceived of in the broadest sense of the term and encompasses a multitude of issues as they pertain to education, from kindergarten to secondary school and college. Because education is undergoing radical if not revolutionary change, the series is particularly concerned with contemporary controversies in education and how they affect both the organization of schools and the content and delivery of curriculum. Authors will endeavor to provide a balanced understanding of the issues and how they affect teachers, students, parents, administrators, and policy makers. Because education has recently undergone and continues to undergo intense changes in both conceptual orientation and organization, the intent of this series is to confront these changes in a way to illuminate and explicate them. In this regard, the aim of the Contemporary Education Issues series is to bring excellent research to today's educational concerns by some of the finest scholar/practitioners in the field while at the same time pointing to new directions. In this vein, the series promises to offer important analysis of some of the most controversial issues facing society today.

—*Danny Weil*
Series Editor

❧ Preface and Acknowledgments

Why this book? How to finance public education in order that all students are provided with adequate educational opportunities that are independent of the wealth of their communities has been a continual challenge for policy makers. Concerned citizens, educators, scholars, legislators, and the courts have all attempted to arrive at viable solutions. The numerous articles, books, publications, studies, and organizations that have been devoted to school finance attest to the gravity with which each has approached this policy challenge. The cross-disciplinary orientations of the writings that have been produced are emblematic of the complexities of education as a social good. Each discipline has relied upon its own sets of paradigms and understandings to frame its approach toward education in general, and school finance in particular. The reader thus frequently has to negotiate him- or herself through various disciplines in order to arrive at a general understanding of the complexity of reform policies and politics in the area of school finance. My experience in studying the struggles in the state of New Jersey to provide a constitutionally adequate education for students from impoverish backgrounds was the impetus behind the writing of this book. My own research took me into the fields of law, political science, sociology, and education. My foray into these different disciplines helped to enlarge my perspective on the subtleties and what appears at times to be intractable difficulties in ensuring that each child in the United States is given an adequate education.

In this book, I attempt to bring together the salient issues that scholars from diverse disciplines have unearthed in their studies of the constitutional and policy journeys that several states and courts have embarked on toward the creation of an adequate education system for all. The central theme pivots on the protracted role of the courts in arriving at constitutionally appropriate remedies to the indisputable stark inequities in educational opportunities, and disparities in educational outcomes that have plagued public education. A primary concern in writing this book is to ensure its accessibility to all who may have an interest in the subject. Thus, deliberate attempts are made to minimize discipline-specific jargon. In addition, the reader is provided with a list of organizations and reference materials that provide easy and readily available information on adequacy reforms.

I would like to acknowledge all the scholars, groups, courts, organizations, and individuals who have committed themselves to this important policy issue. Furthermore, I am grateful to Dan Weil, editor of the ABC-CLIO series Contemporary Education Issues, and Alicia Merritt of ABC-CLIO, for their assistance on this project. The faculty of the Department of Educational Leadership, Management, and Policy in the College of Education and Human Services at Seton Hall University provided the intellectual and moral support that made the completion of this book possible. My thanks to Dan Gutmore, who was my research collaborator on the early studies of the New Jersey reforms. A special note of thanks goes to John Collins for the significant contribution that he made to Chapters 7 and 8. Finally, I must acknowledge my deep sense of gratitude to my daughters, Jody and Ashleigh, for their love, support, and patience.

Chapter One

●◆ Introduction

EDUCATION AND THE DEMOCRATIC IDEAL

The "common school" movement that began in the mid-nineteenth century ushered in a radically different conceptualization of schools than what existed before. Prior to the mid-nineteenth century schooling was linked to religious learning and restricted to elite classes. Although a number of factors influenced the movement, such as the growth of industrialization, urbanization, and immigration, an important impetus was the belief in the principles of democracy. Education, it was argued, was important for the support and sustenance of a newly emerging democratic society. Thus, schooling and the development of civic responsibilities became inextricably intertwined. Public education became the means through which the inculcation of civic values into the masses could be achieved and replaced the disparate forms of schooling that existed prior to the movement. The movement's intellectual influences can be traced to the post-Enlightenment idea of scientific rationalism, which holds that human knowledge can be harnessed to improve human civilization.

The saliency of education to the democratic process and human development received further intellectual support through the work of John Dewey (Dewey 1983). Dewey posited that in order for the democratic ideal to become a reality, human beings must acquire the capacity to think freely, imaginatively, and creatively. Since education is important to the stimulation of individual growth and because the development of the individual's potentiality is necessary for the creation of social communities and good citizenship, Dewey advanced the notion that *universal access to education* by all was important for the survival of democracy. Several contemporary scholars have expanded upon Dewey's ideas. These scholars have suggested that in order for individuals to make choices, to participate meaningfully in decisions that have import for themselves as well as their communities, they must be afforded an educational experience premised on the ideals of democracy (Greene 1995).

Education is not only viewed as an important force in the development of democracy, but in a society premised on notions of meritocracy, education is seen as the vehicle by which individuals are able to attain social mobility and status. It has been argued that education allows individuals through their efforts to enjoy horizontal as well vertical movements from one social class to another, or within a given social class. However, counterarguments have been posited to challenge these assumptions. Race, gender, social class, and educational inequities are posited as constituting structural barriers to individuals' abilities to move freely from one social class or status position to another (Apple 1982; Miron 1996).

In spite of such realities, the idea of democratic citizenship and the right of individuals to an education remain firmly enshrined in many states' constitutions. Although the exact wording and specificity of each state's educational clause may vary, they tend to call for the establishment of a system of free common schools that guarantee that all children will be given a thorough and efficient education or an adequate education (Rebell 2002). According to Rebell, "These provisions generally were incorporated into the state constitutions as part of the common school movement of the mid-19th century, which created statewide systems for public education and attempted to inculcate democratic values" (Rebell 2002, 232).

Concerns have been raised that the educational assurances codified in many states' constitutions have not been substantively met. These concerns have arisen because of noticeable differences in educational outcomes that have occurred for students from different racial, ethnic, language, and social class backgrounds, as well as students who are held to have special emotional, learning, and physical needs. The judicial renderings issued by several states' lower and higher courts have confirmed the constitutional legitimacy of these concerns. What is the evidentiary basis for arriving at these conclusions?

DISPARATE OUTCOMES IN EDUCATIONAL ACHIEVEMENT AND ATTAINMENT

Notwithstanding the evidence that demonstrates a narrowing of the achievement gap between students from different social and racial groups, national as well as state-level data continue to show that educational attainment as well as other indicators of school level behaviors, such as the dropout rate, still pose a problem for certain groups of pupils.

In particular, the performance of African Americans and students of Hispanic descent continue to lag behind that of whites. Similarly, the achievement levels of students from impoverished backgrounds in urban as well as rural communities remain below the levels of students who live in affluent communities. Furthermore, the intersection of these variables—race and poverty—creates a negative cumulative impact on students' educational attainment.

In its annual report on the condition of education in the United States, the National Center for Education Statistics notes that in the year 2000 among the fourth-grade public school population, there was a higher percentage of black and Hispanic students in high-poverty school districts (75 percent or more of students eligible for subsidized lunch) than whites. These high-poverty school districts had higher rates of student absenteeism and lower percentages of students with very positive attitudes toward academic achievement than districts with minimal levels of student poverty (National Center for Educational Statistics 2002). The report also notes that fourth-grade students who were not personally eligible for subsidized lunch but who attended high-poverty schools had lower mathematics scores than those who attended low-poverty schools.

In addition to these trends, achievement data on the National Assessment of Educational Progress (NAEP), available from the National Center for Educational Statistics, reveals differences in performance among students attending central city, urban fringe, and rural schools. These differences are evident in reading and mathematics. The NAEP results for the 2000 academic school year revealed that:

- Students in grades four and eight who attended schools in central cities read at levels below their counterparts in suburban and rural communities, while students attending schools in rural communities in these grade levels had lower reading levels than students in suburban communities.
- Suburban students in grades four and eight perform better in mathematics than their peers in rural and central city communities.
- Students in rural areas perform better mathematically than students in central city school districts.

Data on secondary school persistence reveal patterns of inconsistencies among various racial groups. Between 1972 and 2000, the status dropout rates (that is, the percentage of youths out of school without a high school credential) for whites and blacks declined for the 16–24 age group. However, the status dropout rates for blacks remained higher than that of whites over the three decades. During the same period, the status dropout rates for Hispanic Americans stayed above the rates for whites and blacks. Indeed, Hispanic American youngsters were twice as likely to drop out of school than their peers who were either white or black (National Center for Education Statistics 2002). Similarly, data on high school students' postsecondary plans reflect disparities in trends based on racial affiliation. Trend data on the immediate college transition rates for black, Hispanic American, and white school completers indicate that

- Transition rates remained stagnant for Hispanic Americans between 1972 and 2000.
- The gap between Hispanic American and white students increased between 1972 and 2000.
- The college transition rates for blacks increased between 1972 and 2000.
- The rate of change for blacks increased at a faster pace than the rate for whites, thus narrowing the gap in college enrollment rates for blacks and whites.
- The gap in enrollment rates for students from different socioeconomic backgrounds remained unchanged between 1990 and 2000. Students from more affluent backgrounds were likely to have enrollment rates that were one-and-a-half times greater than students from low-income backgrounds.

ACCOUNTING FOR CONTINUING DISPARITIES IN EDUCATIONAL ATTAINMENT

Several explanations have been proffered to account for these trends. In a comprehensive historical overview of the factors that explain the continuing disparities in educational outcomes, Rossi and Montgomery (1994) identified a number of pervasive social forces that have deleteriously influenced educational attainments and social mobility for some students. These forces represent two broad categories of influences: those arising out of the student's background and those associated with the school environment to which to the student is exposed. Although each set of influence is perceived to have an independent effect, both interact to create a nexus of risk factors that constrain the ability of students from certain social groups to perform well in school.

A number of at-risk factors in a student's background have been identified as potentially harmful to learning (Rossi and Montgomery 1994). These include poor neonatal conditions, exposure to prenatal drug use, structural difficulties in family arrangements, negative peer pressures, negative community influences, and a paucity of community resources. Although the research on these background factors lacks conclusiveness as to the magnitude of each of these factors' effect on learning, there is consensus that all constitute potential risk factors for students (Rossi and Montgomery 1994). With respect to school environment, such factors as the climate of a school, the kinds of instructional practices that occur and materials that are used, the availability of resources, and the rigor of academic standards that are established, as well as the use of ability grouping and tracking are found to significantly relate to how well students perform.

Poverty and the legacy of racism are viewed as two primary causative factors in creating these at-risk conditions both at the individual student level and at the school level. As early as the 1960s James Coleman's landmark study explicated the links between social class and student achievement (Coleman 1966). Students from poor backgrounds lack the social and economic resources as well as opportunity to compete equally with students from affluent backgrounds. Some scholars have suggested that in the case of blacks, the separate and unequal schooling that arose out of de jure segregation resulted in their educational experiences being inferior to that enjoyed by whites (Edley 2002). Thus the vestiges of de jure segregation are thought to have a lingering impact on educational opportunities and outcomes.

RESPONDING TO THE EVIDENCE OF UNEQUAL EDUCATIONAL OUTCOMES

What has been the response of the federal and state governments to the policy challenges created by these differences? The traditional policy responses that have occurred at the federal and state level to equalize educational experiences for all students can be grouped into four categories: legal access guarantees, categorical programs, standard-based reforms, and school finance reforms (which are primarily state-reform initiatives).

Federal Response

Legal Access Guarantees

Orland and Tan (1995) identified three significant legal and legislative decisions that have made an indelible imprint on equalizing opportunities for students in this country: the 1954 *Brown v. Board of Education* decision, the 1974 *Lau v. Nichols* U.S. Supreme Court decision, and the 1975 Individuals with Disabilities Education Act. Prior to 1954, when the Supreme Court overturned the decision rendered by the Court in 1896 in *Plessy v. Ferguson,* blacks were educated in schools that were considered to be inherently inferior to schools attended by whites. The *Plessy* decision upheld the legal practice of "separate but equal facilities," noting that it did not violate the equal protection clause of the Fourteenth Amendment of the U.S. Constitution. By upholding the doctrine of separate but equal, the *Plessy* decision provided the legal anchor on which many states' segregationists policies in the area of education could be supported.

By the turn of the twentieth century, however, several legal challenges to the constitutionality of separate but equal practices were mounted. During the 1930s and 1940s at least three significant victories overturning the irrefutability of the doctrine in higher education were secured. By the early 1950s legal cases seeking to desegregate elementary schools were beginning to be heard by both the lower and upper courts in some states, such as Kansas, Virginia, South Carolina, Delaware, and in the District of Columbia. The cornerstone of the arguments raised by plaintiffs rested on the belief that separate schools violated the equal protection clause of the Fourteenth Amendment. In each of these instances, the lower courts ruled in favor of the defendants. However, in 1952 the Supreme Court agreed to hear the appeal of all five cases, grouping them together as a single case. In 1954 after hearing arguments and re-arguments, the Court rendered its decision. In delivering the opinion for the Court, Chief Justice Warren opined, "Education is the most important function of state and local governments. Compulsory school attendance laws and the great expenditures for education both demonstrate our recognition of the importance of education to our democratic society. . . . We conclude that in the field of public education the doctrine of 'separate but equal' has no place. Separate educational facilities are inherently unequal" (*Brown v. Board of Education,* 347 U.S. 483).

This decision formed the cornerstone of the desegregation movement. It was initially met with fierce resistance, and efforts to desegregate schools were slow. However, the passage of the Civil Rights Act in

1964 provided a strong impetus in speeding up the desegregation of the nation's public schools.

Whether public schools have been successfully desegregated remains an issue of much debate. A study conducted by the Civil Rights Project at Harvard University notes that many school districts are becoming increasingly resegregated, especially in the Southern states. The study *Resegregation in American Schools*, conducted by Orfield and Yun (1999), found:

- Increasing segregation in the South. The percentage of black students in the South in predominantly white schools fell from 43.5 percent in 1988 to 34.7 percent in 1996.
- Increasing segregation in states with substantial black enrollment. The top four states with largest increases in segregation between 1980 and 1996 were Rhode Island (20 percent), Wisconsin (13 percent), Florida(12 percent), and Oklahoma (12 percent).
- Hispanic students attend the most segregated schools, and Hispanic American students in the Northeast attend the most segregated schools. Seventy-eight percent of Hispanic students in the Northeast are in schools that are composed of 50 percent or more minority population.
- Racially segregated schools have the highest levels of poverty. In the 1996–1997 academic years, schools attended by Hispanic and African American students had poverty rates that were two and a half times greater than schools attended by white students.
- Increasing segregation of Hispanic and African American students in suburban schools. African American and Hispanic students enrolled in suburban schools are likely to be in schools in which two-thirds or more of the students are not white.
- White students attend schools where the majority of students are of their own race. White students attend schools where on average 81 percent of the students are white.

Several factors account for these trends. Demographic shifts in the population of many urban centers in the North, "white flight" out of these cities, and court decisions that have granted districts under desegregation mandates unitary status have all contributed to the increasing resegregation of schools. Prior to the 1990s, the courts played an important oversight role in the desegregation efforts of many school districts. Since the 1990s, courts have been granting these districts unitary status, which releases them from court oversight. The granting of unitary status effectively means that students are no longer compelled to attend non-neighborhood schools and are free to return to their neighborhood schools (Weiler 1998). According to Orfield et al. (1997), resegregation has resulted in schools that are overwhelmingly composed of nonwhite poor students.

While *Brown v. Board of Education* sought to provide equal educational access for nonwhite students, the 1973 amendment to the Rehabilitation Act and the 1975 Education for All Handicapped Children Act, renamed the Individuals with Disabilities Education Act (IDEA), granted legal access guarantees to disabled students. Both pieces of legislation provided legal protection for disabled students, granting these children a right to a "free and appropriate education regardless of their disabilities." The law requires states to ensure that the rights of students with disabilities and their parents are fully protected. Prior to the passage of this legislation, children with disabilities were denied access to the same types of education opportunities as those enjoyed by their nondisabled peers. In 1973, when Congress amended the Rehabilitation Act, it became illegal for school districts to deny disabled students access to programs that were available to nondisabled students. The passage of IDEA and its subsequent amendments has expanded significantly access to quality educational experiences for disabled students. In 1997, IDEA mandated that disabled students receive their education in the least restrictive environment. Increasingly the marginalization of disabled students is being eroded. Disabled students are now required to meet the same academic standards as all other students, and their participation in state and local assessments, if allowed by their individual educational plans (IEPs), is mandatory.

In 1974 the U.S. Supreme Court in a precedent decision held that school districts must take affirmative actions to rectify the language deficiencies of non–English-speaking students in order to make available to them the educational experiences that students without such deficiencies enjoyed. The Court issued its decisions after appeals were made to it on behalf of non–English-speaking Chinese students in San Francisco who in an earlier case had argued that the failure of the San Francisco Unified School District to provide services to these students violated the equal protection clause of the Fourteenth Amendment. Whereas the lower court had absolved the district of any responsibility for the language deficiency of non–English-speaking students, the Supreme Court reasoned that students who are deficient in English "are certain to find their classroom experiences wholly incomprehensible and in no way meaningful . . . and are effectively foreclosed from any meaningful education" (*Lau v. Nichols*, 414 U.S. 563). The Court based its decision on Title VI of the Civil Rights Act of 1964, which bans discrimination based on the grounds of race, color, or national origin, and in any program or activity receiving federal financial assistance. This decision was important, since the 1968 Bilingual Education Act did not explicitly require bilingual instruction, provided minimal guidelines for educating students who were limited English proficient, and did not require compliance. The Lau decision and the Equal Education Opportunity Act of 1974 were therefore watershed decisions in the history of bilingual education and formed the basis for the amendment to the Bilingual Education Act in 1974.

Categorical Programs

What other policy and legal avenues has the federal government pursued in order to mitigate the effects of poverty, language deficiencies, and handicapping conditions on student learning? In addition to legal access guarantees, the federal government through the establishment of categorical programs has pursued the twin goals of equalizing educational opportunities and minimizing educational disparities for students who are educationally disadvantaged either because of poverty, language deficiencies, or a physical, emotional, or learning disability. Unlike block grants, categorical programs provide aid that is restricted to a narrow range of services for a specially identified group. In 1965 the federal government instituted one of the largest of such programs: the Title 1 (or Chapter 1) Compensatory Program. The Title 1 program has its legislative roots in the Elementary and Secondary Education Act (ESEA). This act was grounded in the civil rights movement and the Johnson administration's Great Society antipoverty programs. Timar (1994) notes that "the significance of Title 1's origins is that education became part of a larger struggle for social, political, and economic equality. Consequently, the federal interest in education was framed by the language of rights and entitlement. Education became the centerpiece of social policy, integral to the national commitment to social justice through equal opportunity" (Timar 1994, 67).

It is estimated that from 1965 to 2000 this program received over $100 billion in federal funds, with an annual cost of about $8.4 billion per year (Loveless and Ravitch 2000). The Title 1 program focuses on the provision of compensatory services to disadvantaged students. The program does not seek to supplant the regular educational services that these students receive, but rather attempts to provide them with supplemental or remedial assistance in order to compensate for the educational disadvantages associated with poverty. Under the old model, program delivery tended to be restricted to either in-class support or pullout instruction—that is, students receive remedial assistance outside of their regular classroom settings. However, in 1988 (with the Hawkins-Stafford Amendment) and 1994 (with the Improving America's Schools Act), the program underwent significant changes. These changes involved program design issues such as the establishment of schoolwide programs, greater program coordination, increased parental involvement, and more stringent accountability requirements. The shift toward schoolwide programs and program coordination represented a significant departure from the fragmentary tendencies of the old model.

Two other categorical programs provide assistance to special education and bilingual students, respectively. It is estimated that approximately 5.2 million students receive special education services annually, with a cost of $43 billion. Although the 1975 Education for All Handicapped Children Act stated that the federal contribution would be 40 percent of the annual total national cost, in actuality the federal contribution is around 12 percent, or $5.2 billion (Loveless and Ravitch 2000). The bilingual categorical program, in contrast, serves one of the fastest-growing segments of the United States student population. According to some figures, this population is increasing annually at a rate of 10 percent. At the same time, the contribution of federal dollars to the total cost of providing educational services to these students has been declining. In 1980, $262.4 million was set aside for bilingual education. In 1996, that amount decreased to $128 million. Under the Bilingual Education Act, schools are encouraged to provide instruction in English and in the native language in order to help limited–English-proficient students progress through the educational system.

Many in the field of educational policy and school reform have challenged the effectiveness of these categorical programs. In 1991 the federal government commissioned a $25 million study of the Title 1 (Chapter 1) program. The Prospects Study was a four-year national longitudinal study of over 40,000 students who received remedial assistance from the Title 1 program. The study tracked the academic progress of students in grades one, three, and seven beginning in 1991 and concluding in 1994. Although the study design has been challenged, the results were nevertheless instructive about the impact of the program on assisting disadvantaged students to improve their learning. The study found that students who received remedial services through the Title 1 program continued to trail behind their classmates. Furthermore, the study revealed that the initial achievement gap that existed between these students and their affluent counterparts prior to their enrollment in the program did not narrow after four years, but rather increased slightly (Hoff 1997).

Much of the debate on special education has centered on the escalating cost associated with this program. There is a paucity of studies using longitudinal large-scale performance data to measure this program's effectiveness on academic outcomes. The few studies that exist paint conflicting portraits. Hanushek, Kain, and Rivkin (2000) in a 1998 study found that the average special education program significantly adds to mathematical achievement, especially for students who are classified as learning disabled. To the contrary, studies by Thurlow et al. (2000) and Trimble (1998) reveal that the achievement gap between disabled and nondisabled students has been steadily growing across most grades. Thurlow et al. found that on state assessments, the average difference in passing rates between disabled and nondisabled students is about 37 percent, and at the eighth grade, nondisabled students are 2.5 times more likely to meet their states' minimum requirements than are special education students.

The National Center on Educational Outcomes in explaining these differences looked at the impact of school practices on the achievement of special education students (Bielinski and Ysseldyke 2000). Two practices were identified as having a negative impact on the overall performance trends of special education populations. The first practice is the tendency for the highest-achieving special education students to move out of the program into the regular program and for their slots to be replaced by the lowest-achieving students in the regular program who have received a special education classification. The second is the reduction in exemption rates for special education students on state assessments. This trend is seen to add to the size of the achievement gap between special education populations and the regular population. In other words, as more special education students are required to participate in their states' assessment programs, a depression in the overall scores for this population occurs.

Similar debates have occurred over the effectiveness of bilingual education. Findings have been contrary to each other as to whether students have actually benefited from the program. A key methodological issue is the inherent difficulty that researchers have experienced in unraveling the effects of bilingual education on language acquisition. For example, some researchers have concluded that the impact of participating in a bilingual program on language development in English did not differ significantly from being in an English-only academic environment (Baker and DeKanter 1981; Rossell and Ross 1986; Rossell and Baker 1996). Others have found that participation in bilingual educational programs does contribute positively to academic achievement (Greene 1998).

The National Research Council of the National Academy of Sciences recommended that perhaps researchers should focus on identifying the elements of effective programs for language minority students, rather than on large-scale studies aimed at determining whether the program is effective (August and Hakuta 1997). The council felt that this approach would be more useful given the diversity in the language minority student population and the variations in local conditions. Thomas and Collier (2002) in one of the largest longitudinal studies of English-language learners found that they fare better academically if they participate in special programs to learn English at the start of their school careers, rather than attend only mainstream classes.

Goals 2000 Act

These conflicting findings have weakened the faith of the public as well as researchers and policy makers in traditional federal policy approaches toward equalizing educational opportunities and securing positive academic outcomes for disadvantaged students. In light of this and the changing demands on education, the federal government adopted new policy initiatives aimed at ensuring adequate educational opportunities for all students. These approaches went beyond what Orland and Tan (1995) define as the narrow programmatic focus of traditional categorical programs. For example, in 1994, Congress passed the Goals 2000 Educate America Act. This act codified eight national educational goals to be accomplished by the year 2000, and was viewed as a major policy shift in federal education legislation. It provided the framework and impetus for the development of systemic reform at both the state and local level. State and local educational agencies were provided with grants with which to undertake their reform efforts. The eight national educational goals promulgated in the Goals 2000 legislation were:

1. All children would start school ready to learn.
2. The high school graduation rate would be at least 90 percent.
3. All students would leave grades four, eight, and twelve with demonstrated competencies in challenging subject matters, and every school in America would prepare students for responsible citizenship, further learning, and productive employment in the nation's modern economy.
4. United States students would be first in the world in mathematics and science achievement.

5. Every adult American would be literate and would possess the knowledge and skills necessary to compete in a global economy and exercise the rights and responsibilities of citizenship.
6. Every school in the United States would be free of drugs, violence, and the unauthorized presence of firearms and alcohol, and would offer a disciplined environment conducive to learning.
7. The nation's teaching force would be provided with professional development opportunities that would enhance their abilities to prepare students for the twenty-first century.
8. Every school would promote partnerships that would increase parental involvement and participation in promoting the social, emotional, and academic growth of children.

Most of the performance goals of the Goals 2000 Act were not met by the year 2000. For instance, although math scores improved, there was no substantive improvement in reading. Moreover, comparative international data on student performance in mathematics and science indicate that the U.S. students were not first in these subject areas (Hoff 1999). Overall, of the twenty-six indicators of progress, only five showed statistically significant improvement (Hoff 1999). In spite of the failure to meet the performance targets in the Goals 2000 Act, the act was instrumental in reorienting and stimulating the national debate on education.

No Child Left Behind

More recently, Congress enacted the No Child Left Behind Act. This act, signed into law in 2002, represents the most significant amendment to the Elementary and Secondary Education Act of 1965. The No Child Left Behind legislation substantially redefines the role of federal, state, and local school systems in education. Embodied in the act is a four-pronged reform plan: stronger accountability, expanded flexibility and local control, more options for parents, and an emphasis on proven effective teaching methods.

Accountability for Results

- Assessments will be created in each state that measure what children know and learn in reading and math in grades 3–8. Student progress and achievement will be measured according to tests that will be given to every child, every year.
- Data from these annual assessments will be provided to empower parents, citizens, educators, administrators, and pol-

icy makers. The data will be available in report card format for schools and states.

•• Statewide reports will include performance data disaggregated according to race, gender, and other criteria to demonstrate not only how well students are achieving overall, but also progress in closing the achievement gap between disadvantaged students and other groups of students.

Creating Flexibility at the State and Local Levels

•• To cut down on federal red tape and bureaucracy and enhance local control, the number of ESEA programs at the U.S. Department of Education will be reduced from fifty-five to forty-five.

•• Local school districts will be allowed to transfer up to 50 percent of the federal dollars they receive among several education programs without separate approval.

•• States will be allowed to transfer up to 50 percent of the non-Title 1 state activity funds they receive from the federal government among different ESEA programs without advance approval.

•• Up to 150 local flexibility demonstration projects will be created for school districts interested in obtaining the flexibility to consolidate all funds they receive from several programs in exchange for entering into an agreement holding them accountable for higher academic performance.

•• Seven states will have new flexibility in the use of their non-Title 1 state-level federal funds in a variety of categories in the form of waivers from federal requirements relating to a variety of ESEA programs. States participating in the new demonstration projects will be able to coordinate their efforts with local school districts through state-local "flexibility partnerships" designed to make sure federal education funds are being used effectively to meet student needs.

•• Local school officials serving rural schools and districts will have a greater say in how federal funds are used in their schools.

Expanding Options for Parents of Children from Disadvantaged Backgrounds

•• Parents whose children are in failing schools have three options: (a) they are allowed to transfer their child to a better-performing public or charter school immediately after a school is identified as failing; (b) Federal Title 1 funds (approximately $500 to $1,000 per child) can be used to provide supplemental educational services—including tutoring, after-school services, and summer-school programs—for children in failing schools; and (c) parents, educators, and interested community leaders will be afforded greater opportunities to create new charter schools.

Ensuring Every Child Can Read with Reading First

•◆ Federal funding for reading will be increased from $300 million in FY 2001 to more than $900 million in FY 2002. Funding will be linked to scientifically proven methods of reading instruction through President George W. Bush's Reading First plan.

Strengthening Teacher Quality

•◆ States will be required to place a highly qualified teacher in every public school classroom by 2005. The bill also makes it easier for local schools to recruit and retain excellent teachers.

•◆ Smaller programs within the U.S. Department of Education will be consolidated. The bill also creates a new Teacher Quality Program that allows greater flexibility for local school districts.

•◆ In addition to specific funds for teacher quality, local schools can make spending decisions with up to 50 percent of the non-Title 1 federal funds they receive. A local school district can use additional funds for hiring new teachers, increasing teacher pay, improving teacher training and development, or other uses.

Promoting English Proficiency

•◆ There will be a consolidation of the U.S. Department of Education's bilingual and immigrant education programs in order to (a) simplify program operations, (b) increase flexibility, and (c) focus support on enabling all limited English proficient (LEP) students to learn English as quickly and effectively as possible. The new act will focus on helping LEP students learn English through scientifically based teaching methods. All LEP students will be tested for reading and language arts in English after they have attended school in the United States for three consecutive years. Parents will be notified that their child demonstrates limited English proficiency and is in need of English language instruction.

Emerging evidence on compliance with requirements in the No Child Left Behind legislation suggests that many are either being reinterpreted or revisited as the states move forward with implementation. For example, Connecticut, Colorado, and Michigan are revising their academic standards, noting that their current performance standards place poor, minority, and special education students at a disadvantage. Under the No Child Left Behind legislation, states have twelve years to reduce the achievement gap in reading and mathematics between these students and their peers. However, these states contend that the high standards at which academic proficiency are established mitigate against the realization of this goal, and therefore consider the resetting of these standards a necessity. Similarly, some states are experiencing problems in complying with the mandate that families with children in failing schools be allowed to transfer to other more successful schools. States have cited facility problems such as overcrowding to be a major obstacle in complying with this element of the law. There are also issues concerning the requirement that high-quality staff are placed in public schools by 2005. Some of these issues turn upon definitional understandings—that is, what constitutes "high quality"—while others concern the alternate programs that have been established to recruit non-education majors into the profession.

State Reform Efforts

States have also pursued various policy initiatives in ensuring equal educational opportunities and high educational standards for all students. For example, state legislatures have enacted laws governing the establishment of standards for curriculum, teaching, and learning; pursued systemic reform; encouraged the establishment of charter schools and school choice programs through various legislative actions; and engaged in school finance reforms. In addition to these efforts, some states have passed tough legislation—for example, takeover laws that seek to wrest local control from school systems and schools that demonstrate continuous histories of failure.

Systemic Reform Standards-Based Movement

Unlike previous reform efforts in the early 1980s, which approached the restructuring of schools in a piecemeal fashion, the "systemic reform" movement in the early 1990s represented a coordinated and systematic effort to coherently restructure all aspects and levels of schooling under an expanded vision of the role of the states. Proponents of this approach argued that unlike the fragmentary approaches of past reform efforts, systemic reform was likely to result in not only more sustainable results but also more efficient uses of resources (Lewis 1989). This movement was influenced by a number of broad societal factors that led to calls for improving education for all students (Conley 1993). These factors included the changing nature of the economy, concerns with educational equity, and failed educational and social policies, as well as an increase in child poverty (Thompson 1994). In addition, the landmark study "A Nation At Risk," which decried the rising tide of mediocrity in American education, signaled the need for more fundamental reforms.

Title III of the Goals 2000 Act, and in particular the standards-based components included under Title III, provided the broad policy framework for many of the states' systemic reform activities (Council of Chief State School Officers 1998). Thus, states guided by these components developed content and performance standards in the core disciplines. Furthermore, states undertook the development of new curriculum frameworks that mapped curriculum to the new standards. This was especially important in the area of assessment, given the strong emphasis that the standards-based movement placed on accountability (Council of Chief State School Officers 1998). The shift toward standards, and the unprecedented coordination among all aspects of the educational system that was needed if these standards were to be achieved, necessitated changes in almost all facets of the nation's public school system, to include preservice teacher education, licensure, professional development, and district and school operations. Supporters of systemic reform contended that this approach to educational restructuring held great promise for reducing educational inequalities. O'Day and Smith (1993), leading advocates for systemic reform, posited that developing democratic and responsible citizenry is possible only if all students are exposed to rigorous content materials, engage in complex problem-solving learning activities, and are held to high academic standards.

The linchpin of standards-based, or systemic, reform as mentioned above is the alignment of all facets of the educational system. School districts are expected to develop and adopt policies that support the changes brought about by their states' new standards. They are also expected to ensure that local curriculum and assessment are aligned to their states' curriculum and assessment frameworks. At the school level, strong emphasis is placed on teacher professional development and involvement in decisionmaking. Critics of the standard-based movement, however, contend that proponents of standards-based (systemic) reform underestimate the complexities involve in bringing about change. Schools, they assert, are very complex organizational structures, and the assumption that high standards and tougher accountability requirements will result in significant changes is deemed too simplistic.

Problems Encountered by the
Standards-Based Movement

Studies conducted by the Northwest Regional Laboratory show that tougher accountability requirements are related to lower high school completion rates. In particular, dropout rates among African American and Hispanic students are found to increase when the stakes associated with testing are raised (Huggins 2001). A Pew Charitable Trust Evaluation conducted by David and Shields in 2002 on the impact of standards-based reform on district and school level changes reveals that state decisions were not always consistent with districts' goals. Moreover, tougher standards did not result in widespread instructional changes, although they did increase the amount of time teachers devoted to test preparation. Finally, this study found that because of the financial costs involved, few districts were willingly to engage in major overhauls of their professional development programs. Other difficulties plague the standards-based movement as well. According to the national Center for Research on Evaluation, Standards, and Student Testing (CRESST), the lack of clarity and the ambiguity in many of the standards have diluted their potential impact at the local level (Baker and Linn 2000). In particular, the center notes that there is minimal alignment between teacher assessments and the external assessments associated with the standards. Arguably, more disturbing is that some of the external assessments established to measure students' mastery of standards are found to have very little connection to the standards themselves.

Whether the standards-based reform movement will result in greater educational equity for all students remains debatable. The Goals 2000 Act acknowledges that in order for all students to meet successfully more challenging content and performance goals, students must be provided with opportunities to learn. Although voluntary, the act set out a number of opportunities to learn standards. These guidelines provide the basis on which judgments could be made as to the sufficiency and quality of resources, practices, and conditions available for students to reach their states' content and performance standards. The failure of some students to attain their states' content and performance standards is viewed as directly resulting from these students being denied quality opportunities to learn.

School Choice Programs

In spite of the standards-based reforms that have occurred in our nation, for some of the reasons enumerated above, many students attend schools that are described as "failing." Almost all states now provide parents of students in these schools with alternatives. One such alternative is a parent's right to remove his or her child from a failing school and have him or her enroll in a school of their choice. The term "school choice" is omnibus and covers a variety of different plans. However, a common element to most of these plans is that they offer families the ability to choose their child's schools. Evident in the literature on school choice is the saliency of the political environment in determining what form choice assumes in a given state. A quick historical overview of the choice movement reveals that one of its earliest proponents, Milton Friedman, viewed the introduction of marketlike mechanisms in education as a means of rescuing public education from the throes of bureaucratic control and government overregulation (Friedman and Friedman 1981).

The choice movement, however, did not become an important facet of the educational landscape until 1986, when the National Governors' Summit endorsed choice as a means of unlocking the values of competition in the education marketplace. The assumption behind the governors' endorsement was simply that allowing schools to compete for students, teachers, and dollars would be the catalyst for forcing schools to make the changes that are necessary for them to succeed. A number of factors coalesced to support the drive to introduce market-like mechanisms into public education almost three decades after Friedman first introduced the idea. Among these factors were growing concerns over the quality of education in the nation's public schools, the diminishing economic role of the United States in the global economy, a decreasing faith in the public sector and a corresponding increase in faith in the private sector, and a desire to provide middle-class parents with tax breaks (Rofes 1998).

School choice may assume many different forms. *Intradistrict choice* allows students and their families to choose schools within a single public school district; in contrast, *interdistrict choice* allows families to cross district lines. Similarly, *intrasectional choice* restricts choice to public schools whereas *intersectional choice* provides families with both public and private school choices. Two of the most popular and controversial school choice plans are *voucher plans* and *charter schools.* Voucher plans provide a mechanism of funding choice that allows parents to use public funds in the form of cash certificates or scholarships for their children to attend any school of their choice, whether public or private. Objections to voucher plans have been raised on several grounds. First, vouchers are viewed as unconstitutional when they are used to pay for sectarian education. Because they can be used to pay for education in private religious schools, vouchers are taken by some to violate the First Amendment, which proscribes against the commingling of state and religion. Some courts have held that the use of vouchers abrogates the constitutional principle affirming the separation of state and religion.

However, in June 2002 the U.S. Supreme Court in *Zelman v. Simmons-Harris* reversed an appeals court ruling that had earlier found an inner-city Cleveland, Ohio, school voucher program to be unconstitutional. The litigants in the Cleveland case argued that more than 96 percent of vouchers were used toward tuition payments for students to attend Catholic or other religious schools, and that 82 percent of the participating schools during the 1999–2000 school year had a religious affiliation. In a five-to-four majority decision, the Supreme Court ruled that the Cleveland program was established for valid secular reasons and not to promote or inhibit religion. Furthermore, the Court opined that since the Cleveland program represented but only one part of Ohio's multifaceted attempts to provide educational opportunities for students in failing schools, it could not be construed as a direct attempt to promote religion.

Objectors to vouchers also argue that they erode confidence in the public education system. Supporters of this position claim that the use of public funds to finance students' education in religious and private schools sends a strong message of no confidence in public schools. In a slightly different vein, opponents of vouchers point to the exclusive nature of private and religious schools as an example of how the use of vouchers can contribute to the demise of the democratic principles embraced by public education. To support their claim these critics argue that private and religious schools can discriminate against students by electing to reject students if their achievement is poor, or by expelling them if there are disciplinary problems or for any number of arbitrary reasons. These practices, they suggest, are in sharp contrast to what occurs in public schools. They note that public schools are by their very nature inclusive, accepting all students, and it is this inclusiveness that facilitates the democratic ideal.

Not only are vouchers seen as undermining the principle of democracy, as well as confidence in public schools, but they are also viewed as siphoning off much-needed resources from the public schools (Miller 1999; Adelsheimer and Rix 2000). Critics note that many public schools suffer from inadequate funding, resource shortages, and outdated texts and curricular materials. By using public funds to support private and religious schools, these critics suggest that the resource difficulties in public schools are exacerbated.

Supporters of vouchers have discounted many of these arguments (Bast, Harmer, and Dewey 1997). First, they note that voucher programs offer poor students a range of educational options for obtaining a quality education. Offered through a "free educational marketplace and scholarships," these options not only provide families with several benefits but, more important, have the potential to reduce the achievement gap that exists between poor students and their peers (Metcalf and Tait 1999). To buttress their claims, voucher supporters draw upon data that show that private schools tend to evince higher levels of performance than do their public counterparts. An interesting line of argument in support of vouchers has been forwarded by some conservatives and libertarians. The gist of this argument is that vouchers provide the surest way of guaranteeing a separation between school and state (Bast, Harmer, and Dewey 1997). Bast and his coauthors cite the successful use of vouchers in other social policy areas, such as public housing, job-training programs, and health care, and views their use as a "bona fide means of privatizing public service" (7).

Charter schools represent a different form of choice to vouchers, and within the past decade or so, they have emerged as viable educational options to traditional public schools. As was discussed earlier, the No Child Left Behind Act contains a provision that allows for the expansion of and federal support for charter schools in communities with chronically failing schools. In spite of the fact that these schools still remain an area of great controversy in school reform, the charter school movement has gained widespread momentum since the state of Minnesota passed the first charter school law in 1991. Charter schools are public schools that operate under a contract or charter (Weil 2000). Charters can be awarded to any group of citizens or organization(s) as long as their applications meet their states' educational and legal requirements. Funded by public dollars, charter schools enjoy greater autonomy from state oversight than traditional public schools while being held to the same performance and accountability standards as their traditional public counterparts. Advocates for charter schools identify a number of positive features about these types of schools (Collins 1999). For example, their smaller sizes promote greater individualized attention to students. Since these schools tend to function outside of onerous bureaucratic rules, they are more advantageously positioned to offer creative and innovative approaches than the traditional public school setting. Also, they are viewed as viable alternatives for failing schools and as having the ability to stimulate broader improvement in the educational system (Hadderman 1998).

Opponents to the charter school movement have raised a number of objections (Collins 1999). They contend, for example, that the movement promotes economic competition within education, increases privatization of education, drains resources from the traditional public school sector, has a minimal impact on system improvement since only a relatively small number of pupils are enrolled in charter schools, introduces resegregation into public schooling since they are primarily made up of minority students, and are less accountable than are traditional schools. Driscoll reports that courts have failed to side with plaintiffs in instances where charter schools have been legally challenged as failing to comport to the equal protection clause and the establishment clause (Driscoll 2001).

Effectiveness of School Choice Programs

The continuing policy debate over the school choice movement is fueled in part by the lack of conclusive and systematic data as to its impact on student achievement. For example, an examination of the research findings on voucher programs reveals conflicting results, even in instances where the same program is the object of study (Lanese 1999). Although most of these findings have been derived from evaluations of the Milwaukee, Cleveland, and New York programs, studies of other programs have also yielded widely divergent findings (Witte 1998). In spite of the inconclusiveness in the research, some consistent trends have emerged from findings across several studies. For one, most studies have found that the vast majority of voucher students are from low-income families and are disproportionately from black and Hispanic backgrounds. Moreover, the educational level of parents of voucher recipients tends to be higher than that of parents of students who remain in the public schools. With respect to parental satisfaction, voucher parents are described as having higher levels of satisfaction with their children's schools than are other parents (Hausman and Golding 2000).

The effect of these programs on student cognitive and noncognitive behaviors remains unresolved. For example, studies find no difference in mobility and attrition rates among voucher students and non-voucher students in public schools. However, though some studies find no significant impact of voucher participation on student achievement, others reveal significant impact, especially in mathematics (Rouse 1998,

Metcalf et al. 1998, Greene et al. 1997). On another front, issues related to program design, eligibility requirements, and recruitment strategies have stymied researchers' ability to test the assumption that vouchers can improve education through marketplace competition and incentives.

The evidence on the impact of charter schools on student achievement remains similarly unclear. According to Miron and Nelson (2001), the paucity of systematic studies and the mixed results from the research that currently exists constrain our ability to answer definitively questions regarding student achievement in charter schools. Thus, for example, whereas some studies find that students in charter schools demonstrate academic gains, others yield results to the contrary (Lin 2001; Perkins-Gough 2002). The lack of clear evidence to support the assumption that charter schools are likely to positively impact academic outcomes is seen to be partially attributed to flawed data, inadequate research design, and small sample sizes (Lin 2001).

FROM EQUITY TO ADEQUACY:
SCHOOL FINANCE CASES

The quest for educational equity remains an important policy imperative in spite of federal and state reform efforts. Advocates for disadvantaged students in urban and rural communities have argued that income and wealth disparities explain the continuing achievement differences between students attending schools in property-rich and -poor districts. These advocates have increasingly turned to their states' lower and upper courts as the arbiters for what is perceived to be the persistent constitutional depravation that poor students experience. The argument is advanced that the democratic ideals espoused by the common schools movement and codified in many state constitutions are unrealized by students from disadvantaged backgrounds because of the inability of their communities to provide quality educational experiences and opportunities to learn comparable to those evident in affluent communities. Moreover, it is suggested that without adequate educational resources and opportunities, students from poor backgrounds will be unable to meet the academic and performance standards that have been developed by their state legislatures. The active involvement of state lower and upper courts in resolving school finance issues has thus helped to shape the reform landscape of several states' educational systems and to expand educational opportunities for disadvantaged students.

Since the early 1970s, over twenty-five judicial decisions have been rendered in favor of plaintiffs who have challenged their state's school financing systems. These decisions have had a profound impact not only on the way schools are financed, but in some instances on all facets of a state's, district's, and school's operations, as will be shown in later chapters. The school finance movement is typically seen as being distinguishable into three waves, each with its own defining characteristics as to legal theory, methods of judicial analysis, and plaintiffs' success rate (Thro 1994). The first wave covered the period from the 1960s to 1973. Cases brought during this period were based on the equal protection clause of the Fourteenth Amendment of the U.S. Constitution. The litigation theory based on the constitutional doctrine of equal protection states that it is unconstitutional for the government to treat "similarly situated individuals differently without a strong justification" (Underwood 1995).

In 1971 in *Serrano v. Priest,* the California Supreme Court held that the fact that communities with small tax bases were unable to spend as much on their children's education as wealthier communities constituted a violation of the equal protection clause of both the state and federal constitutions. In 1973 the U.S. Supreme Court arrived at a different conclusion. The plaintiffs, who were Mexican American parents in San Antonio, Texas, argued that in spite of the fact that their local property tax rate was 25 percent higher than that of a white neighborhood, they were only able to spend 60 percent of the amount spent by the same neighborhood on education (*San Antonio Independent School District v. Rodriguez*). Citing the equal protection clause, the plaintiffs claimed that since all children have the right to either an equal amount of money or equal educational opportunities, the financing system violated the rights of children in property-poor districts (McMillan 1998). The U.S. Supreme Court ruled that the claims based on the federal equal protection clause were without merit and that the Texas system of financing education did not operate at a disadvantage of any suspect class, since education is not one of those rights that is protected by the Constitution. The Court was reluctant to get involved in school finance cases because of concerns about federalism. The Court was wary about imposing on states what it perceived to be inflexible constitutional restraints that would handicap the continued research and experimentation vital to finding solutions to educational problems (*San Antonio Independent School District v. Rodriguez* 1973, 43). This decision forestalled any further cases at the federal level based on the legal doctrine of equal protection and rang the death knell for plaintiffs who sought federal fiscal relief.

However, the distinction that the Supreme Court made in its ruling with respect to the role of education in the states as opposed to the federal Constitution encouraged plaintiffs to pursue their claims at the state level. The period 1973–1989 thus marked the second wave of school finance litigation. The legal arguments raised during this period were similar to those raised during the first wave; however, relief was sought based on the equal protection clause and the education article in the states' constitutions. Two decisions that emerged as important to the second wave were *Serrano v. Priest* (1976, California) and *Robinson v. Cahill* (1973, New Jersey). In the *Serrano* decision, the court held that education was a fundamental right protected by California's constitution and that the system of funding public education was unconstitutional both with respect to the " provision of services as well as with the geographic distribution of the tax burden" (Verstegen and Whitney 1997, 333). The New Jersey Supreme Court arrived at a similar decision as to the unconstitutionality of that state's mechanism for funding public education. However, the New Jersey Court arrived at its decision not on its analysis of the equal protection clause but on that state's educational article, which guaranteed to each child in the state a right to a thorough and efficient education. The court held that the unequal funding that existed among school districts abrogated this right. In spite of these victories, defendants prevailed in most of the cases that were heard during this period. According to LaMort (1989), in ten of seventeen decisions, states' finance systems were upheld by their supreme courts.

State courts experienced great difficulties in applying the equal protection clause to rulings on state finance mechanisms for several fundamental reasons. The first pivoted on issues of local control and separation of powers. These issues raised concerns about the institutional legitimacy of the courts and were largely responsible for courts ruling in favor of the defendants (McMillan 1998; Rebell 1999). The second issue centered on the potential impact that decisions based on the equal protection clause could have on other areas of social needs. Because of the general nature of the equality mandates, courts had trouble in circumscribing these mandates to specific needs and feared that using the equal protection clause as a basis for overturning a state education finance system might set an unfavorable precedent for other areas of social reform. With the demise of the second wave, litigants sought to draw upon alternative legal theories to support their cases.

Starting in 1989, litigants strategically shifted their focus from emphasizing equity and fiscal neutrality to emphasizing equity in quality of educational experiences. This third wave of school finance cases has relied almost exclusively on the educational clauses in the states' constitutions for seeking judicial relief. In many of these third-wave cases, plaintiffs have prevailed. A number of factors were responsible for the pendulum being swung back in favor of plaintiffs. First, because of the specific focus of the education clause, the courts were less concerned about the implications for other areas of law. Second, the third wave of finance cases coincided with the shift toward standards-based school reform as well as the larger concerns about the quality of education in the society. These standards provided the courts with what Rebell (1999) defines as *judicially manageable standards.* These standards allow courts to make judgments as to the core constitutional concepts of adequacy. Thus, according to Rebell, "This core concept focuses on providing students with a set of skills above a minimal reading, writing and arithmetic level, skills that will allow the student to participate in a democratic society and compete in the contemporary marketplace. Although strong emphasis is placed on test scores and other output measures to assess progress toward meeting the standards, ultimately the core adequacy concept is rooted in the fundamental values of educational opportunity" (2).

ROLE OF THE COURTS

The proper role of the courts in educational policymaking and school reform has been the subject of much debate. Two questions are frequently raised with respect to this role (Bosworth 2001). The first is defined as a normative question: What should courts do? The second is an empirical question: What *can* courts do? According to Bosworth, there are two divergent viewpoints on the normative question, What should courts do? The first represents the position held by those who advocate judicial restraint, and the second is held by those who promote judicial activism. Judicial *restraintists* view the proper function of the courts as interpreting the law and applying that interpretation to the case under consideration. From this perspective, courts should not be involved in making independent social policies, nor should they encroach on the powers of the executive and legislative branches of government. Those who define the court's role in more conservative terms are concerned with the violation of the separation of powers. Judicial *activists,* in contrast, see the proper role of the court as redressing constitutional wrongs by devising remedies that have implications for the common good (Glick 1971). These activists are less deterred from interjecting court presence in areas that fall under the purview of the executive and legislative branches by notions of separation of powers. Courts have adopted both positions in their rulings on school finance and reform issues, as will be seen in later chapters.

The second question—and perhaps the more important one—is What can courts do? Can the decisions rendered by courts significantly reform our educational system? Rosenberg's book *The Hollow Hope* (1991) paints a gloomy picture with respect to the courts' abilities to produce significant social reform. Rosenberg identifies three constraints that set structural limits on the ability of courts to generate profound social change. The first is derived from the "bounded nature of constitutional rights, which prevents courts from hearing or effectively acting on many significant social reform claims, and lessen the chances of popular mobilization" (13). The Constitution and the rights that are supported by it bind litigants. Thus, litigants in bringing cases for judicial resolution must base their arguments on one of the following propositions: (1) that one or more of these rights are being violated, (2) that an expansion of a right to a new situation is needed, or (3) that the establishment of a new right is warranted (10–13). As was discussed earlier, plaintiffs in school finance cases based their arguments on one of the two following constitutional provisions: the equal protection clauses in either the United States Constitution or their respective state's constitutions, or the educational clause enshrined in their state's constitution.

A second constraint is perceived as stemming from the judiciary lack of independence from the other branches of government in spite of the principle of separation of powers. Scholars who claim that judicial independence is limited argue that the social reform issues that are brought for judicial adjudication are ones that the other branches of government are either incapable of resolving or are unwilling to resolve. However, the judicial appointment process, the potential fracture that could occur between the judiciary and other branches of government if courts render decisions that are perceived to be unfavorable by these branches, and the ability of these branches to make changes in the legal structure can, it is suggested, influence a court's unwillingness to make an unpopular decision.

The third constraining factor identified by Rosenberg is the inability of the courts without the cooperation of the legislative and executive branches, as well as the public, to enforce the implementation of any of the remedies that they might develop. Courts are viewed as having minimal authority and enforcement powers to compel compliance with court-sanctioned remedies. Furthermore, courts are viewed as lacking the resources, perspectives, and know-how for promoting social change. Of even greater challenge for the courts is the contentious political and social arenas surrounding many of the social issues that they are asked to address. As Rosenberg points out, courts are asked to make decisions on highly contested issues. Any court decision is therefore likely to be met by opposition from one group or another. Under these conditions, implementing a set of court remedies is likely to be fraught with difficulties.

Those who argue that courts are dynamic and can be the catalysts for change counter the notion that courts are severely constrained in their abilities to promote significant social reform. Four lines of arguments are forwarded to support this viewpoint. First, unlike the other branches of government, the judicial branch is viewed as insulated from political pressures and institutional constraints. Because of this relative insulation, courts are better positioned to make decisions about constitutional matters that the public may deem to be unpopular (Rosenberg 1991, 22). Second, many social institutions are seen to suffer from bureaucratic malaise. This stymies their abilities to self-reform. Courts, because of their independence, can coercively force changes in these institutions.

Third, courts are able to play an important role in safeguarding the rights of the politically and economically marginalized citizens from unfair policies. Policymaking, it is suggested, is dominated by political and economic elites; thus the public interest is not always reflected in policies. Because access to the court is not dependent upon economic and political resources, groups that lack resources can have their claims for social reform heard. Thus, as Rosenberg notes, McCann asserts that "the judiciary with no corrupting links to anyone affords equality of both access and influence to citizens more completely than any other institutional form" (McCann 1986, 118). Fourth, the workings of the judicial process ensure that the full scope of information on social issues is "brought to bear on the final decree" (24). Unlike other social institutions, which may be prejudiced in their assessment of information, the judiciary carefully assesses information before it accords it the status of "fact." This impartiality places judges in a strong position to act, and unlike other institutional actors allows them to be more acutely aware of the "ramifications of comparable decisions" (Cavanagh and Sarat 1980, 381–382, as quoted in Rosenberg 1991).

These two radically divergent viewpoints on what courts can do continue to dominate the debate on whether courts can be the catalysts for change in our society. Certainly within the field of education we have seen where court decisions in the past two decades have significantly impacted reforms in the education systems in several states—for example, Alabama, Kentucky, Massachusetts, and New Jersey. Admittedly, while the influence of courts over educational policy may vary both with respect to strength and impact across states, it is safe to say that they have played a pivotal role in the educational policy process in many states. In the ensuing chapters of this book we will examine the impact of these decisions on schools and state departments of education, and their implications for students and their families.

CONCLUSION

Ensuring an adequate education for all children remains an ongoing priority for federal and state policy makers, as well as the courts. The history of U.S. public education is replete with examples of attempts to reform our educational system. In many instances our federal and state governments have spearheaded these reform efforts, but as we have seen within the past fifty years, our nation's courts have come to play an increasingly important role in safeguarding the rights of many students who because of poverty, a disability, or language deficiency are denied an opportunity to quality educational experiences. Many of these court decisions are influenced by the ideals embraced by our democratic society and reflected in our federal and state constitutions. Two important considerations have formed the cornerstone of judicial activism in education reform matters: first, the belief that some issues of educational importance, such as school finance and educational adequacy, have constitutional value and fall well within the purview of judicial competence; and second, that judicial decisionmaking does in fact have legitimacy and will be perceived as such by the other branches of government and the public. Given these beliefs, and the evidence amassed, decisions rendered by the courts have formed a powerful impetus to bring about reforms of our educational institutions.

The present volume frames our understanding of the impact of court decisions on educational adequacy within a policy analysis model that distinguishes five phases to the policymaking process (Dunn 1994). These phases are agenda setting, policy formulation, policy adoption, policy implementation, and policy assessment. Each major chapter in the book corresponds to one of these phases. Chapter 2 describes the evolution of adequacy as a key constitutional and educational concept within the school finance debate (*agenda setting*). It seeks to establish how adequacy as a constitutional claim became an integral part of the political, legal, and educational debate and how it became an important policy as well as constitutional goal that the courts were asked to address. Chapter 3 and, in part, Chapter 4, present a discussion on the various proposed judicial remedies and decisions issued by the courts to the dilemma posed by school financing structures and the corollary absence of a constitutional adequate education (*policy formulation*). How the legislature and executive branches responded to the decisions rendered by state judiciary, and in particular the types of legislative actions that were adopted in response to these decisions, form the nub of the discussion presented in Chapter 4 (*policy adoption*). Chapter 5, which focuses on state education agencies' roles in implementing adequacy decisions, is premised on the fourth phase of the policymaking process: *policy implementation.* Finally, the last major chapter, Chapter 6, assesses the effects of affirmative court decisions on adequacy claims on the lives of schools and students (*policy assessment*). Chapters 7 and 8 provide a reference list of major organizations, resources, and print and nonprint materials that explicitly focus on educational adequacy, school finance, and educational reform.

REFERENCES

Adelsheimer, E., and K. Rix. 2000. *What We Know about Vouchers: The Facts behind the Rhetoric.* San Francisco: WestEd Policy Program.

Apple, M. W. 1982. *Education and Power.* London: Routledge and Kegan Paul.

August, D., and K. Hakuta, eds. 1997. *Improving Schooling for Language Minority Children: A Research Agenda.* Washington, DC: National Academy Press.

Baker, E. L., and R. Linn. 2000. "Alignment: Policy Goals, Policy Strategies, and Policy Outcomes." Center for Research on Evaluation, Standards, and Student Testing (Winter).

Baker, K. A., and A. A. Dekanter. 1981. *Effectiveness of Bilingual Education: A Review of the Literature.* Washington, DC: U.S. Department of Education.

Bast, J. L., D. Harmer, and D. Dewey. 1997. "Vouchers and Educational Freedom: A Debate." *Cato Policy Analysis* 269 (March).

Bielinski, J., and J. E. Ysseldyke. 2000. *Interpreting Trends in the Performance of Special Education Students.* University of Minnesota, National Center on Educational Outcomes Technical Report 27 (October).

Bosworth, M. H. 2001. *Courts as Catalysts: State Supreme Courts and Public School Finance Equity.* New York: State University of New York Press.

Cavanagh, R., and A. Sarat. 1980. 'Thinking about Courts: Toward and beyond a Jurisprudence of Judicial Competence." *Law & Society Review* 14:371.

Coleman, J. 1966. "Equal Schools or Equal Students?" *The Public Interest* 4:70–75.

Collins, T. 1999. "Charter Schools: An Approach for Rural Education." *ERIC Digest* (January):ED425896.

Conley, D. T. 1993. "Roadmap to Restructuring: Policies, Practices, and the Emerging Visions of Schooling." *ERIC Clearinghouse on Educational Management,* ED359593.

Council of Chief State School Officers. 1998. *Status Report: State Systemic Education Improvements.* Washington, DC: Council of Chief State School Officers.

David, J. L., and P. Shields. 2002. "When Theory Hits Reality: Standard Based Reform in Urban Districts." *Educational Theory* 48, 3 (Summer):309–330.

Dewey, J. 1983. "Social Purposes in Education." In Jo Ann Boydston (ed.), *John Dewey: The Middle Works, vol. 15.* Carbondale: Southern Illinois University Press.

Driscoll, J. P. 2001. "Charter Schools." *Georgetown Journal on Poverty, Law, and Policy* 3, 2(Summer):505–511.

Dunn, W. N. 1994. *Public Policy Analysis: An Introduction.* Upper Saddle River, NJ: Prentice-Hall.

Edley, C. 2002. "Education Reform in Context: Research, Politics, and Civil Rights." In *Achieving High Educational Standards for All: Conference Summary National Research Council.* Washington, DC: National Academy Press.

Friedman, M., and R. Friedman. 1981. *Free to Choose.* New York: Avon Books.

Glick, H. R. 1971. *Supreme Courts in State Politics.* New York: Basic Books.

Greene, J. 1998. *A Meta-Analysis of the Effectiveness of Bilingual Education.* Claremont, CA: Tomas Rivera Center.

Greene, J., W. Howell, and P. Peterson. 1997. *Lessons from the Cleveland Scholarship Program.* Cambridge, MA: Harvard University Press.

Greene. M. 1995. *Releasing the Imagination: Essay on Education, the Arts, and Social Change.* San Francisco: Jossey-Bass Publishers.

Hadderman, M. 1998. "Charter Schools." *ERIC Digest* 118 (February): ED422600.

Hanushek, E. A, J. F. Kain, and S. G. Rivkin. 2000. "Does Special Education Raise the Achievement for Students with Special Disabilities?" Texas School Project. Austin: University of Texas.

Hausman, C., and E. Golding. 2000. "Parent Involvement, Influence, and Satisfaction in Magnet Schools: Do Reasons for Choice Matter?" *Urban Review* 32, 2 (June):105–121.

Hoff, D. J. 1997. "Chapter 1 Study Documents Impact of Poverty." *Education Week* (April 16).

———. 1999. "With 2000 Looming, Chances of Meeting National Goals Iffy." *Education Week* (January 13).

Huggins, E. M. 2001. "Maintaining a Focus on Equity in Standards." Portland, OR: Northwest Regional Educational Laboratory.

LaMort, M. 1989. "Courts Continue to Address the Wealth Disparity." *Educational Evaluation and Policy Analysis* 11:3–15.

Lanese, J. F. 1999. A Review of Voucher Program Studies 1998: Cleveland Public Schools, *ERIC Digest*, ED431038.

Lewis, A. 1989. "Restructuring America's Schools." *ERIC Digest*, ED 314820.

Lin, Q. 2001. "An Evaluation of Charter School Effectiveness." *Education* 122, 1 (Fall):166–177.

Loveless, T., and D. Ravitch. 2000. "Broken Promises: What the Federal Government Can Do to Improve American Education." *Brookings Review* 18, 2 (Spring):18–21.

McCann, M. 1986. *Taking Reform Seriously: Perspectives on Public Interest Liberalism.* Ithaca, NY: Cornell University Press.

McMillan, K. R. 1998. "The Turning Tide: The Emerging Fourth Wave of School Finance Reform: Litigation and the Courts' Lingering Concerns." *Ohio State Law Journal* 58:1867.

Metcalf, K., W. Boone, et al. 1998. *A Comparative Evaluation of the Cleveland Scholarship and Tutoring Grant Program.* Bloomington, IN: School of Education.

Metcalf, K., and P. Tait. 1999. "Free Market Policies and Public Education: What Is the Cost of Choice?" *Phi Delta Kappan* 81, 1 (September):65–68, 70–75.

Miron, G., and C. Nelson. 2001. *Student Academic Achievement in Charter Schools: What We Know and Why So Little.* National Center for the Study of Privatization in Education. New York: Columbia University. Occasional Paper. (December).

Miron, L. F. 1996. *The Social Construction of Urban Schools: Situating the Crisis.* Cresskill, NJ: Hampton Press.

Miller, M. 1999. "A Bold Experiment to Fix City Schools." *Atlantic Monthly* 284 (July):15–31.

National Center for Educational Statistics. 2002. *The Condition of Education.* Washington DC: NCES.

O'Day, J., and M. S. Smith. 1993. "Systemic Reform and Educational Opportunity." In Susan H. Furhman (ed.), *Designing Coherent Educational Policy: Improving the System.* San Francisco: Jossey-Bass Publishers.

Orfield, G., M., D. James Bachmeier, and T. Eitle. 1997. "Deepening Segregation in American Public Schools: A Special Report from the Harvard Project on School Desegregation." *Equity and Excellence* 30, 2 (September):5–24.

Orfield, G. M., and J. Yun. 1999. *Resegregation in American Schools.* Cambridge, MA: Civil Rights Project, Harvard University.

Orland, M. E., and A. Tan. 1995. "Securing Equal Educational Opportunities: Past Trends and Coming Challenges." *The Finance Project* 8 (February). Washington, DC: The Finance Project.

Perkins-Gough, D. 2002. "RAND Report on Charter Schools and Vouchers." *Educational Leadership* 59, 7 (April):90–91.

Rebell, M. A. 1999. "Fiscal Equity Litigation and the Democratic Imperative." *Equity and Excellence in Education* 32, 3 (December):5–13.

———. 2002. "Educational Adequacy, Democracy, and the Courts." In *Achieving High Educational Standards for All: Conference Summary National Research Council*. Washington, DC: National Academy Press.

Rofes, E. 1998. *How Are Districts Responding to Charter Laws and Charter Schools: A Study of Eight States and the District of Columbia*. Berkeley: University of California Graduate School of Education.

Rosenberg, G. N. 1991. *The Hollow Hope: Can Courts Bring about Social Change?* Chicago: University of Chicago Press.

Rossell, C., and M. Baker. 1996. "The Educational Effectiveness of Bilingual Education." *Research in the Teaching of English* 30, 1:7–74.

Rossell, C., and M. Ross. 1986. "The Social Science Evidence on Bilingual Education." *Journal of Law and Education* 15, 4:385–419.

Rossi, R., and A. Montgomery, eds. 1994. *Education Reforms and Students at Risk: A Review of the Current State of the Art*. American Institutes for Research. Washington, DC: U.S. Government Printing Office.

Rouse, C. 1998. "Schools and Student Achievement: The Evidence from the Milwaukee Parental Choice Program." *Economic Policy Review* 4, 1:61–70.

San Antonio Independent School District v. Rodriguez, 411 U.S. 1 (1973).

Thomas, W. P., and V. Collier. 2002. "Learning Gap Linked to LEP Instruction." (August). Fairfax, VA: George Mason University Press.

Thompson, J. 1994. "Systemic Education Reform." *ERIC Digest* 90 (May).

Thro, W. E. 1994. "Symposium: Issues in Education Law and Policy: Judicial Analysis during the Third Wave of School Finance Litigation: The Massachusetts Decision as a Model." *Boston College Law Review* 35:597.

Thurlow, M., J. Ysseldyke, J. R. Nelson, and E. Teelucksingh. 2000. *Where's Waldo: A Third Search for Students with Disabilities in State Accountability Reports*. National Center on Educational Outcomes Technical Report 25. Minneapolis: University of Minnesota Press.

Timar, Thomas. 1994. "Program Design and Assessment Strategies in Chapter 1." In K. C. Wong and M. C. Wang (eds.), *Rethinking Policy for at-Risk Students*. Berkeley: McCutchan Publishers.

Trimble, S. 1998. "Performance Trends and Use of Accommodations on a Statewide Assessment: Students with Disabilities in the KIRIS On-Demand Assessments from 1992–1993 through 1995–1996." National Center on Educational Outcomes Report 3. Minneapolis: University of Minnesota Press.

Underwood, J. K. 1995. "School Finance Adequacy as Vertical Equity." *University of Michigan Journal of Law Reform* 28:493.

Verstegen, D. A., and T. Whitney. 1997. "From Courthouses to Schoolhouses: Emerging Judicial Theories of Adequacy and Equity." *Educational Policy* 11, 3 (September):330–352.

Weil, D. 2000. *Charter Schools: A Reference Handbook.* Santa Barbara, CA: ABC-CLIO.

Weiler, J. 1998. "Recent Changes in School Desegregation." *ERIC/CUE Digest* 133 (April):ED419029.

Witte, J. F. 1998. "The Milwaukee Voucher Experiment." *Educational Evaluation and Policy Analysis* 20, 4 (Winter):229–251.

Chapter Two

⬤‹ Educational Adequacy

INTRINSIC EQUALITY

Some constitutionalist scholars have argued that the equal protection clause of the Fourteenth Amendment embodies the moral principle of the intrinsic equality of all human beings (Dworkin 1996). They suggest that the inherent protection of the intrinsic equality and worth of all citizens afforded under the clause implies that any set of actions, beliefs, practices, and circumstances that result in inequalities between individuals are unconstitutional, and as such should be judicially remedied. Thus, for example, social inequalities that flow from differences in wealth and lineage should be subject to judicial adjudication. (Some scholars have taken issue with this strict interpretation of the Constitution by noting that not all inequalities violate the principle of intrinsic inequality. For example, Foley [1998] notes that if all children receive a minimum education, the fact that some children may have better opportunities does not violate the principle of intrinsic equality.) This moral reading of the Constitution is of particular importance to the field of education, where the evidence has unequivocally shown that quality educational opportunities and outcomes are differentially distributed on the basis of wealth, race, disability, and native language status.

There is general agreement that education is of vital import in a democratic and meritocratic society. Several reasons can be invoked to explain this consensus, some of which were enumerated in the previous chapter. However, fundamental to these arguments is the notion that the survival of democracy is contingent upon the creation of a body of citizenry who are able to meaningfully participate in the democratic process, and whose participation is not adversely affected by an inadequate education (Foley 1998). Moreover, the individual's enjoyment of mobility and advancement within the society is predicated upon the attainment of a certain level of education (Gamoran 1994). Educational practices and outcomes that place groups in disadvantageous positions are therefore inimical to promoting democratic citizenry, violate the principle of intrinsic equality, and are moral imperatives for resolution.

If the premise that each individual is intrinsically equal is accepted, how are significant discrepancies in educational outcomes and opportunities reconciled? The past fifty years or more have witnessed attempts by citizens, scholars, policy makers, and the courts to wrestle with this dilemma. These attempts have resulted in the creation of various policy solutions. One issue that has dominated the policy discourse at the state level, both in the legislative and judiciary branches, pivots on the inequities in educational opportunities and outcomes that have been engendered by the reliance on local property taxes as the primary source for funding public education. Advocates on behalf of students residing in property-poor districts have contended that this traditional method of funding public education has disenfranchised these students and has violated their constitutional rights. Although redress at the federal level has been rebuffed, some state supreme courts have ruled on behalf of plaintiffs. (*San Antonio Independent School District v. Rodriguez* is perhaps the most well-known case on this issue.)

A historical tracing of the judiciary's reaction to claims that states' funding systems violate the principle of intrinsic equality reveals a long and tortuous path for plaintiffs. Numerous scholarly articles have been written to explain the legal and constitutional conundrum that plaintiffs and judges have faced on this issue. However, without question, the almost forty years of school finance litigation have helped to substantively redefine the debate around what constitutes an "adequate education" and the relative importance of educational inputs versus educational outputs in school reform.

EDUCATIONAL INPUTS

Is the right to an adequate education a constitutionally protected right? The constitutional claim advanced in *San Antonio Independent School District v. Rodriguez* rested on the argument that the disequalizing effects of the Texas system of funding public education had violated the equal protection clause of the Fourteenth Amendment. Specifically, plaintiffs argued that the equal protection clause of the U.S. Constitution prohibits the quality of public education from being a function of wealth other than the wealth of the state as a whole. The arguments in the Rodriguez case drew upon new legal theories that were advanced in the late 1960s.

That era witnessed the emergence of several new legal theories that formed the conceptual basis for challenging various states' systems for funding public education. Wise (1968), for example, posited that public education was a fundamental interest that could not be un-equally distributed within any state unless a compelling state interest could be made. In seeking to redress the apparent anomalies in educational opportunities created by the unequal distribution of educational resources, Wise suggested that a similar standard to that which governed voting rights should be applied to public education finance—the notion of one scholar, one dollar. Legal-aid lawyers posited a somewhat different conceptual approach to that set forth in Wise's arguments. These lawyers grounded their constitutional claims on a needs-based argument (Minorini and Sugarman 1999b). The premise of this argument was simple and straightforward: all students irrespective of their income backgrounds have the right to have their educational needs equally met. According to Minorini and Sugarman (1999b), this argument raised more questions than answers. For example, how does one fashion an appropriate constitutional definition of "needs"?

Coons et al. (1969, 1970) advanced an alternative legal perspective for repudiating states' public education finance systems. These scholars based their arguments on the inherent inequalities generated by a wealth-based system of funding public education. They contended that education is a constitutionally protected right that is abrogated by the wealth-based discrimination that property-poor districts are subjected to. Because these communities, unlike wealthier communities, have little property wealth that can be taxed to fund public education, the quality of education received in property-poor communities is inferior to that available in property-rich districts. In order to correct what is perceived to be an unconstitutional practice, they proposed that the "quality of education measured by the amount spent, should not be a function of the wealth other than the wealth of the state as a whole" (Minorini and Sugarman 1999a, 37–38).

In spite of what appeared to be promising legal theories for challenging states' finance systems, the U.S. Supreme Court in *San Antonio Independent School District v. Rodriguez* denied the claimants' application for it to use a strict scrutiny analysis, and ruled that wealth was not a suspect class. In applying a "rational analysis," the Court denied the plaintiffs' claim that education was a fundamental right guaranteed and protected by the U.S. Constitution. (In equal protection cases the court can apply either a *rational basis test* or a *strict scrutiny analysis*. When a court applies a rational basis test it seeks to determine whether a law is rationally related to a legitimate state interest. A strict scrutiny analysis focuses on whether a law meets a compelling government interest and whether that law applies to a suspect case such as race or touches upon a fundamental right such as voting. See Safier 2001 for a discussion.)

Moreover, the Court found the plaintiffs' argument that the protection of education was important to the protection of other rights to be without merit. Although the Court in its ruling foreclosed the argument that the right to an education was a federal constitutional matter, it nevertheless left open the door that this argument could be pursued at the state level.

It is important that the Court's ruling in *Rodriguez* not be misconstrued as a disinterest at the federal judiciary level to adjudicate on educational matters. In fact, as discussed in Chapter 1, the Court had in the past, and subsequent to the *Rodriguez* decision, made significant rulings that altered the face of public education. These included the *Brown v. Board of Education, Lau v. Nichol, Pyler v. Doe,* and more recently *Zelman v. Simmons-Harris* decisions. In *Pyler v. Doe,* 457 U.S. 202 9(1982), the Supreme Court held that undocumented alien children in Texas could not be deprived of educational opportunities. In that decision the Court reaffirmed the fundamental importance of education in transmitting values, in helping individuals to lead economically productive lives, and as the mainstay of some of society's basic institutions. However, the Court in *Rodriguez* was unwilling to make a decision that in effect would abrogate a state's structure for funding public education, out of concern that this decision would impact the traditional state/federal relationship. Moreover, the Court did not find that poor students in the state of Texas were being absolutely denied an education.

In spite of this setback, advocates on behalf of students residing in property-poor districts have continuously used their state and local courts to challenge their states' funding structures. At the heart of the debate are two issues: whether under the states' constitutions education is a protected right, and what constitutes educational sufficiency. The debate is made contentious by (1) the fact that there is uncertainty as to the exact correlation between educational input and output, (2) the political tension that inheres in a system of education premised on local control and one that attempts to equalize educational opportunities by centralizing school finance as a mean of reducing per-pupil discrepancies, (3) the difficulties with establishing judicial manageable standards that can be used to guide judicial decision, and (4) the balance that theoretically exists between the judicial and legislative branches (Heise 1998).

Legal scholars, educators, state legislators, and policy makers have assumed different positions as to the validity of each of these concerns. For instance, it has been suggested that the concerns about local control may be misplaced in light of the realities of governance practices and arrangements (Rebell 1995). Rebell posits that while local control is normatively desirable, in reality, educational governance is strongly influenced by state actors. Furthermore, the paucity of resources that exists in poor communities and the inequitable means of funding public education render the concept of local control in poor communities illusory.

Legal challenges continue to mount against many states over what is perceived to be the denial of constitutional rights to poor students. The proposed solutions have oscillated between focusing on inputs or outputs, with the latter concept now being the predominant emphasis. However, since so much of the initial focus in school finance litigation assumed that input solutions constituted the necessary remedies to an untenable system, it is important to understand what these solutions were. What are the necessary inputs that are needed to guarantee a child a quality educational experience?

As early as the 1960s, the education community was unsure as to what these were. Beliefs that educational inputs mattered were challenged by the findings in the Coleman report that asserted that background characteristics were more important than educational resources in determining educational success (Coleman 1966). Juxtaposed with Coleman's findings were the results of other studies and the assumptive positions of opposing scholars that inferred otherwise. The absence of consensus in the academic community, and the judiciary's own lack of knowledge and expertise of the subject matter, placed the Courts in the untenable position of trying to arrive at judicially sound decisions.

These difficulties did not, however, deter advocates of school finance reform, as evidenced by the pervasive legal challenges to many states' funding structures. The policy reforms that school finance reformists advocated for were ones that could ultimately result in a system of school finance in which the level of inputs into poor communities would be quantitatively enhanced. Inarguably, the focus on inputs revolved around the question of how to ensure greater equity in resources. Three concepts loomed large in the early equity discussions: fiscal or wealth neutrality, horizontal equity, and vertical equity.

Fiscal or Wealth Neutrality

The concept of fiscal or wealth neutrality implies that no differences should exist between the education that students receive and the property wealth that supports that education (Berne and Stiefel 1999, 12). This concept was first propounded by Coons et al. (1969) and became central to the legal arguments raised in the Rodriguez case. Does fiscal neutrality imply that communities should be constrained to spend equal amounts on public education? Proponents would answer no. Under wealth neutrality, using the mechanism of district power equalizing (DPE), a state based on a state-aid formula attempts to equalize spending in that state by, if necessary, funding poorer districts at a higher level. Once equality is achieved, communities with state permission can, if they desire, tax themselves at a higher or even lower rate. California was one of the earlier states that attempted to implement district power equalizing. Under California's proposed plan, a district that taxed itself at a specified rate was guaranteed a certain amount of revenue (Minironi and Sugarman 1999a, 49). However, the passage of Proposition 13, which set limits on property tax rates essentially led to the plan's demise. (Proposition 13 significantly curtailed the legislature's ability to raise taxes to fund education. For example, under Proposition 13, property tax rates were limited to 1 percent of the cash value of the property. It also required a two-thirds agreement from the legislature for raising taxes.)

Horizontal and Vertical Equity

The concept of equity is more complex than it appears at first blush, and its legal as well as practical operationalization has been fraught with difficulties. Some of these difficulties stem from fundamental differences in perspective among those attempting to secure equal educational opportunities for all children. (See Berne and Stiefel [1999] discussion. Berne and Stiefel noted in their discussion the inherent difficulties that both concepts suffer. For example, how does one identify and specify students that are equally situated? The question can also be posed for students who are dissimilarly situated.) Distinctions have been made between the notions of horizontal equity versus vertical equity. Horizontal equity holds that children who are similarly situated should be treated equally. Vertical equity, in contrast, specifies that given the differences that exist among students stemming from environmental and other factors, such as state policies, it is legitimate to allocate resources differently to compensate for the inequities in educational opportunities and outcomes that these differences produce (Underwood 1995). For example, special education students may need more resources than nonclassified students to equalize their educational opportunities and outcomes.

In spite of the differences in perspectives, advocates of educational inputs are in agreement that in order to mitigate against the inequities that result from various practices and social factors, resources must be deployed in such a manner that students disadvantaged by these practices have an equal chance of succeeding. Although in school finance litigation these resources have been cast primarily in terms of equitable funds, other equally important inputs such as school facilities, curriculum offerings, class size, and quality staffing have informed the discussion on equitable resources.

The Debate about Educational Inputs

The link between educational input and educational productivity has been less than incontrovertible. Since Coleman's landmark study, scholars have been preoccupied with trying to establish what link, if any, exists between resources and educational outcomes. These studies, referred to in the literature as production-function research, have sought to establish a relationship between educational inputs and educational outputs. The most common inputs examined in this body of research are per-pupil expenditures, school facilities, student-teacher ratios, teacher education, and other administrative factors (Picus 1995). Similarly, typical output measures studied include dropout rates, graduation rates, achievement on standardized tests, and labor market outcomes (Picus 1995).

Hanushek (1989) analyzed the findings in 187 production-function studies that were conducted over a twenty-year period. Based on this analysis, Hanushek concluded that the evidence yielded no significant positive association between student achievement and school resources. Contrary to Hanushek's conclusion, Hedges et al. (1994) in a re-analysis of the same data set determined that increases in average per-pupil spending did, in fact, contribute positively to student achievement. Crampton (1995) arrived at a similar conclusion based on her analysis of per-pupil expenditures and student achievement in New York.

Indubitably, the difficulties in attempting to correlate educational inputs with educational outputs or productivity—as attested by the inconclusiveness of the research—are compounded by the complexity of the nature of educational outcomes. Schools, as we know, produce a variety of outcomes, some of which are less malleable to measurement than others (Grissmer 1998). Schools are responsible for the cognitive, emotional, and social development of the students they serve. Although strides have been made in the measurement of cognitive development, difficulties still abound in the measurement of emotional and social development. Moreover, students' development in these areas is the result of a complex interplay of the processes inherent in schooling, the socialization activities that occur in other social institutions, and the effects of many societal-level problems, such as poverty and racism. Consequently, isolating the independent and unique effects of schools in models of production functions can be a knotty methodological issue for researchers (Hadderman 1998; Picus 2001).

In spite of the methodological difficulties alluded to above, the issue of school productivity still remains of central concern to policy makers and educators. This concern is due in large measure to the move toward tighter accountability requirements, the mounting evidence on poor student performance, and a general concern about efficiency in public schooling (Odden and Clune 1995). Several writers have framed these issues within the context of resource allocation. Monk (1996) and others have suggested that the strategies employed by districts and schools in the allocation of funds influence the returns that are seen in school productivity. For example, Crampton's (1995) study found that expenditures on smaller class sizes and more highly educated teachers were strongly correlated with higher levels of productivity. In a slightly different but related vein, Krueger and Whitmore (2001) estimated that every dollar invested in small class size yielded a return of $2 to society. In comparison, allocations made to services other than core instructional programs are found to obviate the goal of improved student achievement (Odden 1997). Overall, the evidence on whether enhanced resources in poor school districts lead directly to improved outcomes remains inconclusive. Some have argued that larger institutional constraints within these school systems result in additional resources failing to have their intended impact (Hess 1998).

Opportunity to Learn Standards

Notwithstanding the inconclusiveness in the findings gleaned from production function studies, there is general agreement that adequate resources are needed to create effective schools. In the case of students in property-poor districts, there is little disagreement in the policy community that resources must be distributed in a way that is facilitative of equalizing learning opportunities. Persuasive arguments have been raised as to the potential benefits for both the individual as well as the society when educational opportunities are justly distributed. The societal-level impact has generally been cast in terms of a strong democratic imperative, but more recently some have used an economic argument to justify the need to have educational opportunities equitably distributed across all social groups. According to a recent ERIC Clearinghouse on Educational Management analysis of trends and issues in school finance, equalizing learning opportunities for racially disadvantaged students would increase national productivity and add more than $230 billion in national wealth and $80 billion in new tax revenues (Hadderman 2001). However, though there may be agreement on the goal of equalizing learning opportunities for all students, there is dissension on the effective policy approach to adopt in order to achieve this end. This is reflected in the sharp policy debates that predated and ensued in the development of national "opportunity to learn" (OTL) standards in 1994.

The resurgence in school reform activities, and the introduction of more challenging content and performance expectations witnessed during the 1980s and 1990s, spawned great national interest and debate in identifying the learning opportunities that poor school systems needed in order to deliver an education commensurate with these new expectations. In 1994, as part of the national Goals 2000 Educate America Act (PL 103–227), a set of OTL standards was legislatively adopted, although without mandatory force. These standards took into consideration several important educational inputs and processes by promulgating a number of preconditions that needed to be met if poor school systems were to be held accountable for higher performance standards.

Conceptually, the idea of defining and clarifying standards of opportunity to learn is not a novel one. The concept was first introduced into the lexicon of school effectiveness by the International Evaluation of Educational Achievement and was used to define processes that explained differences in mathematics achievement (McDonnell 1995). However, the concept gained widespread attention in the early 1990s during the policy debates that surrounded the Goals 2000 Act. The policy disagreements that emerged in the 1990s revolved around several key points. For instance, some policy analysts objected to the federal government's involvement in setting OTL standards, noting that this action represented an encroachment upon local control (Schwartz 1995). Others, though supportive of the establishment of OTL standards, took a contraposition on whether they should be legislated, suggesting instead that local educational agencies should be given the resources and the latitudes to reform their schools (Elmore and Fuhrman 1995). The cost and feasibility associated with implementing OTL standards, coupled with the fact that they were voluntary requirements for states and local educational agencies, created further grounds for skepticism in the policy community. In spite of the maelstrom that surrounded the standards, they were legislatively included in the Goals 2000 Act.

OTL standards are defined as "the criteria for, and the basis of assessing the sufficiency or quality of the resources, practices, and conditions necessary at each level of the educational systems to provide all students with the opportunity to learn" (Section 3 (a)(7)). In the Goals 2000 Educate America Act, OTL standards were established in the following areas:

- •> Curricula, instructional materials, and technologies
- •> Teacher capability
- •> Continuous professional development
- •> Alignment of curriculum, instructional practices, and assessment with content standards
- •> Safety and security of the learning environment
- •> Nondiscrimatory policies, curricula, and instructional practices
- •> Other factors that help students receive a fair opportunity to achieve the knowledge and skills in the content standards

Whether these standards were successfully instituted, given that they were voluntary for states and local education agencies, remains unclear. Certainly, the evidence on the failure to meet many of the educational goals embodied in the Goals 2000 Act would suggest that even if the standards were implemented, they failed to result in any substantive measurable progress in academic performance. (Refer to Chapter 1 for discussion of some of the debate around the Goals 2000 Act.)

EDUCATIONAL OUTPUTS/ADEQUACY CONSTITUTIONAL CLAIMS AND STATES' EDUCATION CLAUSES

In the post-*Rodriguez* litigation era, the constitutional basis for equity and adequacy claims has been framed primarily within the context of states' equal protection and educational clauses. Early cases drew on data that showed that affluent school districts on average spent at least twice that which was spent by poor school districts, and sometimes four or five times as much (Hadderman 1999; Miller 1999). Using litigation theory that made claims on the basis of states' equal protection clauses, claimants asserted (as was discussed earlier in this chapter) that the doctrine of equal protection in states' constitutions prohibited children in poor districts from being denied quality educational opportunities similar to those enjoyed by children from wealthier communities.

The record of court decisions at the state level on equal protection claims reveals that most decisions went against the claimants. (See Chapter 3 for a discussion of some of these cases.) This pattern was reversed somewhat from 1972 onward, when plaintiffs either based their legal arguments on the constitutional guarantees enshrined in the states' education clause or buttressed their equal protection arguments with reference to the education provision. These claims marked a significant shift in focus from educational *input* to educational *output*. This reorientation forced the Courts and litigants into new constitutional and educational territories as both wrestled with defining what constituted educational adequacy. The academic community was also drawn into the foray as it attempted to provide definitional clarity to the concept (see *Educational Policy Special Issue*, 1994).

The shift away from equity theory to one that was grounded in theories of educational adequacy was prompted by several factors. First, as intimated in the preceding paragraph, courts were disinclined to rule favorably for plaintiffs in equity claims, thereby creating some disquietude among those using equity theory as the foundation of their legal arguments. Second, pronounced disparities between poor and wealthy school districts, not only in terms of funding but also in the needs of their populations and communities, generated concern among school finance advocates about the overall quality of education in the former communities. Third, the political difficulties associated with implementing wealth neutrality and the experiences in California resulted in a deliberate abandonment of this concept (Minorini and Sugarman 1999a). Fourth, the emergence of the standards-based movement and the expectation that all children master a tougher academic program shifted the policy focus away from educational inequality to educational outcomes. Fifth, the waning of race-based litigation over school desegregation issues refocused some advocates' attention to school finance reform as a means of enhancing equal educational opportunities for poor students (Minorini and Sugarman 1999a).

States' education clauses have figured prominently in successful school finance litigation. Unlike the federal Constitution, which does not contain an education provision, each state's constitution—with the exception of Mississippi's—has a provision that provides constitutional protection for education, and imposes an affirmative duty on the legislature for developing a system of free public education. Many of these clauses were inserted into the states' constitutions during the common-school movement of the mid-nineteenth century. Although there are similarities among some states in the wording of their educational clauses, a careful read of the provisions yields standards that vary significantly in their quality, depth of coverage of educational content to be offered, specificity in language, and degree of responsibility imposed on their respective legislatures. Attempts have been made to develop broad frameworks that allow us to compare clauses. However, categorization of the clauses by quality, specificity, and obligations imposed on the legislature varies according to the orientation of those who are evaluating them. In this section, two classification schemas are discussed.

Specifying Educational Quality

States' education clauses differ in the degree to which they describe the quality of education to be delivered by their respective educational systems. According to Jensen (1997), whereas some states have strong quality phrases, others have very weak and vague phraseologies. Jensen found that in at least half of the states' education clauses the standards prescribe a high-quality education for their citizens. These standards are expressed with language such as "thorough and efficient" (New Jersey); "efficient system of high quality" (Illinois); "general, uniform and thorough" (Idaho); "complete and uniform" (Wyoming); and "competent" (Vermont). In contrast, in other states no quality assurances can be detected from the language of the clause. The education standards in these states may be defined by such vague terms as "uniform," as in the case of Florida, or, as are the cases of Alaska, Connecticut, Kansas, Michigan, Rhode Island, and others not mentioned at all.

Goal, Content, Purpose, and Duty

Some state education clauses include language that amplifies the importance of education. For example, Jensen (1997) notes that both Illinois's and Washington's education clauses view the legislature's role in the development of public schools to be its most important function. Similar sentiments can be found in the constitutions of Georgia, Louisiana, and Montana. There are also variations among the clauses as to the degree of specificity in describing the educational content to be offered. New Hampshire's clause calls for the imparting of knowledge in literature, the sciences, the arts, history, and trades. Hawaii, in contrast, obligates its legislature to provide an education that focuses on culture and the study of Hawaiian history. Both Michigan's and Vermont's constitutions require their public education system to provide students with moral and religious knowledge. Finally, some states' education clauses contain language that suggests that the right to an education is paramount to the protection of all other rights. North Dakota's constitution, for example, notes that the continuance of the government, the integrity of the voter, and the happiness of the people all rest on the establishment and maintenance of a system of public schools (See Jensen 1997).

Classification Schema of Educational Clauses

Thro (1989) presents a four-category schema in which states' education provisions can be classified, based on the degree of specificity in their language and the strength of the affirmative duties imposed on the legislature.

Category 1 Clauses: Education clauses belonging to this category are the most vague in terms of standards and impose the least burden on their legislature. Although they do provide for the creation of a system of free public schools, the language describing the quality of the educational content to be offered is minimal. An example of a constitutional provision in this category comes from the state of Oklahoma.

Category 2 Clauses: Constitutions in this category impose a much stronger obligation on their legislatures than those in the first category. Furthermore, they are much more likely to have stronger language than Category 1 constitutions in describing their educational standards, and many of their phraseologies tend to be borrowed from each other. Nonetheless, description of the overall quality of education to be delivered through their educational system remains scanty, and standards are set at relatively minimal levels (see, for example, Kentucky's constitution).

Category 3 Clauses: Category 3 educational provisions are much more specific in their standards and support of education than either Category 1 or 2 clauses. They also tend to contain more original language than Category 2 clauses. According to Thro, these clauses tend to embody a strong and specific education mandate and have preambles that are purposive in intent. Thro cites California's and Rhode Island's constitutions as examples of Category 3 clauses.

Category 4 Clauses: Clauses in Category 4 have the strongest mandates for education, place the greatest obligation on the legislature, and show a greater commitment to education than any of the three preceding categories. These provisions define education as fundamental, primary, and of paramount importance. The constitutions of Georgia and New Hampshire are two examples in this category.

DEFINING EDUCATIONAL ADEQUACY

The constitutional grounding for defining educational adequacy has been lodged in the educational clauses of the states' constitutions. These clauses have been construed as not only providing the basis for viewing education as a state-protected right, but as the normative underpinnings for defining from a constitutional perspective the elements of an adequate education. However, in some states, lack of specificity in language, the absence of clear standards, and the imposition of minimal burden on the legislature serve as constraints on the Courts' and litigants' abilities to rely solely on the education provisions to draw clear inferences on what constitutes an adequate education. Consequently, as Thro (1989) points out, cases involving Category 1 clauses are much more likely to be decided against plaintiffs than are cases based on Category 3 clauses. Nevertheless, states' education provisions form the basic platform upon which theories and definitions of educational adequacy have been built.

In 1973, the court in *Robinson v. Cahill*, 303 A.2d 273 (N.J. 1973), became the first to use a state's educational clause to invalidate a state's system of school finance. The *Robinson* court ruled that in the state of New Jersey, the mechanism for funding public schools precluded students in property-poor district from obtaining a thorough and efficient education. Using the education clause to determine a qualitative standard of education, one that represents a constitutional obligation, in effect allows for an analysis of resources relative to their abilities to contribute to students meeting this standard. Hence, the issue for judicial review becomes: Are students meeting the quality assurances enshrined in their states' constitutions, and how are finance structures connected to these assurances? Thro (1994) identifies a five-step line of inquiry that courts employ in litigating adequacy claims: (1) Is the claim an equality suit or an adequacy suit? (2) In the case of an adequacy suit, is there constitutional language that dictates a specific standard or quality? (3) If there is a standard, how is that standard defined? (4) Using the standard as a benchmark, is a system in violation? (5) If a system is in violation, how does funding contribute to this violation?

Several broad national reform trends that allowed for the development of judicially manageable standards were instrumental in helping the judicial community to rule more soundly on this issue (Rebell 1999a). The systemic and standard-based reforms that began in the mid- to late 1980s and lasted until the 1990s resulted in states developing comprehensive curricular and accountability frameworks, which established the core academic skills that were to be taught, and the standards against which students' mastery of these skills could be measured. The standards-based movement has been exhaustively discussed in literature by several authors. The movement was fueled by a number of forces: the publication of *A Nation at Risk;* the National Governors' Summits, held in 1989 and 1996; and the national education goals. In fact, the 1996 summit was instrumental in setting the stage for a broad policy commitment among the states to the development of tougher academic standards and more stringent assessment systems. These reforms made it possible to link funding structures to more rigorous state curriculum standards and assessments. Several states, either on their own or under judicial duress, used their standards to clarify their constitutional educational requirements. For example, New Jersey used its core curriculum standards, adopted in 1996, to further define the meaning of the term "thorough and efficient education." According to Verstegen (2002, 3), creating a coherent policy environment in which finance structures are linked to state and national standards requires six conditions: (1) the creation of standards and goals that meet constitutional requirements; (2) the development of curriculum frameworks that are linked directly to the standards; (3) the use of instructional and curricular materials that are reflective of the tougher standards; (4) the institution of high-quality professional development; (5) the creation of assessment systems that are well articulated with the curriculum standards; and (6) the implementation of school finance systems that are explicitly linked to the standards.

Adequacy theories therefore implicitly focus on *what students ought to know,* or the output side of the production function equation. The appeal of adequacy theories in contrast to equity or input arguments can be attributed to several factors. First, as a legal doctrine, it is less likely that adequacy decisions, unlike decisions derived from equal protection considerations, will have repercussions (or set precedent) for other areas of social policy (Cover 2002; Rebell 1999a, 14). Second, adequacy decisions are less likely to adversely impact local control to the same extent that equity decisions do. Adequacy remedies focus less on control of spending than remedies that are derived from equity claims. Adequacy as a concept places no restriction on maximum amounts of spending, as implied by some of the equity concepts. As such, it is less threatening to advocates of local control. Third, adequacy, by virtue of its link to challenging educational standards, is more politically palatable, since educational adequacy increases the level of expectations for all students (Rebell 1999a, 14). Fourth, adequacy does not place restraint on education funding. It requires a minimum level of funding but does not impose a ceiling on funding, thereby making it a potentially less contentious litigation strategy than equity claims (Cover 2002).

Adequacy theories are not, however, without limitations. Cover (2002) argues that there are several inherent difficulties that courts face in adjudicating adequacy claims. For one, adequacy claims in effect insert courts more expansively into the realm of education policymaking than equity claims do. Moreover, whereas courts are able with equality claims to use comparative analysis to determine whether disparities in funding violate constitutional rights, adequacy requires a more complex set of analysis. In fact, there is no incontrovertible evidence to suggest that adequacy standards are any easier to interpret constitutionally than equity standards. Given these limitations, there is some plausibility to the notion that has been raised by some scholars that adequacy claims may indeed be less suited to a court's expertise and legitimacy than are equity claims.

What is adequacy? It is clear that the word "adequacy" takes on different meanings in different contexts, evolving and assuming complex nuances over time. The courts, claimants, and academicians have all sought in one respect or the other to resolve its inherent indeterminate conceptual complexities. Ironically, in legal discourse where the concept is most frequently used, adequacy has been framed from a multiplicity of different vantage points. Adequacy has been alternatively examined from the perspectives of paucity of resources, failure to meet some substantive standard, or a combination of both. Within the academic community, one of the earliest attempts to provide definitional clarity was offered by Clune (1994, 377), who proffered a rather simplistic definition by defining adequacy as adequate for student achievement and the full cost of achieving high minimum standards. Clune generated a three-pronged remedial model for achieving the coined term "true adequacy." The model called for a high foundation program that focused on equal spending rather than a guaranteed tax base. It also proposed the creation of compensatory aid and services for less wealthy school districts, and a "performance-oriented education policy" that would define high minimum standards (Clune 1993, 405).

Clune's proposal was polemical for a number of reasons. Elmore (1994) noted, for example, that the model failed to account for problems of productivity in educational spending, and suggested that concerns with educational adequacy must address issues of how schools' base expenditures are spent on staffing, professional development, and curriculum, as well as the extent to which schools engage in cost-benefit analyses. Hess's concerns centered on the model's failure to give weight to pragmatic considerations. He argued that the model not only failed to pay attention to the extant political processes at the federal, state, and district levels but was also bereft of any attempts to elucidate the complex interaction between these different arenas of policy settings (Hess 1994, 561). Hess further agreed with Elmore's observation that the model left obfuscated how expenditure decisions are made at the district and school levels.

The notion of high minimum standards—and achieving consensus on adequacy based on these standards—has also evoked a number of other concerns. As Goertz (1994) aptly pointed out, state standards vary in content and quality. States also differ in how they assess student mastery of these standards. Such variation makes it virtually impossible to achieve a uniform definition of adequacy and a common set of criteria that would allow one to determine when an educational system is adequate. Adequacy thus takes on a relative cast that is influenced by the educational policies that exist within any given state. The inherent relativism in the concept is even more transparent when the court rulings on adequacy claims are examined, a point that will be taken up later in this chapter.

Noticeable shifts in the meaning of adequacy are detectable in subsequent intellectual discourse. For example, Clune in later writings defines educational adequacy as the "widespread availability of properly financed and managed accelerated education programs that produce high minimum educational outcomes for all students" (Clune 1997, 342). With this definition, educational adequacy becomes a less omnibus concept and is linked more directly to the implementation of instructional programs, such as Success for All and Accelerated Schools (Clune 1997). In fact, Clune uses the cost associated with implementing Success for All to project what the cost would be for attaining a minimum level of educational standards. This perspective on educational adequacy—that is, tying adequacy to educational programs—has been looked on favorably by some courts. In New Jersey, for example, the judicially sanctioned remedies in the 1998 *Abbott v. Burke* decision specifically called for the adoption of research-proven whole school reform models (*Abbott v. Burke,* No. A-155–97). Implicit in the *Abbott* decision and Clune's formulation of the concept is the inextricable link between input and output and the artificiality of defining adequacy from the narrow perspective of solely an "output function."

It is instructive to note that whereas adequacy as a theory was developed primarily to address the plight of high-poverty schools, there are other equally important overlapping educational needs for which adequacy theories are relevant. As was discussed earlier in this chapter, claimants were concerned not only with inadequate funding but with the overall quality of education in these school systems. Within many high-poverty school systems are subpopulations of students who suffer from linguistic difficulties as well as difficulties that arise from having a handicapping condition. In these contexts, adequacy must address the inputs that are necessary for these students to meet high academic standards. Adequacy is thus a concept that, although linked to poverty, is also inclusive of other conditions that stymie a student's ability to enjoy, to the same degree as students for whom these conditions are absent, the constitutional entitlements in his or her state's education provision.

The Courts and Educational Adequacy

What is the proper role of the courts in defining adequacy? Some have argued that courts in crafting a constitutional definition of adequacy must be careful not to encroach on the rights of the other coordinate branches of government (Dietz 1996). Although courts have to be concerned with issues of legitimacy, encroachment, and enforceability, the constitutional protection afforded citizens under their states' education provisions necessarily implies that judicial redress is an appropriate forum for resolving matters related to the abrogation of this right. Various state courts have identified standards for defining a constitutionally adequate system of education in their respective states. These standards vary in their depth, scope, and the degree of perceived encroachment on the responsibilities of the other coordinate branches.

Dietz (1996) identifies two polar extremes in judicial action on adequacy claims: one that is differential to the coordinate branches, the other that is intrusive. Courts that defer to the other branches tend to formulate rulings that are very general in their orientation. These decisions provide minimal guidance to the legislature and contain no specific remedies for the plaintiffs. In comparison, courts whose actions are intrusive tend to develop rulings that are very detailed. In these rulings, the legislative branch is provided with strict guidance, and strong directives are issued for legislative and executive action. Some courts that are perceived as activist have been careful to point out that they are not engaged in judicial legislating (for example, Kentucky's Supreme Court). Rather, they construe their role as applying, interpreting, and defining the phrases in their states' constitutions even when these actions run counter to that of the other branches, or when these actions restrain the action of the coordinate branches.

There is no overarching explanatory framework that can help us toward predicting whether a court in its decisionmaking will drift toward activism or restraint. Various rival hypotheses have been postulated to explain judicial behavior in the realm of education policy setting. Swenson (2000) developed an interesting set of propositions to explain judicial decisionmaking, suggesting that:

- Elective courts are more likely to rule that their states' school finance systems are unconstitutional than are appointive courts.
- Courts interpreting a state constitution with a strong education clause are more likely to strike down their school finance systems than courts interpreting a weak education clause.

•➤ Courts are likely to be influenced by the preponderance of rulings in one direction or another.

•➤ In states in which most of public school funding is derived from local sources, courts are more likely to rule against the school finance systems than states with a low reliance on local sources for funding education.

•➤ Where large wealth gaps exist, courts are more likely to find the system of funding public education unconstitutional than in situations where the gap is smaller.

•➤ Courts in states with low per-pupil expenditures are more apt to rule against the structure for funding public education than courts in states with high per-pupil expenditures.

•➤ In states where the legislatures show a willingness to engage in school reform, courts are less likely to rule against the school finance system than in states where the legislatures are unwilling to promote reform.

•➤ Courts in states that have a mass public that embraces a liberal ideology are more prone to rule that the system of funding public education is unconstitutional than courts in states with a conservative mass public. Furthermore, elective courts in states with a liberal ideology are more likely to rule against the mechanism for funding public education than are appointive courts.

•➤ If a state has a Democratic governor, its courts are more inclined to declare its system of funding public education as being unconstitutional than if the governorship is Republican.

•➤ Appointive courts are more likely to be influenced by partisan politics than elective courts.

Confirmatory evidence based on actual court decisions supports only two of the above propositions. Evidence shows that there is a greater propensity for courts to be influenced in their decisions by the per-pupil expenditure of their states and by the dominant ideology of the mass public. Courts are less likely to be restrained in their rulings if there is a low per-pupil expenditure on public education or if the public holds to a liberal ideology (Swenson 2000).

Early Court Decisions

The *Robinson v. Cahill* and *Seattle v. Washington* cases, two of the earliest examples of judicial interjection in defining educational adequacy, proposed very general guidelines for determining an adequate education.

Robinson v. Cahill, 303 A.2d 273 (N.J. 1973), defined an adequate system as one that gives students the skills for competing in the labor market. The court deciding on *Seattle v. State of Washington*, 585 P.2d 71, 1978, was somewhat more expansive with its definition of adequacy. It concurred with the earlier viewpoint expressed by the *Robinson* court but went beyond that ruling by alluding to the development of intellectual prowess and the preparation of students to effectively participate in the political process as hallmarks of an adequate educational system.

More Recent Court Decisions

Later adequacy court decisions demonstrate an even more emboldened stand by the courts in their substantive guidelines for an adequate educational system. The 1989 decision rendered by the Kentucky Supreme Court in *Rose v. Council for Better Education*, 790 S.W.2d 186, became a landmark decision. However, ten years before Kentucky's ruling, the West Virginia Supreme Court in its *Pauley v. Kelly* decision signaled a shift in judicial pronouncements on educational adequacy. The West Virginia Supreme Court in overturning an earlier ruling that went against the claimants in a lower court held that the West Virginia legislature had failed to meet the mandate of the state's educational clause by denying students in Lincoln County a thorough and efficient education (*Pauley v. Kelly*, 255 S.E. 2d 859 [W.Va. 1979]).

Drawing extensively on decisions rendered by courts in other states, and the debates that occurred in many states when their educational clauses were originally framed in the mid-nineteenth century, the West Virginia Supreme Court defined an adequate system as one that legally accomplishes the following: (1) affords every child the opportunity to develop to his or her capacity in (a) literacy; (b) ability to add, subtract, multiply, and divide numbers; (c) knowledge of government; (d) self-knowledge and knowledge of the environment; and (e) work-training and academic training; and (2) affords all students the opportunity to make informed political choices, decide upon their best options in the world of work, and allow them to intelligently choose recreational pursuits, interest in the arts, and social ethics. The court went on to recognize the need for supportive services in the areas of facilities, instructional materials, and personnel, as well as the importance of state oversight in order to ensure efficiency and progress in student, teacher, and administrative competency.

The Kentucky Supreme Court's decision in *Rose v. Council of Better Education* can be seen as one of the most important rulings on an adequacy claim. This decision not only had significant precedent effects for other courts but also gave credence to adequacy theory as a legitimate theoretical argument in school finance cases. In 1983, support for educational reform in Kentucky had begun to mushroom. The Prichard Committee for Academic Excellence, which grew out of an examination of issues in higher education in the state, concluded that the entire system of public education in the state was in need of reform. The Prichard Committee, which was composed of a broad coalition of business representatives, citizen advocacy groups, and community representatives, garnered support for its educational reform agenda from the media, the state's largest education union, and a large cross section of the populace. The committee deliberately chose not to include in its membership elected officials and educators, wishing instead to maintain its independence from these groups. The committee aggressively mobilized support for its educational reform agenda, and by 1987, when the courts became involved in litigating claims against Kentucky's public educational system, there already existed a groundswell of support for reform.

In 1987, a coalition of sixty-six property-poor districts (approximately one-third of all districts in the state) brought their claim for educational reform to the courts. These sixty-six districts had in 1985 formed the coalition Council for Better Education, which was seeking to bring about changes in these underfunded districts. The trial court found Kentucky's system of funding public education to be in violation of the constitutional mandate to provide an efficient system of common schools throughout the state. In 1989, upon appeal, the state's supreme court not only affirmed the trial court's decision but also deemed the entire system of education in Kentucky to be unconstitutional and ordered a major overhaul of Kentucky's educational system. The court found that the fundamental right of each child in the state to an education was abrogated by the unequal and inadequate nature of the educational system.

The court in arriving at its decision was influenced by several pieces of evidence that underscored the appalling state of education in the state. For example, during the 1980s, Kentucky ranked fiftieth among all states in adult literacy, forty-ninth in college attendance, and forty-eighth in per-pupil and per-capita expenditures on public schools. At the secondary level, only 68 percent of ninth graders were able to complete high school within four years. With respect to curriculum and instruction, significant differences existed among school districts. Schools in rural Kentucky had minimal access to instructional supports such as equipment and laboratories, were plagued by large class sizes, and were characterized by deplorable physical conditions (Hunter 1999).

In remedying this constitutional breach, the state supreme court outlined the substantive requirements for a constitutionally sound educational system. These requirements, in addition to programmatic changes, included the following seven standards:

- Sufficient oral and written communication skills to enable students to function in a complex and rapidly changing civilization
- Sufficient knowledge of economic, social, and political systems to enable the student to make informed choices
- Sufficient understanding of governmental processes to enable the student to understand the issues that affect his or her community, state, and nation
- Sufficient self-knowledge and knowledge of his or her mental and physical wellness
- Sufficient grounding in the arts to enable each student to appreciate his or her cultural and historical heritage
- Sufficient training or preparation for advanced training in either academic or vocational fields as to enable each child to choose and pursue life work intelligently
- Sufficient levels of academic or vocational skills to enable public school students to compete favorably with their counterparts in surrounding states, in academics, or in job markets

Since these early decisions, a number of courts have upheld claims of inadequate educational systems in their respective states. These include Alabama, Arizona, New Jersey, North Carolina, New Hampshire, and Tennessee. For example, in 1998, the New Jersey Supreme Court set out an ambitious agenda for reform in the thirty school districts that are classified as special needs. This court, as was noted earlier, was one of the earliest to rule against a state's funding structure based on the constitutional guarantees in the educational clause and has been involved in perhaps the most contentious and longest-running litigation battle over finance reform.

The court in 1998 called for remedies that included a preschool education for all three- and four-year-olds, implementation of all-day kindergarten, implementation of proven effective whole school reform models, the decentralization of governance; the establishment of linkages between schools and community social-services and mental health providers, the reduction of class size in the earlier grades, the creation of a technology infrastructure to support learning, the upgrading of school facilities, and the establishment of new school-based positions such as parent coordinator and dropout-prevention coordinator in all schools (Walker and Gutmore 2000). However, not all adequacy claims have resulted in rulings favorable to plaintiffs. For example, cases brought in the states of Florida, Rhode Island, and Illinois were all decided against the claimants.

Adequacy as a Socially Constructed Concept

Some writers have taken issue with what they view as the scientific, technical (positivist), and minimalist approach toward defining adequacy, arguing that adequacy is a socially constructed concept that is influenced by the political processes that are associated with court decisions, legislations, and ideological movements (First and Miron 1991). These processes, so the argument goes, overlook the valuable contribution that the community can make in arriving at a moral consensus on what constitutes an adequate education. Shunning the traditional notions of input and output, these scholars advocate for a definition of adequacy that is rooted in the value of community and that "could be actualized via community consensus" (427). The emerging definition of adequacy from this process of inclusion is viewed as one that approximates the ideal of inherent fairness and closely aligns with the Jeffersonian belief that not only should education facilitate the democratic ideal but also states should be responsive to the needs of the community (443). Although current definitions of adequacy reflect the values of accountability and responsibility, it is this notion of community that is viewed as missing.

In pluralistic democracies public policy is positively fostered when civic dialogue is encouraged and promoted. In fact, research has shown, that successful civic dialogue can reduce the degree of political opposition to legislative and court actions (Werner 2002; Hunter 1999). Rebell (1999b) notes that judicial orders and legislative actions on adequacy claims encounter the least resistance by the body politic in those states in which the decisions and actions are either preceded by or followed by extensive civic dialogue. Public engagement is thus a critical and necessary ingredient for increasing the probabilities that judicial remedies for educational reforms are complied with, a point that is well illustrated by the fate of the courts' decisions in Kentucky and West Virginia.

Comparisons of the West Virginia and Kentucky reforms reveal that whereas in Kentucky the court's decision made an indelible imprint on that state's educational landscape, this was not the case in West Virginia. In West Virginia, reaction to the court's decision was mixed (Werner 2002). There were individuals both in and outside the state who strongly embraced the court's vision for creating an adequate system of education. Even so, there was a significant group of individuals who viewed the decision as an example of inappropriate judicial activism, and of a judiciary that had seriously intruded into the responsibilities of the other coordinate branches of government. As to be expected, given the concerns about judicial overreach, the decision was met with rancor among the political establishment, with some politicians calling for the impeachment of the judge who penned the majority opinion.

The reforms outlined in the court's plan thus became embroiled in conflict and turmoil. At the center of the conflict was what was perceived to be the exorbitant financial cost of complying with the court's plan. West Virginia's voters were unwilling to meet this cost and on two separate occasions rejected proposals for statewide levies (Werner 2002). Almost a decade after the court issued its ruling, West Virginia's educational system remained unchanged. In 1990, teachers disgruntled with the quality of education in the state, their poor working conditions, and inadequate wages staged the largest strike in that state's history (Werner 2002).

The response of the Kentucky legislature and public to the *Rose v. Council of Better Education* decision stands in sharp contrast to what occurred in West Virginia. As discussed earlier, by the time claims for educational reform were heard by Kentucky's lower and upper courts there already existed a fertile, receptive climate for reform, due in large measure to the mobilizing activities of the Pritchard Committee for Academic Excellence. Not surprisingly, the state's supreme court ruling in 1989 was greeted with widespread support from politicians, education interest groups, the business and media sectors, and citizens. Subsequent to the decision, the Kentucky legislature passed the Kentucky Education Reform Act (KERA) of 1990, which codified the court's decision. Support for the implementation of KERA was orchestrated through concerted attempts to engage civic dialogue about the reforms. Reform proponents marshaled support for KERA by conducting various outreach activities and public information campaigns across the state (Hunter 1999).

A similar process of public engagement occurred in New Hampshire, although efforts to directly mobilize the public remained weaker than what was evident in Kentucky. Following the 1997 New Hampshire Supreme Court's decision in *Claremont v. Merrill,* 703A.dd (N.H.1997), public dialogue and the policy debate around education reform were heightened. Local boards of education held several well-attended debates, radio stations promoted call-in programs on the proposed reforms, the print media devoted considerable space to public opinion, Internet message boards and chat rooms were dedicated to discussions of the reforms, and various public forums and roundtables sponsored by different groups were held in several towns (Dunphy 2001, 35).

Paris (2001) posits that court decisions promoting liberal reform are more likely to be successful if there is coherence between *legal mobilization* and *political mobilization.* Legal mobilization can be defined as "the translation of a desire or want framed as an assertion of rights" (Paris 2001, 639). Political mobilization, in contrast, can be taken to represent those "extra judicial" political activities and practices that occur around an issue or claim. Paris suggests that when these two aspects of reform (legal mobilization and political mobilization) fit well together, the probability is enhanced (other things being equal) that court decisions will be met with success. In the case of Kentucky, Paris argued that success, measured by the degree of convergence that existed between the court's vision for education reform and that held by citizens, politicians, and other interested groups, was achieved by the successful mobilization of public support (Paris 2001, 669).

ADEQUACY AND CURRENT REFORM TRENDS

Is adequacy compromised by current trends in school reform? A growing body of research has begun to examine the possible threats to adequacy that are caused by various policy designs associated with the school choice movement (Sugarman 1999; Huffman 1998; *Harvard Law Review* 1996). Although competition is viewed as a possible stimulus for promoting quality in public education, there are concerns that for a variety of compelling reasons, school choice policy designs may in fact result in a loss of quality in some schools. Some of these design issues focus directly on the impact of the choice movement on conventional schools, whereas other issues reflect the policy discontinuities that stem from the flaws in existing state legislation. Arguments that have focused on the impact of a true free market in education on adequacy and quality have identified four possible reasons why the exercise of choice may adversely effect quality in traditional public schools.

The first identified reason centers on the potential deleterious effects of a loss in revenue for traditional schools. In many states, under existing school choice plans, students who exercise their right to attend a school other than their neighborhood school take with them the cost of funding their education. If a school loses a disproportionate number of students relative to its overall population, that loss in funds could be substantial. Under such conditions, the draining of funds could inevitably exacerbate problems of educational quality. Were this to occur, these schools could end up offering an even more inferior education to that which existed prior to the exercise of choice.

A second reason for suggesting that choice could be inimical to quality and adequacy in some schools derives from the implications for poor schools when their most talented students are siphoned off. Opponents of choice argue that some receiving institutions may engage in selective practices that exclude academically weak students from obtaining a placement in their schools. Although these practices are more likely to occur in nonpublic schools than in public schools, as the latter are required by some state statutes to use a random selection process, the net effect is the same. When a school experiences a loss of its most talented students, its overall climate, morale, and quality of teaching are likely to suffer. In addition, when interdistrict and intradistrict choice policies lead to a widening of the gap between rich and poor districts, this has the potential of resulting in a decline in quality in high-poverty schools. Opponents argue that school choice, by siphoning off the wealthiest and most talented students from the traditional public schools, could unwittingly create a new system of traditional public school education that serves only the very poor, the least talented, and students with the greatest needs (Huffman1998). Indeed, figures published by the U.S. Department of Education (1997) reveal that on average, charter schools are less likely than traditional public schools to enroll students who are limited English proficient or who have a special education classification. Moreover, the concept of choice is rendered null and void in circumstances where poor dissemination strategies and transportation difficulties constrain a parent's ability to exercise his or her options.

Variations among states in the quality of the regulations that govern choice are partially responsible for some of these problems (Huffman 1998). For example, significant oversight policy differences exist among the states. Some states directly assume responsibility for overseeing charter schools, but others relegate that responsibility to local districts (Huffman 1998). Similarly, whereas some states closely regulate admissions and curricular policies—for example, Wisconsin and Minnesota—others, such as California, Colorado, and Arizona, are looser in their regulation of these policies. There also exist significant policy differences from state to state in teacher certification requirements. As Huffman has suggested, the more permissive the legislation that governs the choice movement, the greater the impact on traditional public schools (Huffman 1998).

Not all would agree that the choice movement necessarily threatens adequacy and quality in traditional public schools. Sugarman (1999) suggests that choice may be able to accomplish what decades of school finance litigation have been unable to do. Sugarman advances the argument that a redesign of school funding structures could result in school choice eliminating wealth-based inequalities and creating quality education opportunities for poor students. Drawing on the experiences of Sweden, Sugarman proposes a finance model in which states directly fund all elementary and secondary education in traditional schools and schools of choice, by relying almost exclusively on statewide property taxes. Under this new finance structure, local districts would be bypassed and funds would flow directly from the states to schools. States would establish a predetermined per-pupil cost, with some adjustments upward for students with special needs and those residing in high-cost communities (Sugarman 1999, 137). Local educational spending would be decentralized, with schools free to make funding decisions without onerous regulatory oversight. Families wishing to send their children to more expensive schools would be permitted to do so, under the condition that they assume the extra financial cost for funding that education.

The question as to whether choice advances the quest for securing a quality and adequate education for all students, or hinders that quest, remains largely unresolved. However, if inadequate educational quality emerges as a consequence of school choice, as some writers conjecture is likely to happen, are there any legal recourses for parents, and do the educational and the equal protection clauses in the states' constitutions provide the basis for seeking constitutional redress?

The looseness in existing legislation creates a certain degree of vulnerability for state legislatures to claim constitutional violation based on the equal protection and education clauses. In particular, Huffman (1998) contends that plaintiffs could prevail if they are able to demonstrate that the existing statues on school choice result in either the development of discriminatory practices against some groups or the denial of equal access to educational opportunities, or if these statues result in some students attending inadequate schools. The outcome of *Villanueva v. Carere*, 85 F.3d. 481 (Colo. 1996), certainly indicates that plaintiffs may encounter difficulties in challenging their state's charter school acts on the basis of equal protection and adequacy arguments.

In *Villanueva v. Carere*, a group of Hispanic parents enjoined the courts in Pueblo, Colorado, to prevent the closure of two public schools. The parents alleged that the Board of Education held discriminatory intent when three months after it had granted an application for a new charter school, it announced the closing of the two schools, whose student populations were predominantly of Hispanic backgrounds. The plaintiffs based their charge of discriminatory intent on four allegations: (1) that the Board of Education in arriving at its decision to close both schools had failed to take into account the high quality of the educational programs at the schools; (2) that the board had failed to make adequate arrangements to ensure that the high levels of parental involvement would continue in the receiving schools; (3) that the closures had resulted in overcrowding in the receiving schools; and (4) that the board because of the charter school's desire to have a racially balanced student population had improperly taken into consideration ethnic mix in its decision to close both schools.

Both the district court, which initially heard the case, and the appellate court denied the claims that the Board of Education and the Colorado Charter School Act had deprived parents of their Fourteenth Amendment right to equal protection, and the rights guaranteed by Title VI of the Civil Rights Act of 1964. The district court ruled that the parents failed to demonstrate (1) that the Charter School Act violated the Fourteenth Amendment; (2) that they suffered any discriminatory impact as a consequence of the board's action; or that (3) the board in its decision had intentionally discriminated against them.

Desegregation is also another major policy issue that has been linked in the literature to the adequacy movement, both in terms of litigation strategies and policy approach. The waning of desegregation litigation has spawned the possibility of incorporating the goals of desegregation into the adequacy and equity movements. Desegregation decisions have been concerned primarily with improving racial balance. Findings in the desegregation literature have been mixed as to whether this goal has been realized and whether desegregation has led to positive outcomes for minority students (Mahard and Crain 1983). There has also been some debate in the academic literature about the extent to which the focus on racial integration has come at the expense of promoting educational quality in minority schools (Kazal-Thresher 1993). With the increasing trends toward racially imbalanced school systems, and the expressed concerns about education quality in minority-populated schools, desegregation advocates have begun to explore folding desegregation issues into school finance reforms (Kazal-Thresher 1993). Persuasive arguments have been raised as to the policy and litigation benefits of merging desegregation claims with school finance and adequacy reforms.

An important case in which desegregation and adequacy issues were merged was filed in 1989 in Connecticut. In *Sheff v. O'Neil*, 678 A.2d 1267 (Conn. 1996), a group of citizens filed a complaint on behalf of children attending Hartford and suburban-Hartford schools. The plaintiffs claimed in their suit that Hartford's schools were in violation of the Connecticut constitution because (1) they were highly segregated on the basis of race; (2) that this segregation harmed students; and (3) that children in Hartford were denied an adequate education. In 1996, the Connecticut Supreme Court reversed the initial trial court decision, which had found in favor of the state. The court held that the achievement gap between black and white students was influenced by the handicaps that students in Hartford confronted. The court then directed the legislature to implement appropriate remedial measures.

FUNDING ADEQUACY

How does adequacy gets translated into practice, and what types of finance reforms are needed to achieve educational adequacy? Policy analysts have used various approaches in calculating the financial costs associated with achieving adequacy. A number of researchers through the employment of different statistical approaches have attempted to estimate the cost of achieving adequacy by calculating cost functions that are associated with student and school district characteristics. Some of these approaches include the use of statistical techniques to estimate teacher cost indices (Chambers 1995); defining state average per pupil based on the performance of a subset of schools in the state that have attained certain performance goals (Augenblick, Myers, and Anderson 1997); and using data on per-pupil expenditures, student performance, and various characteristics of school districts to estimate cost functions (Reschovsky and Imazeki 2000).

Relying upon complex statistical modeling to calculate the cost of adequacy may, however, raise some practical policy concerns for legislators. Guthrie and Rothstein (1999) argue that such complex techniques may be very difficult for policy makers to understand and explain to their constituents. An alternative to these techniques is the use of professional judgments, as was done in the state of Illinois, where committees of teachers, administrators, and public officials were convened to determine what resources were needed to ensure an appropriate education. A similar process occurred in the state of Alaska. (See Chambers and Parrish [1994] for a discussion of this technique.) This approach toward estimating the cost of adequacy relies upon the opinions of local and national experts, as well as research findings on effective education programs to determine and specify the level of educational resources needed to achieve adequacy. This approach lacks the obvious objectivity of the statistical model. However, it has been used by certain states in their determination of the cost associated with adequacy (Guthrie and Rothstein 1999).

CONCLUSION

Unquestionably, society has a moral and legal responsibility to ensure that all children receive an adequate education. This responsibility protects not only the society's interest but the interests and rights of the individual as well. Although the exercise of this responsibility is not in dispute, there is disagreement as to whether the law, and in particular the courts, have the "right" to dictate to the coordinate branches how they should provide for an adequate education in their states. Findings on the legal pursuits against the perceived inadequacies of many states' systems of funding public education reveal that while several courts have assumed an affirmative posture with respect to their roles in setting educational policy reform, other courts have been more tentative and conservative. In spite of these differences, the past four decades of school reform litigation have resulted in significant departures in public policy in how deficiencies in educational quality and opportunities are addressed. These policy shifts have often occurred in political and economic contexts that are highly charged.

REFERENCES

Augenblick, J. G., J. L. Myers, and A. B. Anderson. 1997. "Equity and Adequacy in School Funding." *The Future of Children: Financing School* 7, 3:63–78.

Berne, Robert, and Leanna Stiefel. 1999. "Concepts of School Finance Equity: 1970 to the Present." In Helen Ladd, Rosemary Chalk, and Janet Hansen (eds.), *Equity and Adequacy in Education Finance: Issues and Perspectives.* Washington, DC: Brookings Press.

Chambers, J., and T. Parrish. 1994. "State-Level Education Finance." In W. S. Barnett (ed.), *Cost Analysis for Education Decisions: Methods and Examples: Advances in Educational Productivity, Volume 4.* Greenwich, CT: JAI Press.

Chambers, J. G. 1995. *Public School Teacher Cost Differences across the United States.* Washington, DC: U.S. Department of Education, National Center for Education Statistics.

Clune, W. H. 1993. "Equal Education, Equal Funding? The Shift from Equity to Adequacy in School Finance." *The World and I,* 8, 9:389–405.

———.1994. "The Shift from Equity to Adequacy in School Finance." *Educational Policy* 8, 4:376–395.

———.1997. "Building a Systemic Remedy for Educational Adequacy." *Education and Urban Society* 29, 3:342–355.

Coleman, J. 1966. "Equal School or Equal Students?" *The Public Interest* 4:70–75.

Coons, J. E., W. H. Clune, and S. D. Sugarman. 1969. "Educational Opportunity: A Workable Constitutional Test for State Financial Structures." *California Law Review* 57, 2:305–421.

———. 1970. *Private Wealth and Public Education.* Cambridge, MA: Harvard University Press.

Cover, A. Y. 2002. "Is Adequacy More a Political Question than Equality? The Effects of Standards-based Education on Judicial Standards for Education Finance." *Cornell Journal of Law and Public Policy* 11:403–439.

Crampton, F. E. 1995. "Is the Production Function Dead? An Analysis of Educational Inputs on School Outcomes." Paper presented at the Annual Conference of the American Education Finance Association, March.

Dietz, W. F. 1996. "Manageable Adequacy Standards in Education Reform Litigation." *Washington University Law Quarterly* 74 (Winter):1193–1223.

Dunphy, D. 2001. "Moving Mountains in the Granite State: Reforming School Finance and Designing Adequacy in New Hampshire." *Studies in Judicial Remedies and Public Engagement* 2, 4:1–38.

Dworkin, R. 1996. *Freedom's Law.* Cambridge, MA: Harvard University Press.

Elmore, R. F. 1994. "Thoughts on Program Equity: Productivity and Incentives of Performance in Education." *Educational Policy* 8, 4:453–459.

Elmore, R. F., and S. Fuhrman. 1995. "Opportunity-to-Learn Standards and the State Role in Education." *Teachers College Record* 96, 3:433–458.

First, P. F., and L. F. Miron. 1991. "The Social Construction of Adequacy." *Journal of Law and Education* 20, 4:421–444.

Foley, Edward B. 1998. "Rodriquez Revisited: Constitutional Theory and School Finance." *Georgia Law Review* 32 (Winter):475.

Gamoran, A. 1994. "The Impact of Academic Course Work on Labor Market Outcomes for Youth Who Do not Attend College: A Research Review." Paper prepared for the National Assessment of Vocational Education.

Goertz, M. E. 1994. "Program Equity and Adequacy: Issues from the Field." *Educational Policy* 18, 4:608–615.

Grissmer, D. W. 1998. *Education Productivity.* Washington, DC: NEKIA Publications.

Guthrie, J., and R. Rothstein. 1999. "Enabling 'Adequacy' to Achieve Reality: Translating Adequacy into State School Finance Distribution Arrangements." In H. F. Ladd, R. Chalk, and J. S. Hansen (eds.), *Equity and Adequacy in Education Finance: Issues and Perspectives.* Washington, DC: National Academy Press.

Hadderman, M. 1998. "Is There a Relationship between Educational Funding and Student Outcomes?" *ERIC Digest* 119:ED420092.

———. 1999. "Equity and Adequacy in Educational Finance." *ERIC Digest* 130.

———. 2001. *Trends and Issues: School Finance.* Eugene: University of Oregon College of Education.

Hanushek, E. A. 1989. "The Impact of Differential Expenditures on School Performance." *Educational Researcher* 18, 4 (May):45–51.

Hedges, L. V., R. D. Laine, and R. Greenwald. 1994. "Does Money Matter? A Meta-Analysis of the Effects of Differential School Inputs on Student Outcomes." *Educational Researcher* 23, 3 (April):5–14.

Heise, M. 1998. "Educational Opportunity, Hollow Victories, and the Demise of School Finance Equity Theory: An Empirical Perspective and Alternative Explanations." *Georgia Law Review* 32:543–624.

Hess, C. A. 1994. "Adequacy Rather Than Equity: A New Solution or a Stalking Horse?" *Educational Policy* 8, 4:544–567.

Hess, F. M. 1998. "Courting Backlash: The Risks of Emphasizing Input Equity Over School Performance." *Virginia Journal of Social Policy and Law* 6 (Fall):11–45.

Huffman, K. S. 1998. "Charter Schools, Equal Protection Litigation, and the New School Reform Movement." *New York University Law Review* 73: 1290–1327.

Hunter, M. 1999. "All Eyes Forward: Public Engagement and Educational Reform in Kentucky." *Journal of Law and Education* 28, 4:485–516.

Jensen, R. M. 1997. "Advancing Education through Education Clauses of State Constitutions." *Brigham Young University Law Journal* 1:44.

Kazal-Thresher, D. M. 1993. "Merging Educational Finance Reform and Desegregation Goals." *Education Policy Analysis Archives* 1, 7:1–21.

Krueger, A., and D. Whitmore. 2001. "The Effect of Attending a Smaller Class in the Early Grades on College Test Taking and Middle School Test Results: Evidence from Project Star. *The Economic Journal* 111, 1–28.

Mahard, R. E., and R. L. Crain. 1983. "Research on Minority Achievement in Desegregated Schools." In C. Rossell and W. Hawley (eds.), *The Consequences of School Desegregation*. Philadelphia: Temple University Press.

McDonnell, J. 1995. "Opportunity to Learn as a Research Concept and Policy Instrument." *Educational Evaluation and Policy Analysis* 17, 3:305–322.

Miller, M. 1999. "A Bold Experiment to Fix City Schools." *Atlantic Monthly* 284, 1 (July):15–16, 18, 26–28, 30–31.

Minorini, P. A., and S. Sugarman. 1999a. "School Finance Litigation in the Name of Educational Equity: Its Evolution, Impact, and Future." In Helen Ladd, Rosemary Chalk, and Janet Hansen (eds.), *Equity and Adequacy in Education Finance: Issues and Perspectives*. Washington, DC: National Academy Press.

———. 1999b. "Educational Adequacy and the Courts: The Promise and Problems of Moving to a New Paradigm." In Helen Ladd, Rosemary Chalk, and Janet Hansen (eds.), *Equity and Adequacy in Education Finance: Issues and Perspectives*. Washington, DC: National Academy Press.

Monk, D. H. 1996. "Resource Allocation for Education: An Evolving and Promising Base for Policy-oriented Research." *Journal of School Leadership* 6, 3:216–242.

Odden, A. 1997. "Raising Performance Level without Increasing Funding." *School Business Affairs* 63, 6 (June):4–12.

Odden, A., and W. Clune. 1995. "Improving Educational Productivity and School Finance." *Educational Researcher* 24, 9 (December):6–10.

Paris, M. 2001. "Legal Mobilization and the Politics of Reform: Lessons from School Finance Litigation in Kentucky, 1984–1995." *Law and Social Inquiry* 26, 3:631–684.

Picus, Lawrence O. 1995. "Does Money Matter in Education? A Policymaker's Guide." In William J. Fowler (ed.), *Selected Papers in School Finance 1995.* Washington, DC: National Center for Education Statistics.

———. 2001. "In Search of More Productive Schools: A Guide to Resource Allocation in Education." ERIC Clearinghouse on Educational Management. Eugene: University of Oregon.

Rebell, M. A. 1995. "Fiscal Equity in Education: Deconstructing the Reigning Myths and Facing Reality." *New York University Review of Law and Social Change* 21, 4:691–723.

———. 1999a. "Education Adequacy Litigation and the Quest for Equal Educational Opportunity." *Studies in Judicial Remedies and Public Engagement* 2, 2:1–31.

———. 1999b. "Fiscal Equity and the Democratic Imperative." *Equity and Excellence in Education* (December) 32, 3:5–18.

Reschovsky, A., and J. Imazeki. 2000. "Achieving Educational Adequacy through School Finance Reform." CPRE Research Report Series RR-045. Consortium for Policy Research in Education. Philadelphia: University of Pennsylvania Graduate School of Education.

Safier, K. 2001. "The Question of a Fundamental Right to a Minimally Adequate Education." *University of Cincinnati Law Review* 69 (Spring):993.

Schwartz, W. 1995. "Opportunity to Learn Standards: Their Impact on Urban Students." *ERIC/CUE Digest* 110.

Sugarman, S. D. 1999. "Politics, Policy, and Law." In S. S. Sugarman and F. R. Kemerer (eds.), *School Choice and Social Controversy.* Washington, DC: Brookings Press.

Swenson, K. 2000. "School Finance Reform Litigation: Why Are Some State Supreme Courts Activist and Others Restrained?" *Albany Law Review* 63:1147.

Thro, W. E. 1989. "To Render Them Safe: The Analysis of State Constitutional Provisions in Public School Finance Reform Litigation." *Virginian Law Review* 75:1639–1679.

————. 1994. "Judicial Analysis during the Third Wave of School Finance Litigation: The Massachusetts Decision as a Model." *Boston College Law Review* 35:597–617.

Underwood, J. K. 1995. "School Finance as Vertical Equity." *University of Michigan Journal of Law Reform* 28:493–514.

United States Department of Education. 1997. "A Study on Charter Schools: First Year Report." Washington, DC: Department of Education.

Verstegen, D. A. 2002. "The New Finance: Today's High Standards Call for a New Way of Funding Education." *American School Board Journal* 189, 10:1–24.

Walker, E. M., and D. Gutmore. 2000. "The Quest for Equity and Excellence in Education: A Study on Whole School Reform in New Jersey." South Orange, NJ: Center for Urban Leadership, Renewal and Research, Seton Hall University.

Werner, J. 2002. "No Knight in Shining Armor: Why Courts Alone, Absent Public Engagement, Could not Achieve Public School Finance Reform in West Virginia." *Columbia Journal of Law and Social Problems* 35:61.

Wise, A. 1968. *Rich Schools, Poor Schools: The Promise of Equal Educational Opportunity.* Chicago: University of Chicago Press.

Chapter Three

◄ Chronology

Some of the following court citations are taken from Terry Whitney's legislative report, "State School Finance Litigation: A Summary and an Analysis," National Conference of State Legislatures, Denver, Colorado, October 1998; and Mary Moran, "Standards and Assessments: The New Measure of Adequacy in School Finance Litigation," *Journal of Education Finance* 25 (Summer 1999):3–80.

1954

In *Brown v. Board of Education of Topeka,* 347 U.S. 483, 493, the U.S. Supreme Court rules that segregation in the public schools is unconstitutional and orders the desegregation of all public schools.

1960s

Several important legislations are passed, including the Civil Rights Act, enacted in 1964, and the Elementary and Secondary Education Act (ESEA), passed in 1965. James Coleman's influential study is also published during this period. It finds that social background has a pervasive and independent impact on student achievement. New legal theories that would form the cornerstone of legal challenges to school finance systems gain currency.

1973

In *San Antonio Independent School District v. Rodriguez,* 411 U.S. 1 (1973), the U.S. Supreme Court finds that the Texas school-finance system did not violate the Fourteenth Amendment of the U.S. Constitution. In *Robinson v. Cahill,* 303 A.2d 273 (N. J. 1973), the New Jersey Supreme Court holds that the system of financing public school violates the state's education clause that calls for the establishment of a system of public schools that are thorough and efficient.

1974

> The state of Washington's system for funding the public schools is deemed to be constitutional (a similar conclusion is reached in 1975 for the state of Idaho). The U.S. Supreme Court rules that school districts must take affirmative actions to rectify the language deficiencies of non–English-speaking students.

1975

> The Individuals with Disabilities Act is passed, granting legal access guarantees to all students with disabilities.

1976

> In *Serrano v. Priest* (II), the California Supreme Court holds that the state's system for funding public education denies plaintiffs equal protection of the laws. This decision affirms the previous decision in *Serrano v. Priest* (I).

1978

> In *Pauley v. Kelly,* 255 S.E.2d 859 (W.Va. 1979), West Virginia's school funding structure is held to be unconstitutional. Several other key decisions in non-school finance cases are also made during this period.

> Significant legislation affecting the education of special education students is also passed during this decade.

1982

> In *Pyler v. Doe* the U.S. Supreme Court rules that the state of Texas cannot deny the children of undocumented aliens a public education. The New York system of funding public education is found to be constitutional in *Board of Education, Levittown Union Free School District v. Nyquest* (439 N.W.2d 359 (N.Y.1982). The court holds that the system of financing public education is constitutional under the equal protection clause of the U.S. Constitution and under both the equal protection clause and the education clause of the state's constitution.

1983

> In *Hornbeck v. Somerset County Board of Education,* 458A.2d 758

(Md. 1983), Maryland's establishment of statewide qualitative standards is interpreted by the court as signaling a good-faith effort on the part of the legislature to provide a thorough and efficient education for children. The court rules on the basis of this observation that the state's school finance system is constitutional. The court further indicates its unwillingness to interfere with the General Assembly's approach to solving educational problems.

The landmark document *A Nation at Risk* is published by the National Commission on Excellence in Education. Decrying the state of public education in the United States, it quickly becomes influential in the systemic reform movement. The document views educational reform in four areas (curriculum, expectation, time devoted to schooling, and the quality of individuals attracted to the teaching profession) to be imperative if U.S. students are to regain their competitive edge with students in other countries.

Minnesota becomes one of the earliest states to gain widespread support for public school choice programs.

1988

The Hawkins-Stafford Amendment is passed, resulting in significant changes to the Title 1 program, including the creation of schoolwide programs, greater program coordination, and more stringent accountability requirements.

State takeover emerges as a policy strategy for dealing with failing school districts. New Jersey becomes one of the first states to initiate this policy with the takeover of the Jersey City Public School system.

1989

In the *Rose v. Council for Better Education*, 790 S.W.2d 186 (Ky. 1989) decision, the Kentucky Supreme Court rules that the entire public school system of education failed to meet the constitutional requirement for an efficient system of common schools. The court establishes standards in seven core areas and requires the General Assembly to implement a system to continually monitor public education in the state, in order to ensure that the system remains in compliance with the state's constitutional requirement.

The first National Governors' Summit is convened under the auspices of then President George H. Bush. The summit produces a broad consensus among the governors regarding the problems afflicting public education and the strategies that are needed to redress these problems. Along with the White House and academicians, the governors agree upon six national goals.

The debate about educational input versus educational output is refueled by research that suggests that no positive association exists between student achievement and school resources.

EARLY 1990s

The burgeoning of charter school legislation begins. Minnesota, California, Colorado, and Massachusetts all pass charter school legislation during this period.

Systemic reform becomes the major policy approach toward educational change. Standards-based policies in curriculum and assessment, and enhancing teacher capacities, form the centerpiece of the movement.

1990

The Kentucky Reform Act (KERA) is passed, introducing sweeping reforms in the state in the areas of funding, assessment, accountability, and school governance.

1992

In *Carrolton-Farmers v. Edgewood Independent School District* (Edgewood III), 826 S.W.2d 489 (Tx.), the Texas Supreme Court raises concerns about the failure of the legislature to address issues related to student achievement. The court reiterates its concerns with educational results, noting that the mandates, which it had previously endorsed, go beyond monetary issues.

The courts begin to formulate decisions that free local districts from court oversight in desegregation efforts, as evidenced in *Freeman v. Pitts*, 503 U.S. 467 (1992), in which test scores in Georgia's Dekalb County School District are accepted as evidence that the county's black students have made significant academic progress. The district court is ordered to relinquish its supervisory role over those areas in which successful compliance to desegregation mandates has been achieved.

1993

In *Alabama Coalition for Equity v. Hunt* (624 So.2d 107 (Ala.1993), Alabama's circuit court expresses concerns over the quality of course offerings and defines "adequate educational opportunities" as composed of nine elements.

1994

The Goals 2000 Educate America Act is passed. The act codifies eight national educational goals to be met by the year 2000 and delineates a set of "opportunity to learn" standards.

The journal *Educational Policy* devotes a special issue to the concept of educational adequacy.

Education is deemed to not be a fundamental right under Kansas's constitution (*Unified School District No. 229 v. Kansas*, 885 P.2d 1170). The court expresses a reluctance to challenge the standards promulgated by the legislature and state department of education, preferring instead to rely upon their judgment. The court concurs with the state that the School District Finance and Quality Performance Act, passed in 1992, is constitutionally adequate.

1995

The U.S. Supreme Court in *Missouri v. Jenkins*, 515 U.S. 70, permits the use of student assessment as an indicator of education quality. The Court is asked to decide whether federal oversight is still needed in a desegregation case brought against Kansas City. The plaintiffs' case is based on the evidence of poor academic outcomes for black students. The Supreme Court remands the case to the district court, which rules that in spite of increases in per-pupil expenditures, student test scores in Kansas City and St. Louis remain below national norms and the state of Missouri as a whole. (Two years later, the state of Missouri's request to be granted unitary status is denied in part. While the court grants it unitary status with respect to extracurricular activities, it remains under court supervision with respect to educational outcomes, assignment of students, faculty, facilities, and transportation.)

Wyoming's Supreme Court issues its opinion in *Campbell County School District v. State of Wyoming* (907 P.2d 1238). The court finds that unconstitutional differences in educational opportunities arise directly from funding disparities among Wyoming's forty-nine school districts. The legislature is directed to devise and develop policies that will guarantee each student in the state a quality education and to provide the necessary funding to ensure that these policies are properly implemented.

1996

Sheff v. O'Neil, 678 A.2d 1267 (Conn. 1996), is heard by Connecticut's Supreme Court. The court holds that the socioeconomic and racial segregation of students attending Hartford Public Schools has adversely affected their academic performance. In its decision, the court reverses a lower court ruling and orders the other coordinate branches to identify and implement appropriate remedial measures.

The second National Governors' Summit is held. At the conclusion of the summit, the governors decide that by 1998, their states will put in place (a) tough academic standards; and (b) an assessment system for measuring students' mastery of these standards. The business community pledges strong support for the governors' agenda.

1997

Alabama's Supreme Court affirms in *Alabama Coalition for Equity Inc. v. Hunt*, CV-91–0117, the earlier ruling of the circuit court in 1993 and gives the legislature until January 1998 to adopt a reform plan.

Disparities in funding education are reviewed by the Alaska Supreme Court. The court concurs with an earlier lower court decision that plaintiffs failed to show that there were disparities in educational opportunities based on perceived differential treatment of rural and urban districts (*Matanuska-Susitna Borough School District v. State of Alaska*, Supreme Court No. 5–5513.).

Ohio's structure of funding schools is held to be unconstitutional by that state's Supreme Court in 1997 in a 4–3 decision (*DeRolph v. State of Ohio*, 677 N.E. 2d 733). The decision is stayed for twelve months while the trial court evaluates the legislature's response to an earlier decision in 1994, which had also held that the system was unconstitutional.

A class action suit (*Hornbeck v. Somerset County Board of Education,* 458A.2d 758, Md. 1983) brought on behalf of students in Baltimore is settled. The suit claims that students attending Baltimore public schools were denied a thorough and efficient education because of inadequate resources. The settlement, which involves the governor, legislature, state board of education, superintendent of schools, and the plaintiffs, calls for the development of a reform plan similar to Chicago's and the infusion of additional aid.

New Hampshire's system for funding public education is ruled as unconstitutional in *Claremont v. Governor* 703 A.2d 1353. The court rules that education is a fundamental right and that the state has a right to provide a constitutionally adequate public education. The Supreme Court holds that education in many communities lacks constitutional adequacy and affirms the legislature's responsibility to establish standards that comport with constitutional requirements.

In *Leandro v. North Carolina* 488 S.E.2d 249 (N.C. 1997), the North Carolina Supreme Court holds that the state's constitution guarantees each child an adequate education. The court uses outcome-oriented standards to define adequacy. (Plaintiffs in this case had lost an earlier equity claim in the mid-1980s. In the lawsuit filed in 1995, they abandoned equity issues and focused primarily on issues related to adequacy.)

Vermont's Supreme Court rules in *Brigham v. Vermont,* 692 A.2d 384 (Vt. 1997), that the heavy reliance on property taxes to fund schools and the disparities that this causes in educational opportunities throughout the state violates the state's constitution's equal protection clause.

1998

In *Texas v. United States,* 118 S. Ct. 1257 (1998), the court rules that the Texas State Department of Education does not have to obtain federal permission to implement the monitoring elements of the Texas Education Code in underperforming school districts.

The New Jersey Supreme Court in *Abbott v. Burke* (V), No. A-155-97, establishes a set of far-reaching remedies to redress issues of inadequacy in the state's thirty special needs districts. The remedies focus on early childhood education, whole school reform, school based-management, parity funding, and facilities improvement.

Alaska's legislature passes a law that changes the way funding is divided among Alaska's school districts. The law results in a substantial redistribution of funds from rural to urban school districts.

Proliferation of Charter School Acts occur throughout the mid- to late 1990s. By the end of the decade, slightly more than two-thirds of the states have passed charter school legislations.

2002

The No Child Left Behind Act is passed into law, substantially redefining the role of federal, state, and local school systems in education. The act establishes guidelines for accountability, creating flexibility at the state and local levels, options for parents of children from disadvantaged backgrounds, strengthening teacher quality, promoting English proficiency, and increasing funding for reading.

The U.S. Supreme Court in *Zelman v. Simmons-Harris* narrowly reverses an appeals court ruling that Cleveland, Ohio's, voucher program is unconstitutional. The court holds that the voucher program was established for valid secular reasons and does not promote or inhibit religion.

2003

The New York Court of Appeals in *Campaign for Fiscal Equity v. State* rules that all children attending schools in the state of New York are entitled to a meaningful high school education. The 4–1 decision overturns an earlier ruling by an intermediate appellate court that declared that the state was constitutionally required to provide students with an education that covered the skills taught between the eight and ninth grades. (In March 2004 the state-appointed commission on education reform estimates that providing a sound basic education based on the June 2003 decision to every child in the state will cost annually an additional $2.5 billion to $5.6 billion.)

Table 3.1

Key Court, Legislative, and Federal Educational Decisions and Policies: 1954–2003

Year	Decision
1954	*Brown v. Board of Education of Topeka*
1964	Civil Rights Act
1965	Elementary and Secondary Education Act
1973	*San Antonio Independent School District v. Rodriguez* (Texas)
1973	*Robinson v. Cahill* (New Jersey)
1975	Individuals with Disabilities Act
1976	*Serrano v. Priest* (California)
1978	*Pauley v. Kelly* (West Virginia)
1982	*Pyler v. Doe* (Texas)
1982	*Board of Education, Levittown Union Free School District v. Nyquest* (New York)
1983	*Hornbeck v. Somerset County Board of Education* (Maryland)
1983	publication of *A Nation at Risk*
1983	Minnesota school choice program gains support
1988	Amendment to the Title 1 Program (Hawkins-Stafford Amendment)
1989	*Rose v. Council for Better Education* (Kentucky)
1989	first National Governors' Summit on Education
early 1990s	national systemic reform movement
early 1990s	burgeoning charter school legislation
1990	Kentucky Reform Act
1992	*Carrolton-Farmers v. Edgewood Independent School District* (Texas)
1992	*Freeman v. Pitts* (Georgia)
1993	*Alabama Coalition for Equity v. Hunt*
1994	Goals 2000 Educate America Act
1994	*Unified School District No. 229 v. Kansas*
1995	*Missouri v. Jenkins*
1995	*Campbell County School District v. State of Wyoming*
1996	*Sheff v. O'Neil* (Connecticut)
1996	second National Governors' Summit on Education
1997	*Alabama Coalition for Equity Inc. v. Hunt*
1997	*Matanuska-Susitna Borough School District v. State of Alaska*
1997	*DeRolph v. State of Ohio*
1997	*Hornbeck v. Somerset County Board of Education* (Maryland)
1997	*Claremont v. Governor* (New Hampshire)
1997	*Leandro v. North Carolina*
1997	*Brigham v. Vermont*
1998	*Texas v. United States*
1998	*Abbott v. Burke* (New Jersey)
2002	No Child Left Behind Act
2002	*Zelman v. Simmons-Harris*
2003	*Campaign for Fiscal Equity v. State* (New York)

Chapter Four

❧ Legislative Formulations of Remedies

The role of the courts in determining educational policies raises a number of legal, political, and policy questions. For example, questions related to the potential impact of court decisions on constitutional structures, educational policy control, majoritarian interests, and the collective good have been all addressed. These questions are inextricably linked with our understanding of the coordinate branches' response to court-issued remedies that seek to redress the abridgement of a constitutional right. Decisions rendered by federal as well as state courts that implicate major institutional reforms at the state level have historically confronted opposition from the legislative and executive branches. For example, the *Brown v. Board of Education* decision that sought to put an end to de jure segregation faced fierce resistance in many southern and northern states. Similarly, case history on penal and mental health reforms reveals legislative inertia in response to court-ordered remedies (Frug 1978).

In light of past rulings and legislative responses, can the courts force the coordinate branches to remedy instances of constitutional abridgement? As discussed in the preceding chapters, opinions are split on the appropriate role of the courts in social policy setting. One line of argument suggests that in instances where the legislative and executive branches of government have failed either wittingly or unwittingly to safeguard the constitutional rights of the body politic, courts have the constitutional responsibility to ensure that judicial relief is provided. Supporters of this position see an activist judiciary that relies both on the use of traditional and nontraditional judicial tools as necessary for ensuring that the democratic principles on which the society is founded are not compromised by failures on the part of the legislative and executive branches. Juxtaposed with this viewpoint is one that calls for courts to exercise restraint by demonstrating a willingness to defer to the other coordinate branches on matters that are clearly under the purview of these branches. Proponents of judicial restraint suggest that courts lack legitimacy in many social policy areas. Judicial intrusion into these policy areas therefore tends to create a constitutional and political conundrum. Judicial restrainists argue that courts should adhere strictly to a principle of decisional minimalism in cases involving social policy, especially if these cases are potentially controversial (Sunstein 1996). By adhering to the principle of decisional minimalism and narrowly tailoring their opinions, courts leave room for democratic dialogue to occur, and for the other coordinate branches to meaningfully participate in the establishment of social policy. Unquestionably, the stark differences in opinions on the appropriate role of the courts are ideologically and normatively based, and their resolutions are likely to remain illusive.

Over the past fifty years, courts at both the federal and state levels have through their decisions profoundly shaped the landscape of public education. The *Brown v. Board of Education* decision represents the pivotal turning point in this history. Although the federal judiciary has rendered several landmark decisions such as the *Brown* decision, it is at the state level that the effects of court decisions on education policy have been most strongly felt and debated. As we have discussed, state courts have been interjected quite visibly into the area of school finance with the educational clauses that are enshrined in many state constitutions, rendering at least facially the justiciability of school finance issues.

Scrutiny of school finance cases reveals that in virtually all states, courts have been asked to wrestle with this policy issue. The education clauses on which many of these cases are argued are not, however, without inherent difficulties. Their language is nebulous, and even when confronted with parallel clauses, courts in different states have arrived at dissimilar rulings. In fact, the courts are frequently called upon to craft specific and enforceable meanings from these essentially vague educational clauses (Gillette 1996).

Some state courts have questioned the justiciability of school finance issues. These courts have refused to hear these cases on the ground that the legislative branch is the best venue for addressing them. They are also disinclined to concur with plaintiffs' claims that education represents a fundamental right under their state's constitution. Moreover, even if a court consents to hear a school finance claim it may still arrive at a similar conclusion, as can be seen in *City of Pawtucket v. Sundlun*, 662 A.2d 40 R.I. (1990), in Rhode Island.

School finance cases thus raise important issues of interbranch relationship. Specifically, these issues pivot on important constitutional concepts such as the separation of power doctrine, the political question doctrine, the question of majoritarian accountability, and features of the legislative process. These issues either singularly or in their combined net effect help to explain the legislative and executive branches' likely dispositions toward court decisions to effectuate an adequate remedy for violations of state educational clauses. The many rounds of challenges to school finance remedies in several states—for example, New Jersey and Texas—underscore the difficulties that plaintiffs in general, and the courts in particular, have in securing legislative compliance with court decisions for constitutional relief. However, it should be understood that there are other equally important political processes that help contribute to the actualization of constitutional redress of school finance cases. In particular, the degree to which plaintiffs can successfully leverage politically favorable court decisions by mobilizing public and legislative support can help to secure legislative compliance. This issue was discussed in Chapter 2 but will be taken up in greater depth in subsequent chapters.

SEPARATION OF POWER DOCTRINE

The principle of separate spheres of responsibility and unique power among the branches of government can be traced to the writings of the French philosopher Montesquieu, who viewed the separation of power as important to the cause of liberty. The republican form of government, which characterizes the American society, is based on this principle, and it plays a critical role in influencing the structure and interpretation of not only the U.S. Constitution but the state constitutions as well. Under the doctrine of separate power, power and responsibility are distributed among the three major branches of government: the executive, legislative, and judiciary. In theory the separation of power doctrine seeks to constitutionally curb the exercise of excess power by any one of the three. The division of responsibility among the three branches further serves to limit the degree of encroachment of any one branch upon the other. The duties of the legislature are to enact laws, the executive to carry out these laws, and the judiciary to ensure that the constitution and individual rights are protected. However, the judiciary does have the power to decide whether an action on the part of either the legislative or executive branch is unconstitutional, and upon review can overturn such legislation.

State legislatures are given important constitutional responsibilities for education. As we have seen, these responsibilities are enumerated in the states' educational clauses, and they vary across states with respect to the burden of the affirmative duties that are placed upon the legislature. Because education is a state function, and because states have responsibilities for public school financing and educational policy setting, judicial intervention in educational matters tends to raise concerns about the constitutional provisions for separation of powers, and whether there is any constitutional legitimacy for courts to intercede not only in issues related to education but other major public policy areas as well.

In the *Rodriguez* decision, the United States Supreme Court reasoned that the state legislature's efforts at dealing with school finance issues in Texas should be treated with respect. The Court also noted that educational policy is an area in which it lacked specialized knowledge and experience, and cautioned against any "premature interference with the informed judgments made at the state and local levels." These sentiments are echoed in some state court decisions on school finance cases. For example, the Illinois Supreme Court in its decision on an educational adequacy claim opined, "courts may not legislate in the field of public education any more than they may legislate in any other area" (quoted in Blanchard 1998, 239). In January 2002, Alabama's Supreme Court in a 7–1 decision ruled that decisions about how to adequately and fairly fund all of the state's school systems fall under the legislative and executive branches of government, and that courts should not be involved in making these decisions. This ruling was predated by a 1993 ruling by a lower court that found the system of funding public education in Alabama to be unconstitutional, and earlier decisions by the state's highest court affirming the lower court's decision.

Although some courts may recognize education as a state function, as we have seen, they nevertheless have asserted themselves in the debates on what constitutes an adequate education. These courts' decisions might not have resulted in a total usurpation of their respective legislatures' responsibilities, but they have required their legislatures to develop policies that comport with the constitutional meaning of their respective educational clauses.

POLITICAL QUESTION DOCTRINE

At issue is whether a matter remanded to the courts passes the political question doctrine. Essentially, this doctrine holds that some issues are political in nature and their resolution lies with the political branches, not the judicial. The nonjusticiability of a political question is thus closely linked with the separation of power doctrine discussed previously. In determining whether a case involves a political question, the Supreme Court in *Baker et al. v. Carr et al.,* 369 U.S. 186, 209 (1962), outlined six formulations, four of which seem appropriate in the context of this discussion. The court stated that it must be demonstrated that one or more of the following applies: (1) textually the issue is constitutionally committed to a coordinate political department, (2) judicial discoverable and manageable standards for its resolution do not exist, (3) there is a likely impossibility of a court arriving at an independent resolution without exhibiting a lack of respect to one of the coordinate branches of government, and (4) there is an unusual need for unquestioning adherence to a political decision already made. The court noted parenthetically that the mere presence of a political question does not mean a dismissal for nonjusticiability. However, if it can be demonstrated that one or more of the above formulations is inextricably interwoven into a case, dismissal may be warranted.

Some scholars and courts have argued that education reform presents a political question and as such falls outside the proper scope of judicial relief, since textually education is constitutionally committed to the coordinate branches. Education reform and particular school finance issues are viewed as *policy issues* rooted in politics and as politically unjusticiable matters that are ill suited for judicial review. But there are at least two counterarguments that one could reasonably raise to support an alternative conclusion. First, in some states, judges are elected and thus are the subjects of majoritarian influences. Second, although education policy constitutionally falls under the purview of the legislative coordinate branch, the mere fact that the right to an education is contained in many state constitutions implies that in instances when this right is violated, the seeking of judicial relief is constitutionally appropriate and the exercise of state judicial review to decide questions on citizens' right to an education is warranted.

This line of argument is similar to that raised by the Supreme Court in *Baker et al. v. Carr et al.*, in which the court cited several instances when judicial intervention is appropriate when the legislative and executive branches in either fulfilling their constitutional responsibilities or in their failure to fulfill a constitutional duty have violated a constitutional right. The court cited cases in foreign affairs, validity of enactments, and the status of Indian tribes as all instances in which political questions were not beyond the reach of judicial cognizance.

Debatable is whether doctrines on the separation of power and political question doctrines ought to play a weaker role in state jurisprudence in contrast to their role in federal jurisprudence. Blanchard (1998) asserts that these principles function quite differently in state contexts than in the federal contexts, noting that state judiciaries' traditional role as protector of individual rights over majoritarian "tyranny" lessens the potency of arguments against judicial review of school finance issues that are based on the separation of power and political question doctrines. Cover (2002), writing on the relative merit of state courts' involvement in adjudicating educational claims, notes that a number of factors make these courts more suitable for interpreting educational rights than federal courts. Among these are a positive rights tradition in state constitutions, amendment processes, and popular accountability.

MAJORITARIAN ACCOUNTABILITY

The democratic system of government on which American society is founded is based on the notion of majoritarian rule and accountability. The legislature as an elected body is beholden (theoretically at least) to the body polity, which is responsible for their election; and individual legislatures tend to represent the interests of their constituents. Education is a highly conflictual policy area, and redistributive practices in particular tend to heighten the tension between groups that have little political influence and those with strong influences. The increasing legalization of educational issues within states has increased this tension. More and more courts are being called upon to protect the rights of politically marginal groups. Many school finance claims in which the courts have become embroiled have sought to redistribute educational resources to economically marginal groups in order to ensure that these groups' constitutional right to an education is secured.

However, as McUsic (1991) observes, "winning in the court is not the same as winning in the classroom" (p. 315). Legislators tend to be influenced by majoritarian opinions, in particular those that emanate from their constituents. Unpopular court decisions that affect educational policy because of their countermajoritarian undertones may be met with stiff opposition from the legislature and those members of the public who are overrepresented in the political processes in their states. Courts themselves, as it has been pointed out, may also be subjects of majoritarian influence. Unlike federal judges, who are appointed, several states require their judges to be selected through the electoral process; and in those states where judges are appointed, state judges come up for review. It is plausible to argue that judges in their decisions may be somewhat influenced by majoritarian concerns—especially those judges who are elected. Unpopular judicial decisions could lead to electoral defeat for those who author these decisions. This creates a dilemma for state jurisprudence. Legitimation of judicial intervention in educational policy, while being enhanced in states where judges are elected, also constrains judicial decisionmaking since "the more legitimacy judges enjoy to enforce a constitutional claim, the less likely they will be able to shape—rather than just be shaped by—public opinion" (*Harvard Law Review* 1991, 1090).

Yet in spite of majoritarian constraints, many state courts using various judicial tools have issued school finance decisions and fashioned judicial remedies that have challenged education policies within their states.

LEGISLATIVE PROCESS

Why has there been a difficulty in securing adequate legislative response to court-sanctioned remedies? The discussion on majoritarian influence helps to explain why plaintiffs in spite of success in the courts still are unable to secure legislative compliance. Several other explanations can also be offered. First, the legislative process itself is one that is seen to thwart the efforts of less powerful citizens. It has been shown that the greatest influence upon state legislatures comes from those citizens who are wealthy and who are able to wield significant political power. This tendency occurs in spite of the democratic principles upon which our society is founded. Citizens and groups from poor communities or who belong to historically disenfranchised groups are less likely to be represented in the political processes of their states. Even when they do have representation, their political representatives are likely to have lower levels of political incorporation into the major political processes of the legislative body than those from wealthier communities and dominant social groups.

School finance claims are usually brought on behalf of students living in poor communities. These students and their families are unable to exercise the same degree of political influence as their counterparts in wealthier communities. Because their political influence is weak, their ability without a broad-based political consensus to compel the legislative body to comply with judicial remedies is likely to be constrained.

A second feature of the legislative process that tends to militate against successful compliance with the judiciary decision to provide constitutional relief in school finance claims derives from the nature of the remedies themselves. The history of school finance litigation has shown that increased taxation as a means of solving fiscal inequities has been an unpopular policy in several states. State legislators from wealthy communities are disinclined to promote policies that will invoke the ire of their constituencies. According to public choice theory, public officials in their decisionmaking are influenced by incentives, and they seek to maximize their political returns from any given decision (Gillette 1996). As locally elected officials, legislators view as disincentives policies that counter the wishes of their constituents and polices that are likely to threaten their political capital. Thus this very structural aspect of the legislative institution can serve as a barrier to developing statewide responses to highly conflictual educational issues, of which school finance is one example (Heise 1998). Even so, it has been suggested that it is precisely because of this barrier that judicial intervention is necessary.

Gillette (1996) points out that the political market failure that is brought about because of this structural feature of the legislature may require the action of an outside force—the judiciary—in order to prompt legislative action. Absent judicial intervention, the legislative body may remain complacent in finding solutions to statewide educational problems. Gillette suggests that legislators who might have been willing to engage in school finance reform but who were reluctant out of fear of a backlash from their constituents might be more inclined to do so under the umbrella of a judicial mandate. According to Gillette, this enables these legislators to avoid the electoral brickbats of their constituents.

The following section examines the responses of the legislature in five states to court-ordered educational reform. These states, Alabama, Kentucky, New Jersey, Ohio, and Texas, represent contrasting cases of legislature activism versus inertia and defiance. The states also differ in the process that is used to select state judges. For example, judges in Alabama are elected, whereas in New Jersey the governor appoints state judges. The five states also present interesting illustrative instances of the important role that political mobilization—or the lack of mobilization, led by key transacting organizations such as advocacy groups—plays in securing legislative compliance with judicial remedies.

STATE LEGISLATIVE RESPONSE

Alabama

Alabama is an interesting study of how the intersection of gubernatorial politics, special interests, and constitutional constraints can lead to the derailment of educational reform. Alabama's school finance claim falls under the third wave of school finance litigation. In 1991 a statewide class of schoolchildren brought an adequacy and equity claim against the state. The complaint alleged that these students' right to an adequate and equitable education was abridged by the system of school financing. The claim was brought on behalf of students in property-poor school districts by the Alabama Coalition for Equity (ACE), a nonprofit corporation composed of twenty-five school systems and individual parents and schoolchildren, and the American Civil Liberties Union (ACLU), both of which sought declaratory and injunctive relief from the alleged constitutional and statutory violations. In the summer of 1992, the consolidated cases *Alabama Coalition of Equity Inc. v. Hunt* and *Harper v. Hunt* were brought to trial in the circuit court in Montgomery County. The court bifurcated the claim into two parts: a liability phase and the remedial phase. The plaintiffs' claims were based on two arguments: first, that educational opportunity in Alabama was inequitable as evidenced by system-wide disparities in opportunities; and second, that education was inadequate on virtually all measures of adequacy, including the state's own measures. Indeed, at the time the complaint was brought, the Alabama public school system was at the bottom in national rankings on almost all educational indicators.

The deplorable state of public education in Alabama was acknowledged by all parties. In fact, many of the defendants in the case—the lieutenant governor, the speaker of the state House of Representatives, the state superintendent, and members of the state board of education, with the exception of Governor Guy Hunt and the state finance director—concurred with the plaintiffs' contention that the system of education lacked adequacy and was inequitable. These defendants were to subsequently join with the plaintiffs in challenging the constitutionality of Alabama's system of public education.

That public education in the state was in a state of crisis was irrefutable. By 1991, when the claim was filed, Alabama ranked forty-ninth among the states in the percentage of students who graduated after twelve years of school; almost half of the adult population lacked a high school diploma; almost half of all students were enrolled in remedial programs; and of the 700,000 students enrolled in the system, more than 100,000 who were eligible for special education were not provided with adequate services. Infrastructural support to ensure an adequate education was also lacking. For example, school facilities were substandard in several counties. Many counties had schools with leaking roofs, septic tank overflow, insect infestations, and inadequate lighting. In addition, curriculum and textbooks were outdated, and course offerings, especially in math and science, were out of compliance with the state's own standards and requirements that were set forth in the Alabama Education Improvement Act of 1991 (Diffenderfer 1996).

None of these facts were disputed by the defendants. In fact, Governor Hunt noted that Alabama had one of the highest dropout rates in the nation—35 percent. The governor in his deposition also indicated that many students graduated from the system unprepared for college. According to his deposition, more than 40 percent of all graduates from the public schools required remedial assistance prior to the beginning of college level work (Morgan, Cohen and Hershkoff 1995).

Many of these problems were directly linked to the state's failed minimum foundation aid program. Up to 1993, funding of Alabama's public school was governed by the Minimum Program Fund Statute of 1935. In 1939, the legislature froze the local tax effort, which remained unadjusted for over fifty years (Berman and Dunphy 1998). By the time Alabama's school equity and adequacy claim was heard by the circuit court, funding for Alabama's school system remained well below a level that would ensure educational adequacy, and the disparities between communities to raise local funds for schools had widened. Thus, whereas wealthy school districts' local contribution to schooling averaged about $2,200 per student, poor school districts' local share averaged around $150 per pupil (Berman and Dunphy 1998). Moreover, by 1991, almost 60 percent of disbursed state aid occurred outside of the foundation plan.

Indubitably, the failure of the foundation plan was inextricably interwoven with Alabamian politics. By disregarding local property wealth in the disbursement of state aid, the legislature was able to fund at a higher level wealthier communities, which used the aid for fringe benefits and instructional supplies. Funding for children with disabilities was also problematic. State funding for special education was based on total pupil enrollment and not on the number of special education students. This meant that funding bypassed individual students' needs, with schools with large numbers of special education student populations receiving less funding per disabled student than schools with smaller numbers of special education students but with an overall larger student population.

In 1991, Judge Reese took over the case from Judge Monteil, who lost a bid for reelection in 1990. In 1993 the court's liability decision, rendered by Reese, favored the plaintiffs (*ACE v. Hunt,* 1993 WL 204083 (Ala. Cir. Ct. Montgomery County, Apr. 1, 1993). However, in 1991 the court had declared that the 1956 amendment (Amendment 111) to the Alabama constitution, which stated that nothing in the constitution should be construed as creating or recognizing any right to education or training at public expense, was "void ab initio" in its entirety and violated the Fourteenth Amendment. This state constitutional amendment had been fueled by desegregation concerns, which were awakened by the *Brown vs. Board of Education* decision. By issuing this ruling, the way was paved for the court to determine whether the system of public school funding was in violation of the state's educational clause. The court held that Article I, Sections 1, 6, 13, and 22, and Article XIV, Section 256, of the constitution of the state of Alabama had guaranteed to all Alabama school-aged children, including children with disabilities, the right to attend school in a liberal system of public schools with substantially equitable and adequate educational opportunities.

Moreover, the court ruled that the constitution had imposed an affirmative responsibility on the legislature: (1) to establish, organize, and maintain the system of public schools; (2) to ensure that the system of public schools extend throughout the state; (3) to ensure that the public schools are free and open to all schoolchildren regardless of the wealth of the communities in which the schoolchildren reside; and (4) to ensure that adequate educational opportunities consist of a minimum of an education that provides students with the opportunity to attain sufficient oral and written communication skills; sufficient knowledge of economic, social, and political systems; sufficient math and scientific skills; sufficient understanding of governmental processes; sufficient self-knowledge; sufficient understanding of the arts; sufficient training for the world of work; and sufficient support and guidance so that every student feels a sense of self-worth.

Based on these constitutional requirements, the facts presented in the case, and the testimony of expert witness, Judge Reese concluded that there was sufficient factual evidence to rule that the system of public education in Alabama violated the constitutional and statutory rights of the plaintiffs. He enjoined the state to establish, organize, and maintain a system of public schools that comported with the Constitution. When Judge Reese handed down the decision at the conclusion of the liability phase, Governor Hunt faced charges on misuse of public funds and was subsequently forced to step down. Democratic lieutenant governor Jim Folsom Jr. succeeded Hunt for the remainder of the term. Governor Folsom who had sided with the plaintiffs during the trial, demonstrated strong support for the reformation of the educational system. However, between the liability and implementation of the remedies, gubernatorial politics resulted once again in a change of leadership in the state, which threw school reform into a state of upheaval.

In January 1993, Judge Reese established October 1 as the deadline for the remedial phase. The judge ordered both sides to work on a remedial plan that would address the liability order. Defendants who during the liability phase had aligned with the plaintiffs now realigned themselves with the other defendants in the case. Between January and October both sides attempted to come up with a set of remedies that would reform Alabama's ailing public school system. The effort was spearheaded by the A+ Coalition for Better Education. With broad-based representation from different sectors of the community, the coalition had in 1992 drafted a plan titled "A Blueprint for Successful Alabama Schools." During 1993 the organization cosponsored, along with the Alabama PTA, the Alabama Association of School Boards, and the local chambers of commerce, several regional meetings in Alabama's four largest cities (A+ Coalition for Better Education 2003). To gain additional feedback, the organization also held a series of town meetings around the state. These meetings garnered strong support from the public, press, and business sectors.

A+ Coalition mobilizing activities were met with a countermovement that brought together various special-interest groups in the state, including religious organizations and the Alabama Farmers Association. This group voiced strong opposition to the proposals contained in the "Blueprint" and embarked upon developing its own agenda for reforming public education in the state. In addition, the Alabama Teachers Association (ATA)—an initial supporter of the reform measures included in the blueprint—by summer 1993 withdrew its support when ATA's head challenged incumbent Governor Folsom for the Democratic nomination. Educational reform in Alabama thus became inextricably caught up in gubernatorial and special-interest politics.

In spite of the turmoil, reformists met the October deadline imposed by Judge Reese. Thus in October 1993, the negotiated remedial order received sanction from the court in *ACE v. Folsom*, Nos. CV-90–883-R, CV-91–0117-R (Ala. Cir. Ct. Montgomery County, Oct. 22, 1993). The remedies, which mirrored earlier remedies adopted by the state of Kentucky in its own response to the unconstitutionality of its system of public education, included performance-based education, mechanisms for accountability at all levels, professional development, decentralization in decisionmaking, early childhood programs, minimization of nonschool barriers to learning, inclusive special education programs, equitable and adequate funding, technology-based learning for students and teachers, and sound infrastructure.

The remedies were drafted into a legislation called the Alabama First Plan. This plan, which incorporated many of the suggestions in the A+ Coalition's "Blueprint," was the fruition of a special task force on educational reform that was convened by Governor Folsom. The total cost of Alabama First was $2 billion. From the beginning, the Alabama First Plan was shrouded in controversy. Legislators who were not involved in the negotiations that led to the adoption of the remedies were tentative in their support of the legislation. Over time, splintering of support for Alabama First became pronounced as various politicians and special-interest groups began to challenge the reform package as noted by the A+ Coalition:

> Traditional special interests and politicians jockeying for votes began to play on the public's natural anxiety about change. Opponents from the far right clouded the debate by making baseless and outrageous claims. Education associations and unions misled teachers and administrators by distorting tenure issues. Groups that traditionally oppose property taxes fanned the flames of opposition by incorrectly claiming the reform plan would cost an average Alabama family over $1,000 a year. Politics became the driving force, and helpful dialogue about how best to improve our schools became impossible. Support for the Alabama First Plan began to fade. (A+ Coalition for Education 2003, 4–5).

Although the plan was approved twice by the Alabama Senate, it was rejected twice in the Alabama House. The defeat of Alabama First was orchestrated by powerful state organizations such as the Alabama Educational Association, the Alabama Farmers' Association, the conservative interest group the Eagle Forum, and the Christian Coalition. These groups were encouraged in their opposition to the plan by the election of Fob James, a Republican, to the governorship. James was vehemently against education reform both at the state and national level, deeming such efforts to be nothing more than mere social engineering (Carr and Furhman 1999, 159). During his race for the governorship James ran on an antitax and antieducational reform platform, promising to overturn, if elected, Judge Reese's decision. James won the gubernatorial race, and in 1994, the Alabama State House in Senate Resolution 97 requested an advisory opinion from the Supreme Court of Alabama as to whether Section 1 of the Senate Bill 607 findings that the legislature is required to provide schoolchildren with substantially equitable and adequate educational opportunities was constitutionally required. The legislature essentially wanted to know if it was required to follow the order of the Circuit Court of Montgomery County. The State Supreme Court in an advisory opinion answered in the affirmative.

Objection to Alabama First was made on several grounds based on the ideological position of those who opposed the legislation. The Alabama Farmers' Association and the Christian right both rejected any plan to raise taxes and were opposed to the outcomes-based components of Alabama First. The teachers' union was concerned about tenure and accountability issues. Parents, students, and "taxpayers" from wealthy communities also leant their voices to those opposing the plan by initiating legal challenges to the liability order and remedies.

In March 1995, Governor James secretly presented his own plan for remedying Alabama's failing school system to Judge Reese. James's plan was subsequently passed by the legislature in June 1995. The plan had two parts: Bill 466, which established minimum curricular requirements and performance standards; and Bill 468, which introduced a new method of financing public education—the foundation approach—(Diffenderfer 1996). Under the new plan, all foundation aid is sent to the local board of education (LBE) for distribution to local districts. The LBEs are responsible for disbursing funds based on the following considerations: student and school needs, school populations, and the number of special education at-risk and vocational education students (Diffenderfer 1996, 200).

Since 1995, the Alabama State Supreme Court has made significant rulings that have impacted the tenor of school reform in the state. These rulings have been strongly influenced by the court' s expressed concern with judicial restraint, separation of power and the political question doctrines, and what it sees as the constitutional difficulties when the judiciary becomes implicated in school reform. In 1997 in *Ex Parte Governor Fob James,* No. 1950030, the court vacated the remedial order. In that decision the court opined that the circuit court engaged in judicial overreach when it ordered the legislative branch to implement a plan that would create an equitable system of school financing. In 2002 the court held that in its concern for judicial restraint (1) the equity funding case had reached its end, and (2) that because the responsibility for funding Alabama's public schools was entrusted to the legislature, it is the legislature, not the courts, from which further redress should be sought. Thus, it held that the equity funding case was dismissed (Supreme Court of Alabama, 1950030, 1950031, 1950240, 1950241, 1950408, and 1950409, May 2002).

Alabamians in September 2003 rejected a proposal that would have resulted in a major tax restructuring. The proposed tax-restructuring plan would have increased the tax burden on corporations and the wealthy while simultaneously decreasing taxes for the poor, in addition to expanding the sales tax base. The restructuring plan was seen as crucial in stemming the cuts that the public schools were subjected to in both 2002 and 2003 due to a shortfall in the state's budget. With the September defeat of the $1.2 billion tax restructuring plan, state school superintendent Ed Richardson issued this ominous warning: "I would say that we are dismantling public education in the state. You're going to see test scores start to go down, [and] the dropout rate start to go up" ("Alabama Voters Say 'No' to Tax Restructuring and More Education Funding," http://www.accessnet.org). More than a decade after Alabama's public school system was held to be unconstitutional, school reform that would ensure an equitable and adequate education for all of Alabama's public school students remains an illusive dream.

Kentucky

If Alabama's failure represents a case where special-interest politics, judicial disagreement, legislative defiance, and an unfavorable political context stymied educational reform, Kentucky provides us with just the opposite picture. Kentucky is frequently cited as an example where judicial activism and legislative will along with the political engagement and mobilization of the body politic resulted in the successful systemic reform of a state's public education system. Kentucky was also unique in that its racial context placed it in sharp contrast to Alabama and many of the other states in which school finance challenges have been raised (Carr and Fuhrman 1999). In states such as Alabama and New Jersey, school finance claims are inseparable from racial politics. The poor communities and school districts in both states are peopled by poor African Americans and, in the case of New Jersey, Hispanic students. As was noted in earlier chapters, these populations wield less political power and therefore have less influence on the legislature than do their wealthier counterparts. In Kentucky, however, race played a minor role in influencing reform politics, since racial minorities tended to be concentrated in the wealthier cities of the state (Carr and Fuhrman 1999). Consequently, school finance reform was not viewed as an attempt to redistribute monies from wealthier white communities to impoverished minority school districts, as were the cases in New Jersey and Alabama.

Up to 1989, Kentucky (like Alabama) had one of the worst systems of public education in the nation. On almost all national education indicators Kentucky ranked in the bottom quartile of the distribution. For example, Kentucky ranked fiftieth in adult literacy, forty-sixth in percentage of high school students going on to four-year colleges, fortieth in teacher-pupil ratio, fortieth in educational expenditures, and thirty-ninth in high school retention (*Rose v. Council for Better Education*, 790 S.W.2d 186; 189 Ky.). Similar to Alabama, Kentucky's political culture was historically marked by a stiff opposition to increase taxation and change (Pearce 1987).

Concerns about the woeful state of Kentucky's system of public education and the need for reform was expressed as early as 1984, when

Martha Layne Collins, the newly elected governor, proposed a school finance reform package that would have increased taxes as a means of providing additional funding to schools (Paris 2001). However, Governor Collins failed to garner enough legislative support for her proposed reforms, and the legislature subsequently rejected the plan. Discontentment with the system of public education began to foment in the community at the same time that the governor's proposal was rejected. Attempts to create a coalition of concerned school superintendents and school board members began in earnest in 1984. Led by the former chief budget officer for the Kentucky Department of Education, a college professor of school finance, and a lawyer, a group of about sixty-six school districts mostly from the rural areas of the state came together to strategize on pursuing possible litigation against the state of Kentucky. These districts not only lent their moral support to the reform movement but also helped to finance the movement, an act that would be subsequently challenged by the defendants in the case (Paris 2001). In May 1985, the movement was formally incorporated as the Council for Better Education, with support from not only poor communities but wealthier communities as well.

Parallel concerns about the state of education in Kentucky were also being expressed by a second group of citizens, although for slightly different reasons than those espoused by the Council for Better Education. The Pritchard Committee for Academic Excellence, named after its chair, Edward Prichard, was convened in 1980 to serve in an advisory capacity to the State Council on Higher Education. Its membership was drawn from the most influential sectors of the state, such as the business community and key civic organizations. The committee was convinced that the economic development of the state required substantive reform of the educational system. It held several outreach efforts that attempted to foster public dialogue around support for educational reform. These efforts made use of a variety of media, including town hall meetings.

In 1983 the committee organized itself into seven policy area subcommittees. The subcommittees were charged with making policy recommendations in the areas of teaching and teacher education, children and youth services, school finance, vocational education, secondary school reform, school effectiveness, and administration and leadership (Paris 2001). The policy recommendations from the work of the subcommittees were published in a document entitled "A Path to a Larger Life." The report was highly publicized in the state and was subsequently accepted into evidence in the suit *Rose vs. Council for Better Education* (Paris 2001). The report generated public pressure for reform. However, although the legislature agreed in 1985 to adopt some of the recommendations from the report, it failed to provide any sort of funding support out of fear of taxpayer backlash were it to raise taxes (Paris 2001).

Section 183 of Kentucky's constitution calls for the establishment of an efficient system of common schools throughout the state. National educational indicators as well as the findings of the Pritchard Committee revealed that this constitutional obligation went unmet. In 1988 in the Franklin Circuit Court, the Council for Better Education, joined in its claim by the boards of education of the Dayton and Harlan Independent School Districts, and the districts of Elliott, Know, McCreary, Morgan, and Wolfe Counties, filed a claim on behalf of the sixty-six member school districts against John A. Rose, president pro tempore of the Senate; Donald J. Blandford, speaker of the House of Representatives; the governor; the superintendent of public instruction, the state treasurer, and the state board of education and its individual members. The plaintiffs alleged that the system of school financing was inadequate; that too much emphasis was placed on local school board resources; that there were inadequacies, inequities, and inequalities throughout the state; and that the system of education that resulted from these inadequacies and inequities was inefficient and thus in violation of Section 183 of the constitution.

The plaintiffs sought a declaratory judgment against the system of public education, petitioning the trial judge to rule the system unconstitutional and inadequate, and to provide relief by requiring the General Assembly to enact appropriate legislation that would comport with the constitutional requirements of Section 183. In countering the plaintiffs' arguments, the defendants raised issues pertaining to the separation of power and political question doctrines, implying that the court had no legitimate jurisdiction over the case. In addition, the defendants cited several legislative efforts to reform the mechanisms of school financing—for example, the Minimum Foundation and the Power Equalization Programs—and to institute policies that were aligned with the spirit and intent of the constitution.

Evidence provided during the trial overwhelmingly demonstrated Kentucky's failed system of public education. For instance, comparative data examining Kentucky's performance against neighboring states (Ohio, Indiana, Illinois, Missouri, Tennessee, Virginia, and West Virginia) revealed that Kentucky ranked sixth with respect to per-pupil expenditures; sixth with salary for instructional staff, seventh on average classroom salary, seventh in the reliance on property taxes as a percentage of school revenues, and seventh on high school graduation rates.

Up until the time of the trial, the Kentucky legislature had demonstrated a checkered history in its handling of school finance issues. In 1930, the General Assembly passed a law that established an equalization fund that aimed to increase funding to districts with poor educational standards. However, in *Talbot v. Kentucky Department of Education*, 244 Ky. 826, 52 S.W.2d 727 (1932), the legislation was overturned on the basis that it violated Section 186 of the constitution, which required state funds to be appropriated on a per-capita basis. An amendment to Section 186 was adopted in 1941. This set equalization aid at 10 percent; in 1944 this was increased to 25 percent. In 1952, Section 186 was deleted from the constitution. With the elimination of Section 186, the General Assembly now had greater latitude in setting funding levels. The General Assembly established the Minimum Foundation Program, which required districts to levy a minimum real property tax of $1.10 per $100 of assessed value. The Minimum Foundation Program was challenged in court, and in 1965 the court of appeals ruled in favor of the plaintiffs, requiring the assessment of property on 100 percent of its fair cash value (*Russman v. Luckett*, 391 S.W.2d 694). However, the legislature in an attempt to avoid compliance with the court's decision enacted a rollback law. The effect of this bill was to freeze revenues. In 1976 the legislature enacted the Power Equalization Program, which had very little effect in correcting a situation that was made worse by the adoption of the rollback law. Although the legislature contended that the Power Equalization Program would result in more funding for the public schools, in actuality funding levels remained virtually unchanged.

When the case was brought to Judge Ray Corns, Kentucky's educational system was in crisis in many respects. Although there were significant problems in financing, it is instructive to note that the plaintiffs in the case were challenging the system not only on the grounds of inequities in financing but also in terms of educational adequacy. In May 1988, Judge Corns issued the first of three rulings. In his first, he ruled that Kentucky's system of funding public education was unconstitutional and discriminatory and that it violated the equal protection guarantees of Kentucky's constitution. Relying on an efficient common school system to be one characterized by substantial uniformity, substantial equality of financial resources, and substantial equal opportunity for all students, Judge Corns concluded that Kentucky's system of common schools was inefficient and lacking in both adequacy and uniformity. In the May 1988 ruling Judge Corn intimated that he would establish an advisory select committee to provide the court with an advisory opinion on school financing.

In June 1988, the court appointed five members to the select committee and gave the committee until September 15, 1988, to issue a report to the court. Judge Corns was careful to point out that the select committee would function solely in an advisory capacity and that he would take its recommendations under advisement in his preparation of a final judgment. The committee conducted public hearings and presented its report to Judge Corns by the September 15 deadline. The committee's report addressed general issues and principles in developing an efficient public school system. In October 1988, Judge Corns issued his final judgment.

Judge Corns incorporated certain principles of the select committee's report in his final judgment, wherein he elaborated upon his initial interpretation of an efficient common school system by noting that such a system should be "tax-supported, coordinated and provide a system of a free and adequate education to students throughout the state irrespective of fiscal capacity" (*Rose v. Council for Better Education,* 790 S.W.2d 186; 189 Ky.). The final judgment further elaborated on the prerequisite educational inputs that the system would need to ensure adequacy. These inputs were sufficient physical facilities, teachers, support personnel, accountability, supervision, and monitoring of personnel performance. Although the court had established the minimum educational inputs that it deemed necessary for the creation of an efficient system of common schools, it was careful in its order to recognize that the final authority for the creation and maintenance of this system rested with the General Assembly. Judge Corns conceded that the separation of power doctrine precluded him from issuing specific directives as to how Kentucky's schools were to be financed. However, he indicated that in order to ensure legislative compliance, the court would maintain continuing jurisdiction.

Two defendants from the General Assembly, the speaker of the House and the president of the Senate, appealed the circuit court decision of 1988. The appellants raised a number of issues. For example, they argued that the trial judge had erred in declaring that the school system was unconstitutional; that he had violated the separation of power constitutional provision; that the judge had erred when he required that expenses associated with the select committee work be paid by the Kentucky Department of Education; that the trial judge's definition of an efficient system did not comport with the state's educational clause; and that the Council for Better Education did not have legal authority to sue.

The Kentucky Supreme Court in its ruling in 1989 disagreed with several of the arguments raised by the appellants. It opined that the

Council for Better Education as a separate legally constituted organization and the local boards of education, which were part of its constituent membership, had a legal right to sue. Moreover, the court inferred—based on the comments of the original architects of the state's educational clause, legal precedents in case history, and evidence that was entered during the trial—that the General Assembly had failed to create a system of common schools that was efficient, and that the current system was as a consequence constitutionally invalid. The court's pronouncement on Kentucky's system of common schools can be summed up by its observation that

> lest there be any doubt the result of our decision is that Kentucky's entire system of common schools is unconstitutional. There is no allegation that only part of the common school is invalid, and we find no such circumstance. The decision applies to the entire sweep of the system . . . all its parts and parcels. This decision applies to the statues creating, implementing and financing the system and to all regulations pertaining thereto. This decision covers the creation of local school districts, school boards, and the Kentucky Department of Education to the Minimum Foundation Program and Power Equalization Program. It covers school construction and maintenance, teacher certification—the whole gamut of the common school system in Kentucky. (*Rose v. Council for Better Education,* 790 S.W.2d 186; 189 Ky.)

With regard to judicial deference to the coordinate branches for which the appellants argued there was constitutional support, the court ruled that although the trial judge did not encroach upon the legislature's responsibilities, as he did not direct the General Assembly to enact specific legislation, he did intrude upon legislative functioning when he required the legislature to report its progress to him. The court therefore reversed Judge Corn's decision on this issue. The court further held that the appointment of the select committee was improper and that Judge Corns should have relied upon the tools that were available to him in formulating a decision. The court, however, affirmed the trial court's position that the General Assembly must assume the responsibility for the establishment, maintenance, and funding of an efficient system of public education that exhibits the following:

- •◆ Free for all Kentucky's children
- •◆ Available to all Kentucky children
- •◆ Substantially uniform throughout the state

- Provide equal educational opportunities to all Kentucky children regardless of place or economic circumstances
- Is monitored by the General Assembly to assure that there is no waste, duplication, mismanagement, and political influence

The court held that such a system was necessary in order to enable all students in the state to have the opportunity to:

- Acquire sufficient oral and written communication skills that would assist them to function in a complex society
- Acquire sufficient knowledge of social, economic, and political systems that would enable their ability to make informed choices
- Understand governmental processes
- Acquire self-knowledge of his or her mental and physical conditions
- Develop grounding in the arts that would enable each student to develop an appreciation for his or her cultural and historical heritage
- Obtain sufficient training and preparation for advance training

A year after the court rendered its decision, Kentucky legislative and executive branches began to work cooperatively to develop a reform package that would be unprecedented in the history of school finance reform. This interbranch cooperation starkly contrasted with the legislative impasse that existed in 1987 and 1988, when the legislature and the governor failed to agree on a reform package that the governor had introduced during the 1988 regular session (Paris 2001). In response to the 1989 landmark court decision, the governor and legislature established the Task Force on Education Reform. The task force drew its membership from the legislature with eight members from each house and five other executive officials appointed by the governor (Block 2002). The task force divided itself into three subcommittees: curriculum, governance, and finance. The subcommittees held several public hearings in which national and local experts on educational reform, representatives of various interest groups, and ordinary citizens testified (Paris 2001). In April 1990, the Kentucky Legislature passed House Bill No. 940, Kentucky Education Reform Act (KERA). In accordance with the three subcommittees of the task force, the bill consisted of three parts: curriculum, governance, and finance. There was some legislative opposition to KERA. Opposition was leveled against the proposed sales tax increases, the additional burden placed on property-poor districts to attain a minimum level of local contribution, the exclusion of rank-and-file legislators in the decisionmaking process, and the breadth and speed of the proposed reforms (Bosworth 2001). The specifics of KERA and its implications for local school districts and schools will be elaborated upon in Chapter 5.

New Jersey

Court involvement in public education in New Jersey has been contentious and prolonged, and the state has one of the longest histories of school finance litigation in the nation. Unlike Kentucky and Alabama, whose economic and educational contexts prior to litigation placed them in the bottom rankings of all states, throughout its many legal school finance challenges New Jersey had and continues to have one of the highest per capita incomes in the country. In 1997, New Jersey's median income ranked second to Alaska, and in personal income per school-aged children, second only to Connecticut (Lindsay 1998). New Jersey also has one of the highest per-pupil expenditures on public education. For example, also in 1997, New Jersey had the highest adjusted per-pupil spending level, which was more that 47 percent higher than the national average (Lindsay 1998).

However, these figures mask the stark disparities in wealth, educational expenditures, educational opportunities, and educational outcomes that have inevitably arisen from the highly segregated nature of the more than six hundred communities in the state. New Jersey communities are marked by racial, social, and economic homogeneity; as an example, during the 1995–1996 school year, in Newark, the largest city in the state, of 628 students enrolled in prekindergarten only three were white (Orfield 1997).

Not surprisingly local capacity to adequately fund education varies widely from community to community. In the 1989–1990 school year, property-poor school districts, with an average school tax levy of $1.21, spent about $5,017 per pupil on general education programs (Firestone, Goertz, and Natriello 1997). In contrast, the per-pupil expenditure on general education programs by wealthier communities, with a school tax levy of $.60—or half that imposed by poorest communities—was $7,017, approximately $2,000 more than property-poor communities (Firestone, Goertz, and Natriello 1997). Such discrepancies in the ability among local communities to adequately fund their schools are correlated to differential levels of academic performance. For example, in 1995 only 43 percent of eleventh graders in property-poor districts were able to pass all three sections of New Jersey's high school graduation test, compared to 83 percent of all eleventh graders statewide (Lindsay 1998). Reform debates in the state have thus been dominated with concerns about fiscal inequities, lack of uniformity in educational adequacy, and racial politics.

In 1966 a young law clerk named Harold Ruvoldt wrote an article on a little-known 1875 amendment—Article VIII—to New Jersey's constitution (Method 2003). Article VIII affirms that the legislature shall "provide for the maintenance and support of a thorough and efficient system of free public schools for the instruction of all children in the State between the ages of five and eighteen years" (New Jersey State Constitution). Ruvoldt sought to challenge the constitutionality of the state's school financing scheme, and in 1970 he filed a claim against the state contending that the scheme was both inadequate and unconstitutional. The claim was entered on behalf of a young student (Kenneth Robinson) who resided in Jersey City, against Governor William Cahill, the treasurer of the state, the attorney general, the president of the state Senate, the speaker of the General Assembly, the commissioner of education, and the state board of education. The mayors and boards of education in East Orange, Jersey City, Paterson, and Plainfield joined the plaintiff. The township of Berlin in the county of Camden subsequently joined the Robinson case in lieu of proceeding with a similar claim.

Several amicus curiae were entered in support of the plaintiffs. The National Association for the Advancement of Colored People's (NAACP) Education Committee, the American Civil Liberties Union of New Jersey, and the staff attorney from the state office of the Legal Services Department of Community Affairs all supported the plaintiffs' challenge to the state's funding mechanism. Although the initial claim also sought relief from de facto discrimination based on race and color by seeking changes in district boundaries, this claim was subsequently severed from the case.

In 1972, Superior Court Judge Theodore Botter heard arguments from both sides in what came to be referred to as *Robinson v. Cahill*, 62 N.J. 473. Plaintiff attorneys argued that: (1) the state's statutory mechanism for funding elementary and secondary education by its overreliance on local property taxes had resulted in impermissible disparities between wealthy and poor districts; (2) education was a state function that must be afforded to all pupils on an equal basis; (3) whereas some districts enjoyed a thorough and efficient education, others did not; and (4) property owners in some districts were subject to discrimination. Although the defendants in the case concurred that there were disparities in educational spending in the state, they challenged the plaintiffs' contention that these disparities resulted in inequities in educational opportunities and outcomes.

However, evidence entered in the trial, including the results of the State Department of Education's own studies, indicated that differences in educational inputs were strongly related to variations in educational outputs. Furthermore, although the legislature had passed the Bateman Act in 1970, which had sought to provide incentive equalization and minimum support aid to all school districts, including wealthy districts, the absence of full funding resulted in its failure to significantly reduce funding inequities. Hence, Judge Botter held in 1972 that a thorough education was not afforded to all pupils in New Jersey, and that the state's statutory funding scheme failed to meet the state's constitutional standard of a thorough education, which he defined as one that represented more than a minimal or simply adequate education ((*Robinson v. Cahill*, 62 N.J.473; 303 A.2d 273). Moreover, he challenged the politics behind the Bateman Act, noting that there was no legitimate legislative purpose in giving wealthy districts state aid. Judge Botter concluded that the New Jersey system of financing public education violated the equal protection rights guaranteed by both the federal and state constitutions by imposing unequal burdens on taxpayers. Additionally, Judge Botter held that the statues governing the financing of public elementary and secondary schools were violative of the state's educational clause. He ordered the legislature to use state revenues raised by levies that were uniformly imposed to finance a thorough and efficient system of education.

Judge Botter's decision was appealed in 1973. The New Jersey Supreme Court upheld the trial court's finding that the constitutional demand for a thorough and efficient education was unmet by the state's statutory funding mechanism. Defining the constitutional problem primarily in terms of dollar input per pupil, the court reasoned that a system that places 67 percent of the burden for funding education on local districts, which varied in their tax base and in which state aid programs fail to neutralize local inequities, itself denies equal protection to the beneficiaries of that system. The court questioned whether the 1970 act, even if fully funded, would have satisfied the state's constitutional obligation to provide a thorough and efficient education. The court further observed that the state's failure to "clearly delineate the content of a constitutionally mandated educational opportunity coupled with its failure to design a state aid program that would compensate for local districts failure to reach that level had resulted in an educational system that reflected provincial rather than constitutional considerations" (*Robinson v. Cahill*, 62 N.J.473; 303 A.2d 273). The court gave the executive and legislative branches until December 31, 1974, to enact legislation that would be compatible with the constitution, with an effective date of July 1, 1975, for implementation.

Both the executive and legislative branches failed to meet the December 1974 deadline, and numerous motions for relief were filed on behalf of the plaintiffs with the court. However, concerns with separation of power issues prevented the court from directly tinkering with the then-existing statutory financing scheme. Instead, the court gave the legislature more time to correct the constitutional deficiencies through the adoption of new legislation. In 1975 the New Jersey legislature passed the Public School Education Act (Chapter 212). This act contained the following provisions: (1) an increase from 28 percent to 40 percent in the state's contribution to public school funding; (2) a revision to the guarantee tax base formula that would increase the number of districts covered; (3) an elaboration on the definition of the constitutional term "thorough and efficient" to include funds, facilities, teacher quality, curriculum goals, and support programs and services for educationally disadvantaged students; and (4) the creation of a system of accountability that relied on compliance monitoring.

Although the Public School Education Act called for increased state aid, it did not specify the sources from which these additional funds were to come. The political context and climate at the time posed insurmountable barriers to the full implementation of the act; and absent judicial intervention, in all probability the act would have remained unfunded. For example, in November 1975, voters rejected a bond issue that would have raised over $100 million in additional state funds, even though compliance with the funding statutes in the Public School Education Act would have been virtually impossible without new state revenue sources. Wealthy districts were opposed to any notions of redistributing funds from their communities to less affluent ones, and they were equally concerned with the implication of diminished home rule with an increased state presence in educational funding and monitoring. It should be understood that at the time of the *Robinson* decision, New Jersey politics was dominated by local control and weak state politics. Social policy was primarily a function of local government. Thus, the court's decision was viewed as a potential threat to educational governance in the state. The Democratic governor also faced stiff opposition from the Republican legislature, which was vehemently opposed to the introduction of a state income tax, a possible new source of revenue that was being proposed by the governor.

The executive and legislative branches' failure to act, and what the court saw as a confrontation between legislative inertia and a constitutional right, led the court to shut down the public schools in July

1976. In that same month, the legislature narrowly passed an income tax bill. The bill received the minimum votes needed for passing in the General Assembly and only one vote over the minimum in the Senate. The court concurred that facially the Public Education Act met the constitutional requirement for a thorough and efficient education.

Yet, in spite of the passage of the income tax bill and the court's acceptance of the Public Education Act as an effective remedy to the constitutional dilemma that *Robinson v. Cahill* sought to resolve, school reform in the state would not be easy, as attested to by the number of legal claims brought against the state after 1976 and the political fallout that several legislators were to experience. In reality the implementation of the Public Education Act did very little to minimize the disparities and improve parity between wealthy and poor districts. In fact, except for a short period in which it appeared that these disparities were being narrowed, the long-term trend in fiscal expenditures revealed a widening of the gap between these communities. In 1981 the Education Law Center, a nonprofit organization located in Newark, the state's largest city, decided to relitigate the case. This decision was based on the mounting evidence of continued disparities in funding, educational opportunities, and outcomes between property-poor and wealthy districts. The Education Law Center brought its claim on behalf of twenty students attending public schools in Camden, East Orange, Irvington, and Jersey City. Raymond Arthur Abbott, an eleventh grader, was listed as the main plaintiff, and Education Commissioner Edward Burke was listed as the first among several defendants against whom the case was brought. The case subsequently became a class action suit covering all similarly situated students in the twenty-eight poor urban school systems that were originally included in the *Robinson v. Cahill* decision.

In *Abbott v. Burke I* the plaintiffs argued that the constitutionality of the Public Education Act was suspect since there was evidence of continued disparities between property-rich and property-poor districts. The plaintiffs used the standards of the 1975 Bateman Act to identify areas of inequalities between poor urban school districts and wealthy school districts. The evidence showed that there were stark inadequacies when compared to wealthier communities in poor school districts in such areas as instruction, the breadth of program offerings, programs and services for special education students, the qualifications of school personnel, the quality of materials and supplies, and the monitoring of programs. Although the defendants conceded that these disparities existed, they laid the blame not on fiscal inequities but on the failure of these districts to effectively manage their respective local educational systems, as well as their failure to invoke the statutory remedial provisions in the 1975 act. Indeed, the Republican governor, Tom Kean, at the time was able to block the case going forward on just this point: the districts' failure to exhaust the administrative channels that were available for redressing their grievances. Although the complaint was filed in 1981, the case was heard only in 1988, after the New Jersey Supreme Court ruled that the proper venue was at the administrative judicial level (*Abbott v. Burke*, 100 N.J. 269, 495 A.2d 376 (1985)).

In 1988 the administrative law judge who presided over the case ruled that the Bateman Act as applied to these twenty-eight districts was unconstitutional because of its contribution to continued disparities between these districts and their wealthier counterparts (*Abbott v. Burke*, OALDKT.NO.EDU 5581–85). Judge Steven Lefelt concluded that students attending schools in the state's poorest communities did not receive an equal educational opportunity, but rather one that was determined by socioeconomic and geographic location (Walker and Gutmore 2000, 12). The commissioner of education and the state board of education strongly opposed Judge Lefelt's decision, arguing that the 1975 act was constitutional. They claimed that there was no evidence that a relationship existed between property wealth and per-pupil expenditure and that New Jersey's constitution only required students to be given an education that would ensure their ability to participate fully in the labor force.

In 1990 the New Jersey Supreme Court rendered its second Abbott decision (*Abbott v. Burke*, 119 N.J. 287, 575 A.2d 359 (1990)). In that decision, the court upheld Judge Lefelt's decision and ordered the legislative and executive branches to either amend the Bateman Act or introduce new legislation that would ensure parity. The court recommended that the determination of parity should be based on the average per-pupil expenditures in the state's 120 wealthiest and highest-achieving school districts. The court linked increased expenditures to adequate quality educational programs and offerings and issued specific directives to the State Department of Education to identify and implement programs and services that would meet the educational and social needs of students residing in poor communities. The 1990 Abbott decision coincided with the election of Democrat James Florio to the governorship. An ardent supporter of urban education, Governor Florio had been a representative from Camden, one of the counties involved in the *Abbott v. Burke* cases (Carr and Fuhrman 1999).

Perhaps in anticipation that the court would rule in favor of the plaintiffs, Governor Florio and the legislature with the assistance of various technical experts began working on new legislation: the Quality Education Act (QEA), which was passed in May 1990, just two weeks before the court rendered its decision in *Abbott v. Burke II* (Block 2002). The Quality Education Act subsequently became one of the most controversial pieces of school reform legislation to be enacted in the state. Under the QEA, state aid was based on a foundation formula, which replaced the guaranteed tax base formula that was formerly used. The state established a base foundation aid of $ 6,742 per pupil in grades one through five. In seeking to achieve parity, the state restricted aid to the wealthiest districts and increased aid to the poorest. The increase of aid to the neediest districts was accomplished through the use of a multiplier, which added 5 percent to the amount of education aid that they received. In order to fund the new legislation the act included a $2.8 billion tax package. Some of these funds were earmarked for offsetting the anticipated budget deficit, while others were slated to be used for property-tax relief (Corcoran and Scovronick 1995). The Quality Education Act also contained a highly controversial proposal—the ending of decades of direct state payments of the employer's share of teachers' pension and social security.

From the beginning, the Quality Education Act faced stiff opposition. Citizens, politicians, and groups representing those communities perceived to be most adversely affected by the new legislation, as well as antitax groups such as Hands Across New Jersey, staged protests at the state capital. New Jersey's School Boards Association as well as the largest teachers' union in the state, the New Jersey Education Association, joined the voices of opposition to the Quality Education Act. A *Star-Ledger*/Eagleton Poll conducted in July 1990 revealed that whereas 54 percent of those surveyed agreed with the *Abbott v. Burke* decision, only 35 percent approved the Quality Education Act. Approval polls taken during 1990 showed a precipitous drop in ratings for Governor Florio. In fall 1990, incumbent Democrat U.S. Senator Bill Bradley narrowly won his bid for reelection over a relatively unknown Republican challenger (Firestone, Goertz, and Natriello 1997, 2). Thus, by 1991 Democrat legislators worried about the political backlash engendered by the passage of the Quality Education Act attempted to placate wealthier taxpayers by reducing the original amount of state aid from $1.5 billion to $800 million. However, in fall 1991, almost all of the legislators who had supported the tax package lost their reelection bids. Republicans took over the state legislature, and two years later, in 1993, Democrat Governor Florio lost his bid for reelection to Republican Christine Whitman, who ran on an antitax and anti-QEA platform. The powerful teachers' union—the New Jersey Education Association—played an important role in Florio's defeat.

A year later, the New Jersey Supreme Court in *Abbott v. Burke*, 136 N.J. 444, 643 A.2d 575 (1994), held that the Quality Education Act was unconstitutional. The court's ruling was based on two facts: the failure of the state (1) to achieve parity by 1994, and (2) to implement the supplemental support programs that the court had required in *Abbott v. Burke II*. In response to the court's findings in the 1994 *Abbott* ruling, the legislature in 1996 passed the Comprehensive Educational Improvement and Financing Act (CEIFA). CEIFA bore the marks of Governor Whitman's antitax position and her declaration that a "thorough and efficient education" was defined best by educational standards rather than financial inputs. Thus, the legislature laid out in CEIFA a set of substantive educational standards in seven core academic areas: visual and performing arts, language arts literacy, mathematics, science, social studies, world languages, and health and physical education. CEIFA elaborated upon the constitutional definition of "efficient" by outlining a number of educational inputs deemed necessary to meeting the newly promulgated education standards. These inputs included class size, the amount and types of instructional materials and supply, and the ratio of teacher and administrative staff to student. State aid was now linked directly to the newly emerging definition of a thorough and efficient education. In determining what it would cost to deliver an education commensurate with the new interpretation of "thorough and efficient," the state proposed the use of a hypothetical model on which to estimate foundation aid.

CEIFA also contained two additional provisions that directly impacted educational programming in the urban districts: the Early Childhood Program Aid (ECPA) and the Demonstrably Effective Program Aid (DEPA). ECPA funds were targeted for programs that included full-day kindergarten classes, preschool classes, and other early childhood services. The allocation of ECPA monies was tied to poverty levels. For example, districts with a poverty level greater than 40 percent received more funds than those below that level. DEPA provided funds to school districts for instruction, school governance and health, and other related social services (Walker and Gutmore 2000).

Once again, in 1997 New Jersey's highest court ruled that the legislative and executive branches of government had failed to meet the constitutional threshold of providing all students with a thorough and efficient educational system (*Abbott v. Burke*, 149 N.J.145, 693 A.2d 417). The court used three formulations to arrive at its conclusion: (1) whether the standards in the law comported with the constitutional meaning of a thorough and efficient education; (2) whether the resources provided by the state were sufficient for the attainment of a thorough and efficient education; and (3) whether CEIFA adequately met the needs of students in poor urban districts. The court held that the new law met the first test of constitutionality but failed the other two. The court argued that the amount of aid generated by the theoretical model was inadequate for ensuring a thorough and efficient education. It also found that the state failed to conduct any empirical studies of the actual needs of students in these districts, and the aid tied to the DEPA and ECPA provisions in the act were therefore arbitrary. The court ordered that the state attain parity funding by September 1997 and that it take all steps to ensure educational improvement in the special needs districts. The court remanded the case to a lower court for fact finding and specifically for the generation of recommendations that would remedy the educational, program, and facilities disadvantages that students in poor districts in the state confronted.

Superior Court Judge Michael Patrick King forwarded to the New Jersey State Supreme Court in 1998 a comprehensive set of remedies that represented the proposals that were presented by the State Department of Education, the Education Law Center, and national experts on school reform during the six weeks of hearing that occurred in the fall of 1997. In May 1998 the court adopted the recommendations from the Superior Court and issued a landmark decision that outlined a comprehensive reform package (*Abbott v. Burke,* 153 N.J.480, 710 A.2d 450). The reform measures included the adoption of an all-day kindergarten program for all eligible students; the implementation of high-quality preschool programs for all eligible three- and four-year-olds; class sizes no larger than fifteen in prekindergarten, twenty-one in grades kindergarten through three, twenty-three in grades four and five, and twenty-four in grades six and higher. In addition, the reform package included the implementation of research-based effective whole school reform programs, the establishment of school-based governance, the adoption of rich technology plans, enhanced services for bilingual and special education students, enhanced curricular offerings, the implementation of needs-based social and health services, comprehensive state funding for facilities improvement, and adequate state funding for all remedies.

Since 1998, New Jersey has become embroiled in several legal challenges regarding its handling of the reforms. At least five more decisions have been rendered on specific elements to include the preschool components, the facilities remedies, and school budgets. In 2001, James McGreevy, a Democrat, was elected to the governorship. The election of McGreevy signaled the possibility of a closer relationship between the executive and state branches on the one hand, and the *Abbott* districts on the other. In fact, in 2002 the Education Law Center—the nonprofit organization that has led the legal challenges against the state's statutory funding scheme—joined with the state Department of Education in petitioning the court for a one-year stay on increased funding of the *Abbott* remedies. This unusual alliance was created in part because of the severe budget shortfall that the state, like many other states, has been experiencing. The state's largest teachers' union—New Jersey Teacher Association—which initially had strongly opposed the Quality Education Act, sided with the *Abbott* districts in their challenge to the proposed budget freeze. Citing budgetary exigencies, the court allowed the state to keep funding for the 2002–2003 school year at the previous year's level. However, in 2003 the court ruled against the state when it proposed a deviation from the remedies that it had approved in its 1998 decision.

Ohio

In 1923 the Ohio State Supreme Court in *Miller v. Korns,* 140 N.E. 773, declared that Ohio's constitutional provision that guaranteed a thorough and efficient system of common schools implied that with respect to "thorough," no school or district in the system could be starved for funds; and with regards to "efficiency," every school district must have ample number of teachers and sound buildings and equipment that would ensure all students an educational opportunity. More than fifty years after this pronouncement, the state of Ohio and its highest court became embroiled in defining whether the system of common schools met the constitutional mandates in its education clause.

In 1976, the board of education for the city of Cincinnati, its superintendent, parents, students, and the clerk-treasurer sued the state of Ohio, claiming that Ohio's system of school finance violated both the equal protection clause and the thorough and efficient clause of Ohio's constitution (*Board of Education v. Walter,* 390 N.E.2d 813). The plaintiffs argued that inadequate foundation funding and overreliance on property taxes resulted in a system of common schools in which some students were deprived of an equal educational opportunity. Although the plaintiffs prevailed at the trial level, the Supreme Court upon appeal upheld the state's statutory funding mechanism.

However, in 1991, the constitutionality of Ohio's elementary and secondary school finance system was once again challenged. In 1991 in the Perry County Court of Common Pleas, the Ohio Coalition for Equity and Adequacy of School Funding, an organization formed in 1990 with the explicit purpose of challenging the constitutionality of Ohio's school funding, filed a complaint on behalf of Dale DeRolph, five school district boards of education, and other plaintiffs against the State Board of Education, the State Superintendent of Public Instruction, and the State Department of Education, seeking declarative and injunctive relief, and requested (1) that public education be declared a fundamental right; (2) that Ohio's system of financing public education be declared unconstitutional; and (3) an injunction requiring the state of Ohio to provide a system of funding public education that comports with the state's constitution. The plaintiffs in *DeRolph v. State*, 78 Ohio St.3d 193, 194, 677 N.E.2d 733 (1997) also requested that the court retain jurisdiction in order to ensure the state's compliance with the court's rulings should it rule in favor of the plaintiffs. The law firm of Bricker and Eckler represented the coalition.

The trial began in October 1993 and lasted thirty days. During the trial more than sixty-one witnesses testified and 450 exhibits were entered into evidence. Both the plaintiffs and defendants concurred that Ohio's system of public education was inadequate. Indeed, at trial it was brought out that the State Department of Education had called for a comprehensive reform of public schooling with an emphasis on achieving equity, adequacy, and reliability. Swayed by the overwhelming evidence that depicted Ohio's public schools as being plagued by inadequacies in curriculum, facilities, and funding; Judge Linton D. Lewis Jr. ruled in 1994 that Ohio's mechanism for school finance was in violation of Ohio's constitution, and ordered the legislature to propose solutions that would eliminate wealth-based disparities among schools.

Although Ohio's State Board of Education voted not to appeal Judge Lewis's decision, the state attorney general filed notice of appeal in the Fifth District Court of Appeal. Neither side disputed the basic fact that Ohio's system of common schools was marked by deplorability in funding, facilities, and curriculum; however, the Court of Appeals in a split decision reversed Judge Lewis's decision and declared Ohio's system of school funding to be constitutional. In addition, the court determined that Judge Lewis had erred in retaining jurisdiction in the case.

The appellate decision was subsequently appealed at the State Supreme Court level. In 1997 the court upheld the initial trial court judge's decision and declared Ohio's elementary and secondary public school financing system to be in violation of Section 2, Article VI of the Ohio Constitution (*DeRolph v. State* (1997), 78 Ohio St.3d 193). The court reasoned that given the great public and general interest that education poses for the citizenry, leaving the resolution of Ohio's educational problems to the General Assembly would represent an abdication of its responsibilities. Moreover, the court held as specious the argument that laws were presumptively constitutional.

The Supreme Court's 1997 *DeRolph* decision was influenced by what it determined to be the major flaws in the School Foundation Program. The court found that the formula amount in the foundation program reflected political and budgetary considerations rather than a rational understanding of what it actually cost to educate a pupil in Ohio. The court also noted that school districts with high poverty levels were unfairly burdened by the provision, which froze additional aid at a threshold of 20-percent concentration of Aid to Dependent Children (ADC). Thus, a district that had a concentration higher than 20 percent would be forced to carry the extra cost. Another weakness identified by the court was the "tax reduction factors" that were made law by the General Assembly in 1976. The purpose of this legislation was to limit growth of real property tax revenues that could result from an inflation of property values. Under R.C. 319.301, communities in which property values increase because of a reappraisal or update were required by law to apply tax reduction factors. By limiting revenue growth, school districts were forced to introduce additional tax levies—most of which according to the court failed. At the same time, however, in spite of the fact that districts were not able to benefit from an increase in the valuation of properties, the state would charge off the increase in value in the foundation formula. In this case, districts would receive less aid under the foundation formula.

Districts that for a variety of reasons were unable to meet their budgets were further forced to borrow funds. R.C. 133.301 established a spending loan reserve program that allowed districts based upon the approval of the superintendent of public instruction to borrow up to a statutory maximum amount. If districts were still unable to meet their budgetary needs they were required to go to commercial lenders to secure the additional funds. Any district that was unable to repay a commercial loan had the loan amount repaid by diverting funds that it would normally have gotten from the foundation program. The court ruled that the loan program that the legislature of Ohio had enacted was "nothing less than a clever disguise for the state's failure to raise revenue to discharge its constitutional obligations" (*DeRolph v. State* at 202, 677 N.E.2d at 740).

The court's decision was also influenced by the persuasive evidence of Ohio's failure to maintain adequate school facilities. The court heard testimony and reviewed evidence that demonstrated serious health and safety issues in many schools across the state. For example, in Buckeye Local, Belmont County, carbon monoxide leakage led to the hospitalization of three hundred students. At the time the case was heard before the State Supreme Court, almost 70 percent of Ohio's schools had not complied with the 1987 Environmental Protection Agency mandate that required schools to be free of asbestos. In addition to these facilities issues, schools confronted inadequacies of instructional supplies, with some schools implementing a lottery to determine which students would be given a textbook.

The Supreme Court in its 1997 decision ordered the General Assembly to make education funding a priority; to provide all schools with sufficient funds that would allow them to satisfy local, state, and federal mandates; and to ensure that all facilities problems were redressed. In order to give the General Assembly time to develop a system of funding that would be constitutional, the court stayed its decision for twelve months and remanded the case back to the trial judge with directions to the judge to assume jurisdiction.

In response to the court decision the legislature and governor introduced and passed several pieces of key reform legislation, some of which were influenced by the recommendations that emanated from the School Funding Task Force that was established following the court's decision. Indeed, during 1997 the General Assembly enacted a flurry of legislations. For example, in May 1997 the General Assembly created the Ohio School Facilities Commission–Amended Substitute Senate Bill 102. This commission assumed responsibility for the Classroom Facilities Assistance Program, which was initially under the purview of the State Board of Education. The commission was responsible for establishing the Emergency School Repair Program as well as for authorizing funds for major repairs and renovations in the state's largest school districts (*DeRolph v. State* (2000), 88 Ohio St.3d). The legislature, however, only appropriated a fraction of the $10.2 billion—$300 million—that it was estimated would be needed to bring Ohio's school facilities up to standard.

House Bill 215 was signed into law in June 1997. This bill adjusted the basic aid formula amount, provided equity aid, and approved additional funding for facilities, textbooks, SchoolNet and SchoolNet Plus programs (computer-based programs), as well as initiating funding for the Disability Access Program.

In August of the same year, the legislature passed the School District Fiscal Accountability Act (House Bill 412) and the Academic Accountability Act (Senate Bill 55). House Bill 412 required districts to set aside funds for building maintenance, textbooks, and instructional materials, and also to maintain a budget reserve. The Accountability Act delineated standards of performance; required the school report card to report information on school performance, attendance, and graduation rates; implemented a statewide fourth grade reading guarantee (that required all students entering the fifth grade to meet state standards); and required summer and remedial programs for third- and fourth-grade students. Governor George Voinovich proposed a one-cent sales tax to fund the new accountability measures. However, his proposal was defeated in the house, and a year later in 1998 a similar proposal was defeated at the polls.

In February 1998, Ohio's General Assembly passed House Bill 650, which sought to create a new system of funding education. Under the new funding mechanism the controversial loan program was to be phased out, modification to the state basic aid formula was made, and a per-pupil base cost was determined. House Bill 770, passed in June 1998, amended some of the provisions in House Bill 650.

Judge Linton Lewis was called upon in August 1998 to once again settle the constitutional question as to whether the General Assembly had in fact instituted new statutory funding mechanisms that satisfied the thorough and efficient clause. Once again Judge Lewis determined that the General Assembly had failed to fulfill its constitutional responsibilities in spite of the progress that had been made. Judge Lewis in his decision expressed concerns about the facilities and repair program, the failure of the state to place education funding as a top budgetary priority, the continued existence of the controversial forced borrowing program, and the failure of the state to provide funding to support the mandates in the Academic Accountability Act. Judge Lewis's decision was appealed to the State Supreme Court in November 1999.

While acknowledging the strides that the General Assembly had made in fashioning an educational system that was constitutional, the State Supreme Court expressed concerns about several aspects of the legislature's response to its decision in *DeRolph I*. First, the court took issue with the manner in which the cost for an adequate education was determined. In particular, the court expressed perplexity as to why the General Assembly after engaging the services of a school finance expert would without any adequate explanation alter that expert's methodology, thus resulting in a lowering of the base cost of an adequate education. In addition, the court was concerned with the General Assembly's proposal to phase in the base cost of an adequate education over a three-year period, noting that such a proposal would result in schools being funded at a level below what the General Assembly had agreed upon to be the base amount of an adequate education. The court also found to be troublesome several aspects of the Classroom Facilities Assistance

Program as well as the Academic Accountability Act. With regard to the former, the court noted that many schools in Ohio still were in total disrepair and posed serious harm to the safety and health of students. Although the court commended the General Assembly on its attempt to introduce academic standards in Ohio's system of education, it did not feel that the legislature had gone far enough. It noted that more work needed to be done to strengthen Ohio's system of public schools. Moreover, the court was bothered by the fact that many of the mandates were not fully funded by the state, thus forcing districts to absorb these costs by reverting to either passing additional levies or borrowing from lenders. Ironically, the State Supreme Court's observations on many of these issues were buttressed by the findings from Achieve Inc., a group that had been appointed by Governor Bob Taft in 1998 to study Ohio's schools. In spite of the *DeRolph I* decision, Achieve Inc. found persistent problems with school facilities and a lack of clear system-wide academic standards. Ohio's Supreme Court in a split decision thus found on May 11, 2000, that the core constitutional remedy that it had required in *DeRolph I*—a systematic overhaul of school funding—had not been achieved by the various pieces of legislation that the General Assembly had passed between 1997 and 1999.

Ohio's Supreme Court is an elected one and is subject to the same types of electoral politics that ordinary politicians are. Not surprisingly, therefore, the continuous tensions between the court and the legislature became the fodder for political backlash against some of the judges who sided with the majority decision. Legislators, perhaps hopeful that one of the sitting judges would lose his or her bid for reelection, failed to move on the court's 2000 decision. In fact, as early as 1997, the Speaker of the House and the Senate president had introduced two bills (HJR 17 and SJR 4) seeking to provide a constitutional amendment that if passed would have vested the final authority of what constituted a thorough and efficient education in the legislature.

In 2000, Justice Alice Resnick, a Democrat and the author of the court's 2000 decision, was opposed in her reelection bid by Terrance O'-Donnell, a Republican. Both the U.S. and the Ohio Chambers of Commerce opposed Justice Resnick's reelection, and together they spent an estimated $10 million in attacking her, sponsoring numerous advertisements that insinuated that Justice Resnick was influenced in her decisions by trial lawyers and labor unions. (The Ohio Election Commission later found probable cause to conclude that these advertisements violated state election laws.) Ohio's teacher associations, trial lawyers, and labor unions supported Justice Resnick, and although these groups were outspent by 5–1, she won a landslide victory. Following her reelection, the General Assembly once again began to address the issue of school funding.

However, with a shortfall in state revenues, the legislature found itself in a dilemma: how to fund the education budget, which it had passed in the biennium budget. The governor and the legislators agreed that instead of raising taxes, funds secured from cutbacks in other areas would be used to meet the education budget, a decision that proved to be unpopular. In 2001, the State Supreme Court was faced with rendering a decision on the continued legal struggles between the plaintiffs and the state. Confronted with public outcry over the cuts in popular programs, and with debates in the press regarding the legitimacy of the court's role, the court became the subject of intense political and media pressure (O'Brien 2003).

The third *DeRolph* decision rendered by the court reflected the influence of these pressures. Although the court ordered the state to implement remedies that would satisfy the tests for constitutionality in *DeRolph I* and *II*, it stated that it would no longer retain jurisdiction (*DeRolph v. State* (2001), 93 Ohio St. 3d 309, 325, 754 N.E.2d). According to Chief Justice Moyer, the author of the decision, the court's decision to relinquish jurisdiction represented an attempt to eliminate the "uncertainty and fractious debate" occasioned by its continued role in the case (*DeRolph v. State* at 311, 754 N.E.2d 1184). The dispute was turned over to mediation on November 16, 2001. On March 21, 2002, the court-appointed mediator informed the court that both parties were unable to reach agreement, and the case was once again placed before the court. On December 11, 2002, the court issued its fourth decision. In a 4–3 ruling the court found that the state had failed to meet the mandates of *DeRolph I* and *II*. However, by March 2003, Ohio's continuing budget woes forced Governor Taft to cut state funding for Ohio's 612 school districts. The Ohio Coalition for Equity and Adequacy of School Funding sought an order from Judge Linton Lewis requiring the state to comply with the *DeRolph IV* ruling. But on May 16, 2003, by a 5–2 vote, in spite of a final order that determined that Ohio's school funding system was unconstitutional, the Ohio Supreme Court issued a writ that prevented Judge Lewis from conducting any further proceedings in the *DeRolph* case.

Texas

Texas's legislature became embroiled during the 1990s with the politically charged and contentious issue of reforming its system of school finance. During this period, race and class cleavages were brought into sharp focus as the legislature sought to comply with the State Supreme Court's mandate for the establishment of a constitutional system of school finance. School finance issues have long dominated the state's legislative politics, going back to as early as 1879, when Texans demanded reforms in the organization and financing of schools (Walker 1988). In 1836 the state's constitution imposed an affirmative responsibility on the legislature to make provisions for the support and maintenance of public schools that would result in a general diffusion of knowledge. In 1876 in Article 7, Section 1 the legislature went further, calling upon the legislature to create an efficient system of public free schools. However, like so many other states, Texas found itself with a system of free public schools that was neither efficient nor able to attain in a uniform manner the general diffusion of knowledge across all social and racial classes.

The state's system of public schools garnered national attention in 1973, when the U.S. Supreme Court upheld the constitutionality of the system used to finance them, while simultaneously advising the legislature that the system was in need of improvement. The Court's decision was in response to a lawsuit brought in 1968 on behalf of Mexican American students attending school in the Edgewood Independent School District in Bexar County. In *Rodriguez v. San Antonio Independent School District*, 411 U.S. 1, 93 S.Ct.1278 (1973), the plaintiffs claimed that the school-finance system was unconstitutional under the equal protection clause of the Fourteenth Amendment of the U.S. Constitution.

In the immediate aftermath of the Rodriguez decision, the Texas legislature passed a number of important bills. House Bill 1126, passed in 1975 and shortly thereafter renamed the Foundation School Program, created a State Equalization Aid program that sought to equalize spending across districts. In 1977, Senate Bill 1 was enacted by the legislature, approving aid for vocational and special education personnel under the State Equalization Aid program. A Select Committee on Public Education was established in 1983 under HCR 275. Governor Mark White appointed H. Ross Perot, a businessman from Dallas, to chair the committee. In 1984 the recommendations from the Select Committee were included in HB 72, an important piece of reform legislation. HB 72 required the creation of prekindergarten programs for four-year-olds from impoverished backgrounds, summer bilingual programs for preschoolers, a maximum class size of twenty-two students in kindergarten through the fourth grade, a state-funded career ladder for teachers, a "no-pass, no-play" rule for extracurricular activities, an expansion of the foundation program, and an Enrichment Equalization Allotment to replace the State Equalization Aid program (Texas State Legislature 1990).

Yet in spite of these legislative efforts, disparities in funding and educational opportunities linked to wealth-based differences among districts remained pronounced. These disparities were exacerbated by the downturn in the Texan economy, increasing enrollment, and attenuation in the interest level and commitment of the legislature to school reform (Bosworth 2001). Not surprisingly, by 1984, advocates on behalf of students in property-poor communities turned once again to the judicial system for relief. Plaintiffs had initially delayed filing suit until the passage of HB 72, which was promised to be a sweeping reform of public education in the state. Judge Harley Clark of the 250th Judicial District Court in Travis County was the trial judge. The plaintiffs were the Edgewood Independent Schools District, sixty-seven other school districts, and individual school children and their parents. Several of the plaintiff-intervenor school districts were from the rural areas of the state. The defendants in the case were the state of Texas, the commissioner of education (William N. Kirby), and other state officials. The Mexican-American Legal Defense and Educational Fund, which received support from the Intercultural Development Research Association (IDRA), represented the plaintiffs, who sought a declarative judgment that would proclaim the financing system to be in violation of the Texas constitution.

During the trial, the judge heard testimony regarding the broad educational disparities between property-rich and property-poor districts that were linked to differences in the abilities of the districts to raise revenue. In April 1987, Judge Clark held that under the Texas constitution, the equal protection rights of pupils in property-poor districts were being denied and that the legislature had failed in its constitutional obligation to create and maintain a system of efficient and free public schools (*Edgewood Independent School District v. Kirby,* 362, 515 250th District Court, Travis County). The judge, however, failed to find that there was any ground to the plaintiffs' claim of racial discrimination. Judge Clark argued that in its failure to ensure that each school district had the same ability to raise and spend equal amounts per student either through local taxation effort or by legislative appropriation, the system of financing had violated Article I, Sections 3 and 19, and Article VII, Section 1 of the constitution. The judge stayed the injunction until September 1, 1989, thus providing the legislature with time to devise a remedial plan.

However, on December 14, 1988, in a 2–1 decision the Court of Appeals reversed the trial court decision (Court of Appeals 761 S. W.2d 859). The court opined that the question as to whether the Texas system of schools was efficient or inefficient was a political one not suitable for judicial review. The court noted that the constitution provided no guidance to it or to any other court for that matter, on how to arrive at a determination of what is efficient or inefficient. The court also found, similar to the earlier *Rodriguez* decision, that education was not a fundamental right under Texas's constitution. The court cautioned, however, that its decision was not to be construed as affirming the system of school finance.

This ruling was appealed to the State Supreme Court, which on October 2, 1989, unanimously overturned the appeals court decision and upheld in part the initial trial court's findings (*Edgewood v. Kirby*, 777 S.W. 2d 391). The constitutional review of whether the system violated the state constitution was based on data for the 1985–1986 school year. The data revealed that whereas the wealthiest districts had $14,000 of property wealth per student, the poorest districts had approximately $2,000 per student, resulting in a 700 to 1 ratio between the value of taxable property in the wealthiest district and district spending per student. Moreover, the average property wealth in the one hundred wealthiest districts was twenty times greater that the average property wealth in the one hundred poorest districts. Even within counties, the disparities between poor and affluent districts were stark. For example, the Edgewood Independent School District had about $38,854 in property wealth per student, compared to Alamo Heights in the same county, which had $570,109. In order to carry its share of educational funding, which at the time was about 50 percent (the state absorbed about 42 percent, and the remaining differences were provided by other sources), property-poor districts had to tax high and spend low, whereas their more affluent counterparts were able to tax low and spend high. Additionally, about one-third of Texas school districts, mostly in poor communities, were unable to meet the state-mandated standards for maximum class size that were promulgated in HB 72.

The court held that the system was neither financially efficient nor efficient in the sense that it provided for a general diffusion of knowledge. Although it neither offered specifics as to what the legislature should do nor recommended that taxes be raised, the court made clear that remediation of the current system was long overdue and that it intended to ensure that whatever remedy the legislature enacted would be constitutionally efficient. Recognizing the complexity and the challenges that the legislature would face, the court modified the trial court's decision and stayed the effect of its injunction until May 1, 1990. However, the court made it clear that should the legislature fail to develop a plan by the May 1 deadline, the injunction against the distribution of state funds to the schools would be invoked.

The lack of specifics in the court's decision created fertile ground for differences among various constituents as to what it meant by the term "efficient." Governor Bill Clements argued that efficiency implied a quality education, noting that the state was spending more than $13 billion on education; the staff director of the Task Force on Public Education interpreted the issue to be equal access to funds; and another member of the same task force argued that the constitutional issue was one of adequacy of state support (Texas State Legislature 1990). In the state legislature, response to the court decision fell along party lines. When the special session on school finance was convened in 1990, some liberals and moderates of the Democratic Party suggested that a possible remedy should entail the infusion of more money into the school finance system. This approach was endorsed by some of the traditional education interest groups, such as the school boards, as well as by both the dominant teachers' and administrators' associations in the state (Bosworth 2001). However, it was difficult for the legislature to agree upon what the amount should be. Some Republicans, in particular the governor, were averse to raising taxes. A compromise Senate Bill 1 involving an additional $555 million based upon a half-cent increase in the sales tax was ultimately reached. This bill failed to pass at the end of the third and fourth special sessions of the House. At the fifth special session, on May 2, 1990, a school finance bill was passed by both houses of the legislature, despite opposition from the Hispanic Caucus. On May 22, 1990, the governor vetoed the measure. The May 1 deadline came and passed without the state being able to come up with a remedy that was approved by all the involved parties.

Thus, in May 1990 the case was referred to Judge Scott McCown of the 250th District Court, who had replaced Judge Clark. Judge McCown gave the legislature additional time to settle its members' differences. On June 7, 1990, the first legislative remedy was signed into law by the governor. Senate Bill 1 was based on the goal of creating a system in which there was 95-percent equity—thereby excluding the richest 5 percent of the districts. The bill essentially left unchanged the existing system of funding the public schools.

The plaintiffs went back to the district court, contending that Senate Bill 1 was still constitutionally deficient. Judge McCown sided with the plaintiffs' contention and found the new financing statute to be unconstitutional. However, he vacated the State Supreme Court injunction that prohibited the financing of public education under the old structure and denied the plaintiffs any further injunctive relief. Both the plaintiffs and the defendants in the case were unhappy with his decision, albeit for different reasons. In fall 1990 the State Supreme Court took up the case once again.

The court issued its second opinion on the school finance case on January 22, 1991 (*Edgewood v. Kirby*, 804 S.W. 2d 491, 66). The court found that (1) the district court exceeded its authority by vacating its injunction and foreclosing consideration for further injunctive relief; (2) the statute remained unconstitutional because of its failure to remedy causes of the wide opportunity gaps between rich and poor districts; (3) the state constitution did not provide a barrier to the general concept of school district tax base consolidations; and (4) local tax revenue could not be recaptured by the state for purposes of educational equalization. The court concluded that Senate Bill 1 was fundamentally flawed because of its failure to restructure the system and "to provide a direct and close correlation between a district's tax effort and the available resources available to it"(*Edgewood v. Kirby*, 777 S.W. 2d at 397). The majority opinion was controversial both within the court and outside it. In particular, the court's finding that tax-base consolidation was not constitutionally invalid evoked much consternation, splintering the unanimity among the justices that had been evident in *Edgewood I* and creating criticism of the court by the media and legislators.

In fall 1990, Democrat Ann Richards was elected governor. Devising a politically feasible solution to the court's findings became a Herculean task for the newly elected governor and the General Assembly. In 1991 the Senate Education Committee under the leadership of Carl Parker devised a plan that would create twenty superdistricts within the state (Bosworth 2001). Both the Senate and Governor Richards approved the plan. However, the House developed an alternative plan, which proposed the creation of two hundred districts rather than the twenty superdistricts in the Senate plan. In April 1991 the Texas General Assembly passed Senate Bill 351, and Governor Richards signed it into law. The legislative remedy in Senate Bill 351 required the creation of 188 County Education Districts for taxation purposes only. It capped per-pupil property wealth and proposed the redistribution of revenues derived from local property tax. Senate Bill 351 represented a compromise among the parties, fuelled largely by their collective desire to untangle themselves from the court and its threats.

The property recapture plans in Senate Bill 351 required a constitutional amendment. Opposition to the bill steadily grew among the middle and wealthier classes of the state. In a state in which class and racial boundaries are sharply drawn, the outrage that Senate Bill 351, or the Robin Hood Plan (as it was euphemistically referred to), spawned was therefore not surprising (Carr and Fuhrman 1999). A group composed of more than 160 of the wealthiest school districts vociferously opposed to the redistributive elements of HB 351 sued the state, asserting that the state ad valorem tax was in violation of Article VIII, Section 1-e of the constitution, which prohibits the state from levying ad valorem taxes on properties. The case was first heard by Judge McCown, who ruled that the redistribution component of Senate Bill 351 was not unconstitutional. McCown thus upheld the constitutionality of the legislative remedies in the bill. Judge McCown's decision was later overturned by the Texas Supreme Court in its third *Edgewood* decision, *Carrollton-Farmers Branch I.S.D. v. Edgewood I.S.D.*, 826 S.W.2d 489 (Tex. 1992).

In its decision, the court held that HB 351 had created an unconstitutional ad valorem tax. Further, the court noted that "an efficient system of education requires more than an elimination of gross disparities in funding; it requires the inculcation of an essential level of learning by which each child in Texas is enabled to live a full and productive life in an increasingly complex world" (*Edgewood III* at 525–526). In reinforcing this point, the court underscored the need for the legislature to articulate the requirements of an efficient system not only in terms of funding but also with regard to educational results.

With the State Supreme Court ruling that Senate Bill 351 was unconstitutional, members of the legislature proffered a variety of solutions to the constitutional conundrum in which they had found themselves. Proposals to have the constitution amended to both deal with the ad valorem issue as well as to weaken the influence of the courts were floated. In 1993 the Fair Share plan was passed after partisan wrangling in the House. The plan sought a constitutional amendment that would in effect provide constitutional legitimacy to Senate Bill 351. The plan was put on the May 1, 1993, ballot for ratification by the citizens of the state.

Political mobilization around the upcoming elections pitted supporters of the plan against opponents. Not surprisingly, those who felt that they stood to lose the most—the wealthier members of the state—took their case to the press, supported in part by the national Republican Party (Bosworth 2001). Interestingly, some of the larger businesses in the state became strong advocates of the constitutional amendment. In May 1990, the plan was defeated 63 percent to 27 percent. Support for the plan broke down primarily along race and economic lines (Reed 1997). With the voters' rejection of the County Educational District Plan, the legislature was once more confronted with the task of developing an appropriate remedy that would satisfy constitutional requirements.

In 1993, through the passage of Senate Bill 7, the legislature created a two-tier system of financing in which Tier 1 provided a basic allotment and Tier 2 represented an equalized enrichment. In addition, the bill capped taxable wealth in a district, limited local property tax rates, and provided wealthier districts with five redistributive options for sharing their wealth with poorer districts. Both poor and wealthy districts were critical of the reform measures in the bill and challenged the bill once more in court based on constitutional grounds. Property-poor districts claimed that total equalization was not attained, that capital and facilities projects were left underfunded, and that the foundation aid was lowered, thus forcing them to use Tier 2 funds in order to meet state accreditation standards. Wealthy districts challenged the constitutionality of Senate Bill 7, asserting that they were illegally forced to redistribute revenue and that the bill contained provisions that needed voter approval.

In 1995 in *Edgewood IV,* the Texas State Supreme Court upheld the lower court finding that Senate Bill 7 was constitutional (*Edgewood I.S.D. v. Meno,* 917 S.W.2d 717). The court reasoned that an efficient system did not require equality of access to revenue at all levels, nor did the concept of efficiency prohibit districts from generating additional funds by raising taxes. In spite of the fact that the system was found to be constitutionally valid, challenges continue to be raised against various elements of the current funding structure. In 2001, four wealthy districts sued, arguing that the system had in fact resulted in the creation of an unconstitutional state ad valorem tax. The trial court dismissed the case, and the court of appeals affirmed. However, the State Supreme Court reversed the trial court and the court of appeals decision and remanded the case back to the trial court.

INSTITUTIONAL REFORM: THE EFFECTS OF POLITICS, JUDICIAL DURESS, AND SOCIAL JUSTICE

Education is a highly conflictual policy area. As the preceding cases demonstrate, achieving institutional reform is made more difficult by divided governments, interest group politics, public opinion, and the political atmosphere created by court decisions. Whether, absent judicial intervention, institutional reform would have occurred in several of these states is difficult, to know. Yet, as the discussion has shown, even under judicial duress, these states, with the exception of Kentucky, were unable to devise constitutionally satisfactory remedies within a reasonable time frame. Redistributive public policies tend to fragment the body politic. Policies that are directed toward restructuring educational inequities in the area of school finance because of their perceived redistributive characteristics tend to pit various social groups against each other. As was seen in Alabama, New Jersey, and Texas, these differences coalesced over race and wealth. However, there are also important ideological differences that such policies can evoke. Although these differences may find expression in partisan politics within the legislature, they are also transparent in the public debates that occur, and in the intensity and density of interest-group politics.

For legislators and judges the political costs of these policies can be very high, as was evident in both New Jersey and Ohio. Yet, in addition to the political cost of policies there is an alternative question that must be addressed: What role should consideration of social justice play in issues related to educational adequacy and equity? Some argue that the very state constitutions on which many of the court decisions are based obligate state legislators to principles of social justice. Application of these principles requires these legislators by virtue of the authority invested in them by the voters to create structures and arrangements that safeguard the rights of all citizens irrespective of race, wealth, or any other distinguishing characteristic.

Advocates on behalf of reforming states' public education systems and in particular the statutory mechanisms that govern the financing of these systems and the judges who have sided with these advocates view reform as not only representing a constitutional obligation but a moral imperative as well. The language of many of the courts' decisions underscores the saliency of establishing a system of education in which all children are given an equal opportunity to meet the constitutional guarantees in their states' educational clauses. As we have seen from our examination of five states, institutional reform of states' educational structures requires more than a restructuring of the mechanism of funding. Several of the remedies involve the provision of programs and curricular offerings, the articulation of educational standards, and the development of accountability structures that ensure that all children are provided with an adequate education.

REFERENCES

A+ Coalition for Better Education. 2003. *For the Sake of Our Children: The Future of Alabama's Public Schools. A Five-Year Report.* Montgomery, AL: A+ Coalition for Better Education.

"Alabama Voters Say 'No' to Tax Restructuring and More Education Finding." http://www.accessnet.org (accessed December 2004).

Berman, J. C., and D. Dunphy. 1998. "Building Plans for Reform: Alabama's School Finance Litigation." *Campaign for Fiscal Equity: Studies in Judicial Remedies and Public Engagement* 1.

Blanchard, M. D. 1998. "The New Judicial Federalism: Deference Masquerading as Discourse and the Tyranny of the Locality in State Judicial Review of Education Finance." *University of Pittsburgh Law Review* 60:149–230.

Block, S. 2002. "Comparing the Adequacy of New Jersey and Kentucky Court Mandates, Statutes, and Regulations to Remedy Unconstitutional Public Education." Dissertation, Seton Hall University, South Orange, New Jersey.

Bosworth, M. H. 2001. *Courts as Catalysts: State Supreme Court and Public School Finance.* New York: State University of New York Press.

Carr, M. R., and S. H. Furhman. 1999. "The Politics of School Finance Reform in the 1990s." In Helen F. Ladd, Rosemary Chalk, and Janet S. Hansen (eds.), *Equity and Adequacy in Education Finance: Issues and Perspectives.* Washington, DC: National Academy Press.

Corcoran, T., and N. Scovronick. 1995. "More Than Equal: New Jersey's Quality Education Act." *Journal of Education Finance* 17:83–119.

Cover, A. Y. 2002. "Is 'adequacy' a more 'political question' than 'equality'?: The Effect of Standards-based Education on Judicial Standards for Education Finance." *Cornell Journal of Law and Public Policy* 11:403–439.

Diffenderfer, M. 1996. "Riding the School Finance Litigation Wave: Alabama's Remedy May Not Be Enough." *West's Education Law Quarterly* 5, 2:204–224.

Firestone, W., M. Goertz, and G. Natriello. 1997. *From Cashbox to Classroom: The Struggle for Fiscal Reform and Educational Change in New Jersey.* New York: Teachers College Press.

Frug, E. 1978. "The Judicial Power of the Purse." *University of Pennsylvania Law Review* 126, 4:715–794.

Gillette, C. P. 1996. "Reconstructing Local Control of School Finance: A Cautionary Note." Capital University Law Review 25:37–50.

Harvard Law Review Note. 1991. Unfulfilled Promises: School Finance Remedies and State Courts. *Harvard Law Review* 104 (March):1072–1092.

Heise, M. 1998. "Schoolhouses, Courthouses, and Statehouses: Educational Finance, Constitutional Structure, and the Separation of Powers Doctrine." *Land and Water Law Review* 33:281–327.

Lindsay, D. 1998. "Quality Counts '98." Special Issue supplement. *Education Week.* January 8.

McUsic, M. 1991. "The Use of Education Clauses in School Finance Reform Litigation." *Harvard Journal on Legislation* 28:307–328.

Method, J. 2003. *School-Financing Struggles in New Jersey's Public Schools: A Biennial Report of New Jersey, 2002–2003.* Asbury Park, NJ: Asbury Park Press.

Morgan, M. F., A. S. Cohen, and H. Hershkoff. 1995. "Establishing Education Program Inadequacy: The Alabama Example." *University of Michigan Journal of Law Reform* 28, 3:559–598.

O'Brien, M. T. 2003. "At the Intersection of Public Policy and Private Process: Court-ordered Mediation and the Remedial Process in School Funding Litigation." *Ohio State Journal on Dispute Resolution* 18:391–438.

Orfield, G. 1997. *Deepening Segregation in American Public Schools.* Harvard Project on School Desegregation. Cambridge, MA: Harvard University Press.

Paris, M. 2001. "Legal Mobilization and the Politics of Reform: Lessons from School Finance Litigation in Kentucky, 1984–1995." *Law and Social Inquiry* 26, 3:631–684.

Pearce, J. E. 1987. *Divide and Dissent: Kentucky Politics, 1930–1963.* Lexington: University of Kentucky Press.

Reed, D. S. 1997. "Court-ordered School Finance Equalization: Judicial Activism and Democratic Opposition." In *Developments in School Finance.* Washington, DC: National Center for Education Statistics, U.S. Department of Education.

Sunstein, C. R. 1996. "Constitutional Myth Making: Lessons from the Dred Scott Case." Occasional Paper Number 37, University of Chicago Law School, Chicago, IL.

Texas State Legislature. 1990. "An Introduction to School Finance." Special Legislative Report, Number 157. Austin: House Research Organization, Texas State Legislature.

Walker, B. 1988. *Equity in Texas Public School Finance: Some Historical Perspective.* Austin: Texas Center for Educational Research.

Walker, E., and D. Gutmore. 2000. *The Quest for Equity and Excellence in Education: A Study on Whole School Reform in New Jersey.* South Orange, NJ: Center for Urban Leadership, Renewal, and Research, Seton Hall University.

Chapter Five

➻ Role of State Education Departments

Although the constitutional authority and responsibility for education resides with the legislative and executive branches of state governments, the actual implementation of educational decisions made by these branches ultimately becomes the responsibility of state departments of education. These agencies vary widely in their structures, and though they are the linchpins of states' educational policies, the many policy challenges that they face, coupled with factors related to capacity and organizational functioning, tend to raise questions about their abilities to be effective governance and administrative units within the wider state apparatus.

The past fifty years have seen a remarkable shift in the balance of power over control of educational policy between local school districts and state legislatures and bureaucracies. Court decisions, federal policies, interest-group politics, and evidence furnished by the scholarly community have all resulted in states assuming greater primacy in educational policy decisionmaking. This ascendancy of state involvement in education has juxtaposed arguments for a more decentralized system of public education against those that call for more a centralized system. Many of the court decisions that were discussed in the previous chapters have contributed to this tendency of increasing centralization in contemporary education policy, as states' contribution to financing public education has steadily risen over the years, and as more courts require their respective states to comply with the constitutional guarantees in their education clauses. However, the strengthening of state education policy activities raises questions as to the efficacy of state departments of education to effectively meet the challenges that this spawns. The sluggishness of these bureaucracies and the contradictory nature of their internal goals and regulations lead some to question whether they are able to be responsive and flexible in meeting the needs of local school communities (Hadderman 1988).

Prior to the 1960s, state education departments played an important and focal role in their states' system of public schools, although local educators eclipsed their overall influence on public education. The passage of the federal Elementary and Secondary Education Act (ESEA) in 1965 was instrumental in bringing these agencies into the centerpiece of federal educational policy—as signified by the proportion of their operating budgets (almost 80 percent) that was assumed by the federal government (Institute for Educational Leadership 2001). The fact that the ESEA and the subsequent amendments to it required states to approve local educational agencies' requests for federal funds to support programs for disadvantaged, bilingual, and special education pupils meant that these departments became an important conduit in the distillation of federal policies. The early to mid-1980s witnessed a significant demise in these agencies. This was occasioned by the downturn in the federal and state economies, which deleteriously affected the budgets of many departments of education. In addition, the perceived crisis in public education engendered by the landmark report *A Nation at Risk* led further to these agencies' relegation to a tertiary role in education policy; as legislatures, governors, and the business sectors inserted themselves more visibly into the education policy arena (Institute for Educational Leadership 2001).

State departments of education were catapulted back onto the policy stage with the advent of the standards-based and systemic reform movements that were spearheaded at the state level. Although states have historically attempted to influence educational practices at the local level, these second- and third-wave reform movements necessitated significant changes in "the states' leadership roles, strategies of influence and policy tools" (Cohen 1990, 271). With the renewed interest in state education policymaking activities, a flurry of articles was written on the organizational and paradigmatic shifts that departments of education needed to make in order to effectively lead the new reforms. (See for example, the policy statements by such organizations as the Consortium of Policy Research in Education.) Since that period the major policy shifts that have occurred at the federal level—specifically, the enactment of the No Child Left Behind legislation—has once more resulted in these organizations assuming a central role in federal education policies. How state departments of education will cope with these new demands has become a subject of inquiry. State education departments differ in their capacity, administrative, and governance structures, all of which impinge on their abilities to successfully cope with the increasing complexities of educational policies. Historical insights into the evolution of the institutional roles of state education departments reveal an ongoing struggle by these organizations to align their internal capacities with the pressure of reform that emanates from the increasing centralization of educational policy that we have seen over the past century (Timar 1997).

HISTORICAL PERSPECTIVE ON STATE EDUCATIONAL SYSTEMS

The emergence and development of state educational agencies has historically confronted opposition from local interests in many states. The inbred ideology of democratic localism that characterized the early development of schools and which was shared by many citizens made any attempt on a state's part to centralize education policy an anathema. Not surprisingly, the trajectory of these agencies' development reveals the contestation that has occurred between them on the one hand, and local communities on the other, over educational governance and administrative responsibilities. Unlike the experience in Europe, the early development of schools in the United States was largely a local phenomenon unaccompanied by any parallel development of a centralized system of administration. (For example, in Europe highly centralized systems were developed in parallel to the establishment of schools.) Schools tended to reflect local political, cultural, and economic needs. Hence, the political culture as well as the structure of schooling that characterized the early development of public education rendered difficult the establishment of state educational systems premised on principles of republicanism (Kaestle 1983; Timar 1997).

Creation of a centralized system of schooling and the development of corollary structures to support that system emerged during the mid-nineteenth century (Kaestle 1983). The reform movement of this period sought to introduce consistency and standardization into a system that hitherto was premised on just the opposite. State authority during the early stages of the reform movement rested primarily on law and specifically in the establishment of the legal underpinnings for a system of public schools. However, the ability of states to influence schooling still remained relatively weak.

ESTABLISHMENT OF STATE EDUCATION DEPARTMENTS

State education departments were established during the nineteenth century, essentially as a by-product of the Progressive era. These departments' assumption of administrative duties provided the conditions for a new institutional framework for education (Timar 1997, 240). State education departments during this historical period were modeled after the bureaucratic archetype and were controlled by professionals who sought to isolate them from the influence of politics. This intent was consonant with the trend toward professionalism that was clearly evident, for example, in the fields of teaching and school administration (Tyack 1974). States such as California and New York played a key leadership role in the creation and centralization of educational bureaucracies. The following case from New York illustrates some of the organizational tensions that occurred as states sought to centralize administration from the early twentieth century up to the 1960s.

New York State Department of Education: An Illustrative Case

New York developed its system of public schools under the common school law of 1812. In 1904, under the unification act, the commissioner of education for the state became the chief executive officer of the regents. The commissioner's responsibilities were largely administrative; that is, organizing the department and supervising elementary and secondary education. This supervisory responsibility was later extended to higher education. Various laws and statues also vested legal authority in the commissioner of education (Folts 1996).

At the beginning of the twentieth century, the New York State Department of Education had few experts in the area of elementary education. Its focus was primarily on secondary education, an emphasis that existed until the 1950s (Folts 1996). The department was deemed by local districts to be authoritarian, as it continued to see its role as an inspectorate with school inspectors responsible for scrutinizing very carefully the educational activities that occurred in local school districts.

The 1930s through 1940s saw an expansion in the department's scope of activities. However, studies of the department conducted during this period reveal its failure to implement organizational and operational changes that could assist it in meeting the challenges of its expanded role. The regents inquiry that was conducted between 1935 and 1938, as well as later investigations undertaken between 1947 and 1951, indicated that the department continued to engage in practices that were dictatorial with respect to the local educational agencies. Moreover, these studies continued to identify operational problems within the department. These organizational problems were magnified during the 1960s when the New York Education Department like other state departments around the country was confronted with an expansion of functions brought about by the National Defense Act of 1958, the Manpower Training Act of 1962, and the Elementary and Secondary Education Act of 1965 (Folts 1996). As a result of these federal initiatives, the department went through a major reorganization, which resulted in a further consolidation of its administrative hierarchy (Folts 1996). However, during the late 1970s state and federal funding support began to dwindle. In 1980 there was a 30-percent decrease in the number of State Department of Education employees, attributable directly to the funding woes that bedeviled the organization.

This brief insight into the history of New York State's education department illustrates three important points about the early development of education departments up to the 1960s. First, the fissure between the centralized tendencies in state education administrative policies and local control of schools evident in New York State typified the experiences of most states. Second, the unfavorable light in which bureaucrats were viewed was not isolated to this state, but represented a pervasive sentiment held by most local educators. Third, the vulnerability and susceptibility of New York's department of education to trends in national policies and the effect of this on its administrative and organizational functioning was an important issue for all departments of education and still remains one of some saliency.

Effects of National Education Initiatives on State Education Departments during the 1950s and 1960s

Several important national initiatives during the 1950s and 1960s influenced the organizational and administrative contours of departments of education. These initiatives were previously alluded to in the discussion on New York State's Department of Education. In 1958 a key piece of legislation, the National Defense Education Act, was passed. Title III of the act provided funding for educational programs at the elementary and secondary levels in the sciences, math, and foreign languages; and additional funding to the departments for building their capacities to effectively supervise teachers in these curricular reform areas. States did not assume leadership over the reform initiatives spawned by the act; instead, this role was filled by private scientists and teachers (Marsh and Gortner 1963). What the departments of education did was to promulgate guidelines and other forms of communiqués to the local districts, as well as review local districts' applications for federal funds. Their overall role was thus more administrative in nature (Timar 1997). Some states were able to take advantage of the provision in the act that set aside funds for curriculum supervisors in science, math, and foreign languages in spite of the many obstacles that were faced. Hence, by 1960 there was a sixfold increase across several states in the number of curriculum supervisors in these content areas (Timar 1997, 247).

The civil rights movement of the 1960s and 1970s and the policy backlash that the movement engendered provided a new set of imperatives for state education departments. These new imperatives centered on meeting the educational needs and protecting the rights of students from disadvantaged backgrounds, different racial and language backgrounds, and with exceptional learning and special education needs. Several key legislative acts, for example the Elementary and Secondary Education Act, the *Lau* decision, and court decisions on desegregation and statutory school finance systems, were instrumental in significantly altering the balance of power between local school districts and state departments of education. These policy changes were also critical in their impact on the organizational landscape of many departments of education. State education departments' organizational and administrative structures became more segmented, with subunits' responsibilities becoming more specialized and technical in orientation. This ossification of responsibilities within particular subunits reflected the new policy directions at the national level (Timar 1997). Examination of contemporary state education politics reflects the homologous relationship that exists between education and postmodernity. Globalization and the complexity of postmodern social life have shaped the spheres of influences upon state departments of education. Thus, the departments' functions have become increasingly fragmented and diffused. Not surprisingly, the effect of these changes can be seen in state governance structures, policy emphasis, and policymaking functions.

In summary, the evolution of state education departments and their changing institutional roles can be understood from three analytical perspectives that have historical overtones (Timar 1997). The first perspective locates these organizations within a framework in which the emphasis is on democratic localism. This typified the early beginnings of these organizations in the nineteenth century. During this period, state education departments enjoyed virtually no centralized power, there was minimal internal differentiation with respect to tasks and responsibilities, and they functioned within a context that lacked coherence (Timar 1997, 253). The second period witnessed an increase in the centralization of these organizations' powers within a political context of consensus. This period went from the turn of the twentieth century up until the 1960s and characterized what Timar defines as centralization within an integrative model of institutional organization. From the 1960s up to the present, state education departments have operated within a political context that is characterized by disaggregate and competing interests among different groups. The marketization and privatization of public education has resulted in the education system becoming less monolithic and more fractured. At the same time the shift in political control over education policy that is associated with the federally imposed standards of the No Child Left Behind legislation has helped to change the institutional role of state departments of education.

STATES' EDUCATION GOVERNANCE STRUCTURES

Table 5.1 presents a profile of the governance structures in all fifty states and in the District of Columbia and Puerto Rico. All states with the exception of Wisconsin and Minnesota have a state board of education. Minnesota represents an interesting case of the effects of public and legislative backlash when state boards attempt to introduce unpopular policies. In 1998, the nine-member board that was appointed by the governor was criticized for writing a diversity rule requiring districts to reduce education disparities between students of different racial and ethnic groups. This rule was intended to replace a 1988 rule on multicultural and diversity issues. The board's decision to reexamine the issue of diversity and multiculturalism was sparked by data that revealed sharp achievement gaps between whites and nonwhites, and evidence that schools in the state remained fairly segregated.

Opposition to the proposed policy was broad based. Both the governor and members of the legislature urged the board to reconsider its proposal, whereas members of the public, conservative organizations, and school districts opposed the rule for a variety of reasons. For example, educators in Minneapolis and St. Paul, who educate most of the state's minority student population, were concerned with the administrative strain that the new rule would impose on their districts. Given the lack of widespread support for the rule, the legislature approved in 1998 a bill that called for the dissolution of the board on December 31, 1999, and a transfer of its rule-making powers to the state's education commissioner. Although the diversity rule became the final catalyst for the board's demise, the marginalization of the board and the erosion of its policymaking function began long before 1998. For instance, as early as 1973 the legislature had stripped the board of its authority over teacher licensure, and in 1983 it transferred the board's power to appoint the commissioner to the governor.

Among states that do have a state board of education, membership on these boards tends to range from a high of twenty-one in Pennsylvania to a low of seven in Alaska, Delaware, Florida, Montana, New Hampshire,

Table 5.1

States' Education Governance Structures

State	Number on State Board of Education	Length of Term (in years)	Selection Process	Selection of Chief State School Officer	Official Role of Chief on State Board
Alabama	8 elected members and the governor	4	Elected	Appointed by the State Board of Education	Secretary and Executive Officer
Alaska	7	5	Appointed by the governor	Appointed by the governor	Executive Officer
Arizona	10	4	Appointed by the governor and confirmed by the Senate	Partisan ballot	Executive Officer
Arkansas	12	6	Appointed by the governor	Appointed by the State Board of Education	Agent, Ex-Officio Member
California	11, including a student member	4, 1 year for the student	Appointed by the governor	Nonpartisan ballot	Secretary and Executive Officer
Colorado	8	6	Partisan ballot	Appointed by the State Board of Education	Secretary
Connecticut	9	4	Appointed by the governor, approved by the House and the Senate	Appointed by the State Board of Education	Secretary
Delaware	7	6	Appointed by the governor, approved by the House and the Senate The president serves at the pleasure of the governor	Appointed by the governor	Executive Secretary
Florida	7	4	Appointed by the governor	Appointed by the State Board of Education	
Georgia	13	7	Appointed by the governor	Elected statewide	Chief Executive Officer
Hawaii	13	4	Nonpartisan ballot	Appointed by the State Board of Education	Executive Officer

continues

Table 5.1 continued

State	Number on State Board of Education	Length of Term (in years)	Selection Process	Selection of Chief State School Officer	Official Role of Chief on State Board
Idaho	8	5	Appointed by the governor	Nonpartisan Ballot	Executive Secretary and voting Ex-Officio Member
Illinois	9	6	Appointed by the governor	Appointed by the State Board of Education	Chief Executive Officer
Indiana	11	4	10 appointed by the governor, 1 by the elected CSSO	Partisan ballot	Chairman and voting Member
Iowa	9	6	Appointed by the governor	Appointed by the governor	Executive Officer
Kansas	10	4	Partisan ballot	Appointed by the State Board of Education	Executive Officer
Kentucky	11	4	Appointed by the governor	Appointed by the State Board of Education	Executive Secretary and Executive Administrator
Louisiana	11	4	3 appointed by the governor, 8 elected	Appointed by the State Board of Education	Executive Officer and Secretary
Maine	9	5	Appointed by the governor	Appointed by the governor	
Maryland	12, including a student member	4	Appointed by the governor	Appointed by the State Board of Education	Chief Executive Officer
Massachusetts	9, including a student member	5	Appointed by the governor	Appointed by the State Board of Education	Board Secretary and CEO
Michigan	8	8	Partisan ballot	Appointed by the State Board of Education	Chairman
Minnesota	N/A	N/A	N/A	Appointed by the governor	N/A
Mississippi	9	9	5 appointed by the governor and 4 by the legislature	Appointed by the State Board of Education	Executive Secretary
Missouri	8	8	Appointed by the governor	Appointed by the State Board of Education	

continues

Table 5.1 continued

State	Number on State Board of Education	Length of Term (in years)	Selection Process	Selection of Chief State School Officer	Official Role of Chief on State Board
Montana	7	7	Appointed by the governor	Partisan ballot	Ex-Officio Member
Nebraska	8	4	Nonpartisan ballot	Appointed by the State Board of Education	Executive Officer
Nevada	10 non-voting student members	4	Nonpartisan ballot	Appointed by the State Board of Education	Executive Officer
New Hampshire	7	5	Appointed by governor	Appointed by the State Board of Education	None
New Jersey	13	6	Appointed by governor	Appointed by governor	Secretary
New Mexico	10	4	Appointed by the governor		
New York	16	5	Appointed by the legislature	Appointed by the State Board of Education	Chief Executive Officer
North Carolina	13, including 2 voting ex-officio members	8	Appointed by the governor	Partisan ballot	Secretary and Chief Administrative Officer
North Dakota	7	6	Appointed by the governor	Nonpartisan ballot	Executive Director and Secretary
Ohio	19	4	11 elected by nonpartisan ballot, 8 appointed by the governor	Appointed by the State Board of Education	Secretary and Administrative Officer
Oklahoma	7	6	Appointed by the governor	Partisan ballot	Chairperson
Oregon	7	4	Appointed by the governor	Nonpartisan ballot	Administrative Officer
Pennsylvania	21	6	17 members appointed by the governor, 4 elected	Appointed by the governor, confirmed by the senate	Chief Executive Officer
Puerto Rico	7	5	Appointed by the governor	Appointed by the governor	Ex-Officio Member
Rhode Island	11	3	9 appointed by the governor, 2 elected	Appointed by the State Board of Education	Chief Executive Officer

continues

Table 5.1 continued

State	Number on State Board of Education	Length of Term (in years)	Selection Process	Selection of Chief State School Officer	Official Role of Chief on State Board
South Carolina	17	4	16 appointed by the legislature, 1 appointed by the governor	Partisan Ballot	Secretary and Administrative Officer
South Dakota	9	4	Appointed by the governor	Appointed by the governor	Executive Officer
Tennessee	10, including a student member	9	Appointed by the governor and confirmed by the General Assembly	Appointed by the governor	Required to be present at State Board of Education meetings
Texas	15	4	Partisan ballot	Appointed by governor	Executive Secretary
Utah	15	4	Nonpartisan ballot	Appointed by the School Board of Education	Executive Officer
Vermont	9, including a student member	6	Appointed by the governor and approved by the Senate	Appointed by the School Board of Education and approved by the governor	CEO and Secretary
Virginia	9	4	Appointed by the governor	Appointed by the governor	Secretary
Washington	11	4	9 elected by local board members, 1 elected by private schools	Nonpartisan ballot	Ex-Officio Member and Executive Officer
West Virginia	9	9	Appointed by the governor	Appointed by the State Board of Education	Chief Executive Officer
Wisconsin	N/A	N/A	N/A	Nonpartisan ballot	N/A
Wyoming	11	6	Appointed by the governor	Partisan ballot	Ex-Officio Member
District of Columbia	9	4	5 by non-partisan ballot, 4 appointed by the mayor	Appointed by the State Board of Education	Ex-Officio Member

Source: Extracted from data compiled on State Education Governance Structure by the National Association of State Boards of Education and revised in January 2004. National Association of School Boards of Education, Alexandria,VA.

North Dakota, Oklahoma, Oregon, and Puerto Rico. The average length of time for service on state boards is about five years. A variety of selection methods are used by the states in constituting their boards. According to the Education Commission of the States there are four general governance models that describe both the selection process for state boards as well as the selection of the chief state school officer (CSSO). In the first model, the state board is appointed by the governor, and the board in turn selects the chief state school officer. This model is used in the states of Arkansas, Connecticut, Florida, Illinois, Kentucky, Maryland, Massachusetts, Missouri, New Hampshire, Vermont, and West Virginia. In the second model the state board is elected by either a partisan or nonpartisan ballot, with the board responsible for appointing the CSSO. The following states are examples of this structure: Alabama, Colorado, Hawaii, Kansas, Michigan, Nebraska, Nevada, and Utah. Eleven states use a third model, in which the board is appointed by the governor and the CSSO is elected. These states are Arizona, California, Georgia, Idaho, Indiana, Montana, North Carolina, North Dakota, Oklahoma, Oregon, and Wyoming. States such as Alaska, Delaware, Iowa, Maine, New Jersey, South Dakota, Tennessee, and Virginia are governed by a fourth model. In this model the governor is responsible for appointing both the state board and the chief state school officer. (According to the report, few minority group members have been appointed or elected chief state school officer.)

There are a few states with unique governance structures that include a combination of two or more of the above models. For example, Louisiana uses both an elective and appointive process in selecting members to its state board, with the board in turn responsible for the appointment of the CSSO. In Mississippi, both the governor and the legislature decide membership on the board, with the governor responsible for appointing five members and the legislature appointing four. Mississippi's chief state school officer is then appointed by the board. The legislature or governor in both New York and Pennsylvania is responsible for appointing board members. However, whereas in New York the state board appoints the CSSO, in Pennsylvania the governor selects the CSSO and four state board members are elected. In Wisconsin, although, there is a chief state school officer and there is no state board of education. Various arguments regarding the relative advantages and disadvantages associated with each of the governance structures can be made. Ideally, having state boards and the CSSO independent of the executive and legislative branches may be one way of helping to reduce the influence of partisan politics on their functions. In reality, however, it is extremely difficult to insulate boards and CSSOs from political pressure, as attested by the experience of several states. For example, Illinois represents one case where political wrangling and the jostling for power and influence by the governor has fractured the relationship between the executive branch and the board. Prior to 1970 the state superintendent was an elected position. In 1970 the legislature statutorily changed the governance structure by creating a nonelected state superintendent and giving the responsibility for selecting the CSSO to the appointed board.

The board itself later became the subject of criticism, with the most recent coming from Democratic governor Rod Biagojevich. Governor Biagojevich in his 2004 state of the state address proposed, among other things, transferring the board's policymaking authority to his office and creating a direct report from the board to the governor (Aguilar 2004). He has also proposed removing the selection of the CSSO from the board and turning that responsibility over to his office.

Illinois is not the only state where politics and gubernatorial interests produce contestation over educational policy and governance. State boards of education in North Carolina, Michigan, Wisconsin, and Delaware have also seen their policymaking functions weakened by the legislative and executive branches. In 1996 Michigan's Republican governor John Engler by executive order transferred power from the elected state board to the appointed schools chief. Governor Engler's order was seen as a way of regaining control of the board when its composition shifted from a 6–2 Republican majority to a 4–4 split (Johnston 1999). In Wisconsin, the State Supreme Court overturned a 1996 law that if left to stand would have changed that state's school chief's position from an elected to an appointed position, with the governor responsible for selecting the CSSO. Policy conflict has also existed between state boards and the chief state school officer. In 1993 California found itself embroiled in a bitter legal dispute between the elected school chief and the appointed state board over policy authority (Johnston 1999). A California court later decided in favor of the board, but by 1997 both parties were back in court seeking judicial resolution to the question as to which of the two had the ultimate responsibility for establishing the direction of education in the state.

States' governance structures have undergone significant changes since the early decades of the twentieth century. In 1930, for example, more than two-thirds of chief state school officers were elected. That number has been dramatically lowered since then, with the number of elected CSSOs now standing at around fourteen (Usdan 2002). Similarly, in 1983 only five CSSOs were appointed by governors; in 2002, governors appointed the CSSO in nine states (Usdan 2002).

Generally, proponents of a governance structure in which governors are given some degree of control over the selection process argue that this would help to alleviate the acrimonious relationships that tend to develop between governors and boards, especially in contexts where the board and CSSO are selected without gubernatorial input. Moreover, it has been argued that with governors now being held more accountable for educational policies, having boards and CSSOs that are favorably predisposed toward their elected governors' educational agenda enhances the possibility that a governor's policy agenda will be favorably acted upon. Critics have pointed out, however, that gubernatorial appointments of CSSOs can lead to much instability in a state's top educational leadership position.

Irrespective of the mechanisms that may be used to constitute a state board or to select a CSSO, and in spite of the variations in policymaking functions across these boards, there are certain general responsibilities that most boards are required to fulfill. Boards typically have regulatory and advisory functions. They are generally responsible for establishing instructional and curricular standards, setting standards for teacher licensure and other certificated requirements for administrators, promulgating regulations that govern education of pupils such as safety and health codes, and providing advice to the executive and legislative branches on educational matters. State departments of education in turn have the oversight responsibilities for ensuring that policies adopted by their boards are implemented.

INFLUENCES ON STATE SCHOOL
BOARDS AND EDUCATION AGENCIES

Over the years the policymaking functions of state boards of education and the oversight responsibilities of state departments of education have become vulnerable to diverse spheres of influences emanating from both within and outside state government. As intimated previously, the reform movements of the 1980s and 1990s have resulted in education becoming a top policy issue for the executive and legislative branches. Prior to the standards-based and systemic reform movements the executive branch's involvement in setting the policy agenda for education was minimal with a few exceptions, notably in the state of Arizona, where that governor during the early 1980s assumed an active role in reshaping the direction of that state's public education.

However, with the advent of the standards-based movement and the governors' summits on education that have been held, governors have become more directly involved in educational policy. Education remains a primary concern of the electorate, and many candidates vying for the governorship position within their states use education as one of their major campaign platforms. The emerging trend is thus one where governors have been interjecting themselves quite openly in the educational debates that are occurring at both the national and state levels. Hence we see that the executive branch's influence upon state boards and state education departments has become more pervasive.

Another important sector that has exerted a visible influence on education policy is the business sector. This sector has played a pivotal role in helping to guide the direction of states' educational policies. For instance, Ross Perot in Texas was influential in helping to shape educational policy in that state during the early 1990s. In fact, from a historical perspective, the private sector has always had an influence, either overtly or covertly, on educational policy. The early organizational development of state departments of education was, for example, emblematic of the corporate style of Weberian management and structure. However, the pervasiveness of corporate involvement in public education intensified during the 1980s when it became evident that America's competitive edge in the global economy had waned. Many business leaders considered the poor skills of the American workforce as a major contributory factor for this decline (Kearns 1988). In the 1980s and 1990s, businesses and organizations such as the National Alliance of Business played an important public role in helping to shape not only state reform agendas but also local school districts' reform initiatives. For example, Chicago's reform act of 1988 was influenced by the business sector, which was able to capitalize on its institutional strength and its legacy of activity in school reform dating back to the 1800s (Shipps 1998).

The influence of corporations on education occurs not only through the political process but through ideas, theories, and concepts that have been sometimes freely transferred from the corporate world into the world of schools. For example, the marketization of education that has occurred since the 1980s is based on principles of economics. Critics such as Apple (1988) and educational organizations such as the Association for Supervision and Curriculum Development (ASCD) have cautioned educators about the deleterious effects of allowing corporate special interest groups to dictate educational policies (Association for Supervision and Curriculum Development 1989). Yet notwithstanding this caution, the imprint of corporate influence on educational policy can be seen in many states throughout the country.

The policies and policymaking functions of state boards of education and state education departments have also been the subjects of influences that have arisen from the nexuses of advocacy groups that surround several policy areas, not only school finance but other areas such as the choice movement and special education. In the case of groups that coalesce around school finance issues, we have seen in the previous chapters that in instances where these groups have been able to successfully litigate their challenges to states' statutory funding mechanisms, their actions have helped to reshape educational policy in their respective states. Moreover, activist courts through the tenor of their decisions have been able to influence not only the creation of new educational policies but also, in some instances, the organizational and administrative functions of state educational agencies.

An increasingly important influence upon state policymaking activities in education are the media. As demonstrated in the previous chapter, the media have played an instrumental role in shaping and articulating the positions of various interest groups' responses to court decisions, and in furthering the mobilization efforts undertaken by some of these groups. However, the media have played a larger mediating role in helping to frame the public discourse on educational policy. Most major newspapers, for instance, routinely publish articles on educational issues, and leading editorials are written on state and national educational policies. Newspapers have been referred to as exercising a "secondary leadership" position in their impact on educational policy; indeed, the politicization of educational issues during recent decades has steadily resulted in this sector becoming more increasingly involved as a key stakeholder in the education policymaking process.

Such diverse fields of influences upon state boards of education and state education agencies have served to surreptitiously enlarge the number of stakeholders to whom these organizations are latently accountable. This differs significantly from their early beginnings in the nineteenth century and up to the 1960s, when they functioned primarily as protectors of the status quo, and when the normative model was based on political and social consensus. The increasing complexity of education policy and national politics since then has strained the organizational and regulatory, as well as policymaking, functions of these organizations and has changed the pattern and modes of interactions between state education departments and local communities.

SYSTEMIC REFORM AND A NEW PARADIGM FOR STATE EDUCATIONAL AGENCIES

As early as the 1980s the Education Commission for the States acknowledged the salient role of state government in leading and sustaining school-level improvement. The commission advocated for a strong level of support for educational improvement by the executive and legislative branches to be reflected in improvements in states' accountability mechanisms, quality statewide implementation strategies, a cogent theory of educational change, and congruence between local needs and state programs (Furhman, Huddle, and Armstrong 1986). These recommendations became important backdrops to the standards-based reforms that dominated educational policymaking activities during the 1990s.

Beginning in the 1990s a new approach to educational reform found expression in the policies that states adopted. The standards-based, or systemic reform, movement attempted to introduce changes in curriculum, governance, and alignment of policies. Unlike the first and second waves of reforms that occurred during the 1980s, which were fragmented, piecemeal, and uncoordinated, the systemic reforms of the 1990s sought to improve the quality of public education by fashioning an unprecedented alignment among all facets of public education.

The first wave of reform was characterized by a series of legislative mandates that unfolded in a top-down heavy-handed manner with minimal policy coherence (Murphy 1990). The second wave, which focused primarily on the organizational restructuring of public education in the policy areas of teacher professionalism, community and parent involvement, and devolution of authority-making decisions, also suffered from the same policy fragmentation that characterized the first set of reforms (Firestone et al. 1991). Systemic reform stood in sharp contradistinction to these earlier reform efforts. It should be noted parenthetically that this reform movement also occurred at the same time that important court decisions were being handed down in school finance cases. Hence, some state reform efforts—for example, New Jersey and Kentucky—represented a confluence of two forces of changes: the broad reform movement of the time, and the specific court directives regarding an adequate education. In fact, as was discussed in Chapter 2, the systemic reform movement provided courts and litigants with one framework that could be used to determine the elements of an adequate education.

The standards-based reform period has been exhaustively studied. Although these studies found evidence of great variability among the states in the degree to which standards-based reform was implemented, three common features to the systemic reform movement have been found to exist in most states (Massell, Kirst, and Hoppe, 1997). These are (1) the introduction of more stringent and rigorous academic standards; (2) the alignment of policies in curriculum, accountability, and teacher certification with the more stringent and rigorous academic standards that were adopted; and (3) the decentralization of educational governance at the local level, which allowed for a greater degree of participation by teachers and parents in educational decisions.

A brief overview of the movement's origins reveals that it was spawned and supported by interest groups representing professional organizations, such as the National Council of Teachers of Mathematics and the American Federation of Teachers; the business sector through the Business Roundtable; government funding sources such as the National Science Foundation; and representatives of school districts. These groups formed an unsteady alliance that ultimately unraveled and splintered when states began developing policies that would affect the implementation of the reforms (Massell, Kirst, and Hoppe 1997). As pointed out in Chapter 1, dissensus emerged around several aspects of the reforms. Disagreement existed about the potential effectiveness of this reform strategy, and problems occurred with the implementation of the accountability systems that were an integral component of the reforms. In addition to these difficulties, the increasing centralization of educational policy that necessarily inhered in the movement became the fodder for further tensions, which helped to fragment support for the reforms.

In spite of the difficulties that the movement encountered, the complex reform strategies that were associated with systemic change and the demands that this imposed upon localities necessitated changes in the manner in which state departments of education viewed their institutional responsibilities. A recurring theme that rang through this period was the need to build capacity at both the state and local levels. It was assumed that the regulatory and administrative orientation of most state departments of education would prove insufficient and incapable of providing state and local actors with the skills that were needed to effectively implement the reforms.

CAPACITY BUILDING AND STATE DEPARTMENTS OF EDUCATION

Capacity-building questions have long dominated the discourse on the organizational functioning of state education departments. As was noted previously, the curricular reforms of the 1950s and the federal educational initiatives of the 1960s were both cognizant of the need to provide resources to the departments in order to assist them with the new challenges that these reforms brought. Discussions on state education agencies' capacity-building efforts were also evident during the 1970s.

For example, Goddu (1972) proposed a model premised on a responsive linkage system that would aid state education departments in their ability to disseminate information to local agencies. Goddu suggested that capacity building for dissemination would require three types of efforts: (1) more state education staff, (2) more systematic information sources, and (3) more information access and utilization mechanisms. The systemic reform initiatives of the 1990s occurred at a time when the internal resources of many state departments of education were decimated because of the budget deficits that many states experienced during this period. In response to the decline in federal and state funding and the severe financial difficulties that they experienced during the early and mid-1980s, some state education agencies coped with these difficulties by either failing to fill positions that became vacant, eliminating positions once someone retired, or closing programs entirely (National Institute of Education 1982). In some states, such as Utah, part-time technical consultants were hired on an hourly basis with no fringe benefits to assume the responsibilities that full-time employees would have normally fulfilled (National Institute of Education 1982).

It is instructive to note that a refocusing of federal policy, and in particular the consolidation of categorical programs that was required by the passage of the Education Consolidation and Improvement Act (ECIA) of 1981, also severely impacted state education agencies. Passage of this act resulted in a retrenchment of staff and a major reorganization of many states' education agencies. Some policy analysts have argued that the cutback in federal funding as well as the consolidation movement in the early 1980s during the Reagan administration represented attempts by the federal government to assume a less intrusive presence in state and local education matters (see National Institute of Education 1982; Benderson 1984). This argument receives some validation when we examine federal funding for education during the Reagan years. According to Benderson (1984), the Reagan years brought with them a decline of about 2.4 percent in federal contribution to education.

Yet, in spite of the daunting circumstances in which many state education departments found themselves on the eve of introducing systemic reform, it was apparent that if the systemic reform initiatives were to be successful, capacity building at all levels of the educational system, from the state policy context to the local classroom level, would need enhancement. Capacity can be defined as the existence of a set of pre- and extant conditions that are necessary for the effective implementation of a policy. It is an important factor that helps one to understand the relationship between policy adoption and policy implementation. A policy's survival is contingent in part upon the institutional and organizational capacity that exists at all levels of the educational system. Consequently, successful implementation requires that a level of capacity exists to support a policy's desired outcome. Within the context of the systemic reform movement, this implied that such classroom factors as teacher skills, student motivation to learn, and curriculum materials that were in tandem with both higher academic standards and more stringent accountability requirements needed to exist (Massell 1998). At the state, district, and school levels, developing organizational structures and practices that could support classroom level changes became imperative.

State departments of education consequently were expected to develop policy and organizational infrastructures that would result in a number of important outcomes: first, the provision of technical support to local school actors; second, the establishment of directions and guidelines for professional development; third, the promulgation of standards in teaching, training, licensure, and certification requirement; fourth, the creation of new promotion and graduation requirements; fifth, the development of curriculum frameworks and the policies that govern the use of such frameworks; sixth, the development of social services; and seventh, the establishment of regulations that guided instruction, school governance, and organizational issues at the district, school, and classroom levels (Massell 1998, 3–4).

These recommended changes were supported by prior discussions in the scholarly community on the implementation models that tend to characterize state-led or top-down reform efforts. Odden and Anderson (1986), for example, identified four distinct yet interrelated stages to state-initiated reform, each with its own unique characteristics and features. The initiation stage requires an identification of readiness among schools with external pressure for change emanating from the state or district. During this start-up phase, awareness training and technical support from external experts for district and school level personnel are required. Collaborative decisionmaking is encouraged, and attempts are made to fashion a fit between local needs, local buy-ins, and states' implementation efforts. Phase two represents the beginning of implementation. Resource support is needed, adequate training of all actors involved in the reform is required, and coordination of state, district, and school activities is a necessity. Phase three represents the latter stages of implementation. School-level personnel are engaged in developing the skills that are embedded in the reforms. Continual support from technical experts is still warranted, particularly when problems arise. In the final phase, the reforms become integrated into the institutional and organizational life of the school.

Several comparative studies investigating the capacity-building efforts of state education agencies during the implementation of standards-based reform have been undertaken (Hertert 1996; Lusi 1997; Massell 1998). The comparative perspective adopted by these studies allows for an understanding of the degree of variability in state-level responses and emphasis. Indubitably, in order to promote successful implementation of standards-based reforms, state education departments themselves needed to transform their internal operations, and in particular the regulatory and monitoring focus, that undergirded their external relationships with local school districts.

These studies found that states varied significantly in how they responded to the complex challenges that this posed. Moreover, local districts' reactions to state-led efforts differed across the country. Massell's (1998) cross-state comparison revealed that most education departments' efforts in spite of some differences were influenced by four capacity-building strategies. First, state education departments relied upon an external infrastructure to provide technical assistance and professional development. Departments of education utilized their regional/county service centers and nongovernmental professional organizations to deliver services to schools. Given the previous discussions on the shrinking internal resources both in terms of personnel and money that these bureaucracies confronted, the reliance by some states upon the regional centers represented a rational organizational response. States such as Maryland were found to spend million of dollars in establishing Regional Staff Development Centers. (It is estimated that between 1995 and 1998, Maryland spent $3 million in establishing these centers.) Although there was a general reliance upon these centers, how these centers were used varied from state to state. In some states the centers were used to serve their reform goals, whereas others relied upon the centers to provide services for targeted programs and populations (Massell 1998). For instance, both Maryland and California regional centers provided support to low-performing schools. Massell reports that in Kentucky, for example, these intermediate structures were used as means of encouraging districts to pool resources.

State education departments also drew upon the expertise of networks, more formalized professional organizations, and institutions of higher education for capacity-building activities. These activities were primarily concentrated in the areas of professional development training and curriculum development and alignment. For example, teacher networks and those associated with other educational experts were used to provide professional development for teachers, support to failing schools, and assistance to districts in their efforts to align their curriculum to their states' content standards (Massell 1998). The state of California's experience in this area is particularly noteworthy. California in its attempt to change teachers' instructional practices relied upon an elaborate system of teacher networks that provided intensive subject matter professional development. The California initiative was known as the Subject-Matter Projects. These networks of teachers were supported by state funding on a three-year funding cycle. The project modeled itself on the University of California–Berkeley writing project.

In addition to teacher networks, states relied upon the expertise of professional associations in the content areas to assist them with capacity building. The contribution of these associations was similar to that of the teacher networks. Professional associations were used to provide professional development opportunities for teachers, and to assist the states with the development of curriculum and assessment policies. Finally, institutions of higher education were relied upon for the support that they could provide in the areas of professional and curriculum development.

The second major capacity-building strategy that most states engaged in involved the establishment of professional development and training standards. Enabling teachers at both the preservice and inductive stages to possess the necessary competencies to effectively teach more rigorous academic content became a priority activity for many states. For example, New Jersey required one hundred hours of continuing professional development for all teachers. Colorado instituted standards that called for ongoing comprehensive professional development. Minnesota developed performance-based licensing, and Michigan and Kentucky redesigned their accreditation processes. Many states offered guidelines on standards for professional development; in some states teacher accreditation systems were redesigned, and in others new requirements for preservice teaching and education were instituted (Massell 1998, 7).

The third strategy that states employed during the standards-based period focused on the development and dissemination of curriculum frameworks and materials. These materials were linked to the new academic content standards that were adopted. Finally, instituting new approaches toward school-level planning and decisionmaking that focused on yearly school improvement became the fourth capacity-building strategy that was embraced by many states.

How did local districts respond to these state-initiated activities? One study that addressed this question found that districts' responses were a function of their internal capacity to handle change (Hertert 1996). Districts that were high capacity but also highly involved in education politics in their states were less critical of their states' reform efforts. These districts were able to capitalize on their political connections in order to influence their states' policy developments. High-capacity districts with low levels of involvement in education politics were less favorable in their evaluations of the state-led reform. These districts tended to focus on their own internal reform agendas. Because of their internal technical strengths and fiscal buoyancy, these districts were able to have successful student achievement while insulating themselves from the reform pressures that emanated from their states. Most districts had neither the fiscal buoyancy, internal technical expertise, nor political access to enable them to adequately influence or insulate themselves from the pressures associated with state reforms (Hertert 1996, 384). These districts tended to be highly critical of state reform efforts, particularly from the vantage point of lack of coherence and misfit with local needs.

Continuing Issues with State
Education Departments' Capacities

The No Child Left Behind (NCLB) legislation introduced by the Bush administration has brought into sharp relief the continuing capacity problems that state education departments confront in disseminating and implementing policies that are generated at either the federal or state level. Signed into law by President George W. Bush in January 2002, after receiving bipartisan support, the NCLB act has significantly broadened and strengthened the state and federal roles in education. The act spells out a complex set of requirements in the areas of student progress and accountability, school choice and the provision of supplemental education services, teacher and paraprofessional quality, and the use of scientifically based research to improve teaching and learning. These requirements are expected to result in the attainment of the five performance goals identified in Table 5.2.

The NCLB act has been the subject of intense criticism from states and their governors, professional organizations representing those involved in public education, institutions of higher education, the media, and local school districts and parents. Criticisms have been leveled at the lack of federal funding to support the cost that states must incur to meet the complex requirements embodied in the act; the potential for some elements of the act to weaken public education in general; the overreliance on test-score performance to make substantive judgments about schools without consideration of the myriad technical factors that may influence test performance; the unrealistic timelines

Table 5.2

No Child Left Behind Performance Goals

Goal 1: By 2013–2014, all students will achieve high standards, at a minimum attaining proficiency or better in reading/language arts and mathematics.

Goal 2: All limited–English-proficient students will become proficient in English and reach high academic standards, at a minimum, attaining proficiency or better in reading/language arts and mathematics.

Goals 3: By 2005–2006, all students will be taught by highly qualified teachers.

Goal 4: All students will be educated in learning environments that are safe, drug free, and conducive to learning.

Goal 5: All students will graduate from high school.

---

associated with many of the provisions; the academic expectations for some subgroups of pupils, for example, special education students, who are expected to achieve at the same rate as other students; the requirement to determine whether teachers are highly qualified; and the intrusion on state rights.

Since the act's passage, at least twelve states have passed resolutions that call on Congress to either amend or repeal the law. These states have objected to spending state funds to carry out federal policies, with opposition cutting across party lines. For example, in February 2004, both Republican and Democratic legislators from Oklahoma passed a resolution calling for an overhaul of the law. In March 2004, more than 138 eastern Pennsylvania superintendents voiced their opposition to certain provisions of the law before a senate committee in Washington (Dillon 2004). Powerful Republican legislators in some western states have also voiced their concerns about the potential negative impact that some provisions could have on small rural districts. For example, in small rural districts where there is a shortage of science teachers, legislators saw as unworkable the requirement that a high school teacher responsible for teaching more than one science subject needed to hold certification in all of the subjects (Dillon 2004).

Faced with growing public discontent over several aspects of the law, President Bush and his secretary of education, Rod Paige, have been forced to embark on a campaign to mobilize support for his education policy. President Bush had to intervene to prevent the Utah legislature from acting on a passed legislative resolution that sharply criticized the law and that signaled Utah's intent not to participate in the No Child Left Behind programs. Furthermore, in order to diffuse the mounting criticism that the act has evoked, the U.S. Department of Education has relaxed regulations governing the testing of special education and limited-English students as well as the provision governing teacher certification. On March 15, 2004, the secretary of education issued new guidelines regarding the highly qualified teacher requirement. These guidelines were influenced by the mounting criticism against the impracticality of the certification requirements, especially in communities that face a teacher shortage. For example, science teachers in rural districts who teach multiple science subjects no longer have to be fully certified in each subject that they teach. They are also given an additional three years to meet the "highly qualified" mandate.

State Education Departments' Responsibilities under NCLB

The No Child Left Behind law requires state education departments to assume new roles while maintaining some of the traditional functions that they perform. Listed below are the major functions that state departments are expected to perform in the implementation of the law. First of all, states were required to submit by January 2002 a consolidated application that included acceptance of the five performance goals. With respect to student progress and accountability, states are federally required to implement a single accountability system, determine the adequate yearly progress that is made by schools, implement a system of rewards and sanctions, and implement an assessment system in science.

The school choice and supplemental services provision requires states to create a list of providers who can offer educational supplemental services to students in failing schools. They are also required to monitor the effectiveness of these providers. Under the provisions governing teacher and paraprofessional qualifications, states are required to set annual measurable goals for districts and schools; to provide assistance to schools that fail to meet these goals for two consecutive years; and to ensure that Title 1 paraprofessionals hired after January 8, 2002, meet the new federal requirements. States also are expected to ensure that their support to schools as well as their applications for federal funds are informed by scientifically based research.

State Responsibilities under No Child Left Behind Act of 2002

Program Consolidation

- Develop a consolidated state application for the major federal formula grant programs.

Student Progress and Accountability

- Implement a single accountability system based on challenging standards in reading/language arts and mathematics to be administered every year in grades 3 through 8 and in one grade level in high school.
- Develop a system that measures student progress by determining adequate yearly progress made by all subgroups of pupils based on the same starting point for all students and all schools.
- Develop a system of sanctions and rewards tied to school performance.
- Implement a science assessment annually, in at least one grade at the elementary, middle, and high school levels.
- Produce an annual report card.
- Annually assess the English proficiency of students learning the English language.
- Ensure the distribution of state results before the beginning of the next school year.
- Participate in the biennial state level NAEP assessments of 4th and 8th grades in reading and mathematics.

School Choice and Supplemental Educational Services

- Ensure that students in previously identified schools are offered school choices.
- Annually report the number of students and schools that participate in public school choice.
- Identify and provide a list of state-approved providers based upon objective criteria.
- Monitor the quality and effectiveness of the supplemental services and programs offered by state-approved providers.

Teachers and Paraprofessional Qualifications

- Set annual measurable goals for each school district and schools, including annual increases in the percentage of highly qualified teachers and the percentage receiving professional development to become highly qualified.
- Provide technical assistance to districts that fail for two consecutive years to meet annual increases in highly qualified teachers.
- Ensure that Title 1 paraprofessionals hired after January 8, 2002, meet new federal requirements that require them to have a high school diploma; complete two years of study at an institution of higher education; or obtained at least an associate's degree; or meet rigorous standard of quality through a formal state or local assessment.
- Must use scientifically based research to inform technical assistance provided by state-established support teams.

Scientifically Based Research

- State application for federal funds must describe how proposed activities are informed by scientifically based research.

States have been able to make progress in some areas, but capacity issues have stymied progress in others (Center on Education Policy 2003). A major study of all fifty states' implementation efforts the first year after enactment of the NCLB act found that states' efforts were more successful in those areas where they had prior experience (Center on Education Policy 2003). Particularly, because of most states' prior involvement in assessment, states were found to have made faster progress in implementing some aspects of the standards and assessment requirements than other areas of the law; for example, identifying providers for supplemental educational services, complying with the requirements for teacher and paraprofessional qualifications, and scientifically-based research.

Interviews conducted with state officials underscore how severe budget constraints and staffing issues imperil state efforts to take on the new roles that have been thrust upon them. State officials are expressly concerned with whether they have the expertise and personnel to provide technical assistance to failing schools (Center on Education Policy 2003, 12). For example, the Center on Education Policy study found that in one large state, budget cuts and hiring freezes resulted in the department's staff being halved. This dramatically altered the department's composition. Whereas, before the budget cut, subject matter specialists staffed the department, in the advent of cuts most personnel became generalists, who while being able to assist in the field are deemed, according to state officials, unable to carry out federal policy because of their lack of subject matter knowledge (Center on Education Policy 2003, 13). State education departments have also confronted capacity problems stemming from the failure of the U.S. Department of Education to provide timely feedback to their queries; technical assistance with some of the more difficult requirements, for example, the supplemental services provisions; and complete information in a timely manner, for example, information that would serve to clarify the teacher and paraprofessional qualifications section of the law. More important, states' capacities to support the ambitious goals of the NCLB act have been hampered by inadequate federal funding.

Questions as to the efficacy of the policy instruments that the federal government has employed to assist states in meeting the many complex goals of NCLB are thus legitimate ones to raise in light of the preceding discussion. Moreover, the organizational and financial strains that many state education departments are experiencing in implementing the act would seem to suggest that the signature educational policy of the Bush administration could well be in jeopardy.

POLICY INSTRUMENT CHOICES OF STATE EDUCATION DEPARTMENTS

The foregoing discussion on capacity building brings to the fore the distinction between the traditional and nontraditional policy instruments that states as well as the federal government rely upon. Like other agencies engaged in public policy, state education departments make important decisions regarding the specific policy tools that they will employ to promote educational goals. These decisions are influenced by a number of considerations, including pressure from various organized interest groups; input from the legislative, executive, and judicial branches of government; the opportunity costs associated with a given choice; the consequences of their actions; and the convergence between the adoption of a particular instrument and policy and ideological preferences (Feiock and Stream 1998). In this decisionmaking context, the opportunity costs associated with a given choice of a policy tool refer to the organizational, institutional, and fiscal constraints that the enacting agency confronts as it seeks to make decisions regarding how best to implement a policy. As we saw in the earlier discussion on state education agencies' responses to the standards-based movement, states chose to rely upon an external infrastructure to provide support to local schools rather than to engage in an expansion of staff roles within their own bureaucracies to serve as direct providers.

Understanding the role that state education departments have played in promoting educational adequacy necessitates an examination of the types of policy instruments and the combination of instruments that are used to pursue adequacy goals. Writings in the field of public policy have stressed the importance of examining the tools that are used by governmental agencies, and in particular, the mix of policy tools that are utilized in the service of policy attainment. Critics have argued that there is a tendency for policy analysts to focus only on a single instrument and to view instruments as mutually exclusive. However, the use of multiple instruments and their interaction effects are thought to provide a much clearer picture as to how policy makers seek to induce compliance to policy goals. Attempts have been made to classify the many policy instruments that policy makers have at their disposal. Although some instruments may be idiosyncratic to a particular policy domain, there are some that are generic to most fields of public policy. These are the use of regulations and incentives, the provision of information and technical support, the enactment of administrative reform, and the employment of what is termed direct government supply or financial support for programs (Feiock and Stream 1998).

The policy tool choices of state education departments and the extent to which they elect to exercise these choices will have important consequences for local school districts. Research has shown that state departments of education use certain policy instruments to a lesser or greater degree within certain school contexts and are also inclined in general to rely upon some policy tools more frequently than others. For example, high-needs school districts are much more likely to be the subjects of monitoring and oversight than are school districts with lower needs (Consortium for Policy Research in Education 1992). State education departments are also more likely to use regulations and monitoring as their major policy instruments than other tools. The overuse of some tools may, however, be counter to the ultimate goal of a given policy.

Local school districts can influence the policy instrument choices of their state education departments. School districts with a high degree of representation in their states' political process are much more favorably positioned to influence the policy instrument choice of state education agencies than are those with little or no influence. As was noted in Chapter 4, legislative officials are very concerned with the political consequences of the choices that they make, and the fear of public backlash brought about by pressure from organized interest groups will help to determine their choice of policy tool.

Policy tools can thus be viewed as strategic structures insofar as they are used by state education departments to provide and deliver resources to schools (Walker 2004). These tools tend to be aligned to policy goals, and departments of education can be selective in the types of tools they use. These structures are key to understanding the interactions between state education departments and local schools, and they serve as environmental buffers between the departments on the one hand, and local schools on the other. The ensuing pages present the major policy tools that state education departments utilize in the implementation of adequacy reforms. Examples from states engaged in reforms that are brought about by court decisions on educational adequacy are provided.

Regulations

Regulatory mechanisms seek to ensure uniform compliance to policy goals. State departments of education have traditionally relied upon the use of regulations to bring about conformity to state education policies and to influence practice in the field. Regulations describe the procedures and standards that govern local school districts and their member schools in complying with statutory requirements or some other form of legal decree. Regulations typically fulfill three purposes: (1) they ensure the implementation of a statute (which is a law enacted by the legislative branch of the government) or judicial decree whose terms and conditions for implementation have been determined by a prior authority; (2) they provide interpretations of a statute or decree whose imprecision in its initial formulation might not have anticipated changes that are brought about by enactment; and (3) they provide clarification and elaboration in instances where a statute or decree lacks sufficient detail to explain and describe the necessity for certain actions (Kerwin 1999; Block 2002). Guidelines for writing state regulations are sometimes spelled out by the state legislatures in governing administrative codes. Legislatures may require that regulations are written clearly, unambiguously, and comprehensively; are easily readable; provide clear definitions as well as enough detail so as to produce the intended consequences; and avoid long convoluted sentences (Martineau 1991; Block 2002).

The increasing centralization of educational policy has brought in its wake a growth in state regulatory activities. Typically, these regulations represent one of three types: they govern inputs, processes, or outputs (Consortium for Policy Research in Education 1992). Regulatory statements on inputs focus on resources, such as teacher credentialing and expenditures. Process regulations set guidelines for instruction, including course offerings, curriculum content standards, and school organization. Regulations on outputs establish accountability requirements at both the system and individual levels; for example, targeted performance goals for students and schools. Prior to the early 1990s regulations tended to focus primarily on inputs and processes. The standards-based reform movement, court decisions on educational adequacy, and the passage of the No Child Left Behind legislation have all resulted in a proliferation of regulations that are concerned with educational outputs.

Local educators frequently look askance at state as well as federal education regulations, viewing them as unwarranted encroachments upon local decisionmaking. But regulations are frequently used by state and federal policy makers as means of influencing educational practice, although according to some researchers it is difficult to link regulations to good practice (Consortium for Policy Research in Education 1992). State education agencies tend to face the compounding problem of enforceability of the regulations that they promulgate. State departments of education are not properly staffed to monitor the degree of compliance with state regulations among schools and districts. They frequently rely upon district and school submissions of written documentation to determine the degree to which adherence with state regulations has taken place at the local level. At times, state education agencies are also unable to assess in a reasonable way the effectiveness of a given set of regulations on desired practices. The disconnection between the policy goals that a given set of regulations purport to support and the inability of state education departments to determine whether these goals have been attained have resulted in what is termed regulatory unreasonableness (Consortium for Policy Research in Education 1992). Regulatory unreasonableness represents a situation in which the means for determining whether a regulatory goal has been attained assumes greater saliency than the goal itself. It is exemplified by a focus by state education actors on "formalistic, legalistic, standardized inspection processes" (Consortium for Policy Research in Education 1992, 3).

Many states in response to successful school finance litigation have utilized regulations to codify court-sanctioned remedies. Purportedly, these regulations are designed to elaborate on standards and procedures that are commensurate with the spirit and intent of the court's ruling. State education departments make use of a variety of strategies in developing these regulations. In direct response to the *Rose v. Council of Education* decision the Kentucky legislature convened the Kentucky Commonwealth Task Force on Education Reform, which relied extensively on public hearings and consultations with national experts in its development of the regulations that were later codified in the Kentucky Education Reform Act.

The experience of New Jersey indicates that when states develop regulations that fail to meet the requirements outlined in a court's decision, courts have the power to nullify these regulations. For instance, the New Jersey State Supreme Court ruled in 2002 that the state's preschool standards did not meet the requirement of "substantive educational standards" and directed the state education department to reexamine the regulations and the state's preschool policies in light of its decision (*Abbott v. Burke*, 2000). To be fair, some courts in their adequacy decisions have crafted their rulings in language that lacks sufficient specificity and clarity to enable state education departments to readily and easily understand what the policy implications are. Under these circumstances, state policy makers and departments of education are left to speculatively interpret the meaning of the decision.

The policy-implementing environment is, however, rendered unstable when regulations are constantly being revised, either because they fail to comport with a statutory or judicial requirement or because they are so poorly written as to create ambiguity among schools (Walker 2004). In either case, the frequent revisions of regulations can lead to a subversion of the policy goals that the regulations undergird. Yet, state education departments tend to rely extensively on regulatory mechanisms to promote educational adequacy. In both Kentucky and New Jersey, two states that were profiled in Chapter 4, local school actors were critical of the overuse of regulations to guide the implementation process of their respective court-sanctioned reforms (Lusi 1997; Walker 2004). In both states the overregulation of the implementation process was antithetical to the intent of the reforms, which emphasized local decisionmaking and local identification of particularized need.

Incentives

Unlike regulatory mandates, which seek to compel compliance behaviors congruent with a policy goal, incentives are used as policy tools by state education agencies to induce rather than force behavior. One of the earliest systematic examinations of the role of incentive structures in promoting educational reform was undertaken by a group of economists who formed the Panel on the Economics of Educational Reform (PEER). (The Pew Charitable Trust underwrote the work of the panel.) The panel's work occurred during the early 1990s and was later published (Hanushek 1994).

Drawing on economic principles, PEER advocated the use of performance-incentive systems as a means of stimulating the efficient use of educational resources, decentralizing and deregulating the management of education, and enticing educational improvement through inducements. Incentive systems are viewed to be of two kinds: those that operate within the existing structure of school systems, and those that fundamentally result in an alteration of existing structures. The first framework focuses on student performance and links incentives directly to desired student outcomes. These include performance contracting, performance-based incentives, and school-based management. Incentive structures that seek to alter the basic structure of schools rely on the exercise of choice by families. These structures are premised on the following assumptions: one, that they allow families, rather than school administrators, through the exercise of choice to determine a good education; and two, that choice serves as an incentive for poorly performing schools to improve (Hanushek 1994, 103–104).

Incentive Systems that Operate within Existing Schools

Performance Contracting

Under performance contracting, independent companies and firms are hired to perform specific services within the public sector. Because the relationship is contractual, rewards or incentives are built directly into the contract and are contingent upon the attainment of the specific measurable goals that are delimited in the contract. States and the federal government have throughout the years relegated some of their responsibilities to private companies. Privatization can assume two forms: divestiture or deregulation. Under divestiture programs the government transfers completely a function, agency, or asset to a private company. In the case of deregulation the government turns the responsibility for delivery of services over to a private firm while retaining responsibility for other areas.

Privatization in public education tends to follow the second model, that is, independent firms are hired to deliver a particular set of services or goods. One of the earliest experiments with privatization occurred in the 1960s in Texarkana, Arkansas (Jost 1994). In Texarkana, the Office of Economic Opportunity contracted with Dorsett Education to deliver reading and mathematics services to potential dropouts. The contract specified that the company would only receive remuneration if student performance showed improvement (Jost 1994). Within two years, the Texarkana project was expanded to more than one hundred school districts. Data on student performance revealed that there was no significant, substantial improvement in students' reading and math achievement. Since then, several school districts and states have entered into arrangements with private companies. Most notable are the experiences of Dade County in Florida, and Baltimore, Maryland. Results on the effectiveness of for-profit companies in influencing student achievement has been mixed.

Opponents to performance contracting and other forms of privatization practices within public education have marshaled a number of arguments in support of their position. First, the argument is posited that unlike other areas of public service, education is a function that states are required by their constitutions to fulfill (Brown and Contreras 1991). This constitutional mandate implies that states have an affirmative burden to ensure that all children have access to a free quality education, which allows them to be responsible and productive citizens. Second, the notion of the common good that is shrouded in the states' educational clauses is seen to be obscured by privatization, since the latter seeks to satisfy individual interest. Third, critics further argue that the economic motives that underlie privatization could result in an erosion of the quality of education for different pupils (Hawley 1995). For example, admission policies could result in the exclusion of students from less-advantaged backgrounds and of different ethnic cultures from schools that are privately managed.

Nevertheless, some states in complying with court decisions regarding the implementation of appropriate remedies to ensure educational adequacy have permitted districts and schools to contract out services to private providers. This is particularly the case where capacity issues stymie the ability of districts to comply fully with a remedy. For example, in response to the court remedy that all three- and four-year-olds should be enrolled in quality preschool programs, the New Jersey Department of Education allowed districts impacted by the *Abbott v. Burke* decisions to hire private preschool community providers to provide these services (Walker 2003).

Performance-Based Incentives

The arguments for performance-based incentives are inextricably woven with notions that accountability within public schools ought to be based on student achievement. Moreover, it is posited that the use of incentives based on student outcomes has a greater chance of improving schools than the use of other policy instruments, such as regulations, since performance incentive structures are more likely to encourage educators to comply with policy goals (Hanushek 1996). Two behavioral theories, *expectancy theory* and *goal-setting theory,* both of which attempt to understand individual motivation to engage in specific behaviors, have been drawn upon to explain the likely success of performance-based incentives (Kelley et al. 2000). According to expectancy theorists, individuals are likely to engage in task behaviors when they hold strong beliefs that they can be successful in accomplishing the task. Goal-setting theories postulate that the more specific and clear goals are, the stronger the motivation on the part of individuals to comply with the goals. Kelley et al. (2000) argue that incentives are likely to be effective motivators if the following conditions are satisfied: (1) teachers hold firm beliefs that they can achieve a specific goal, (2) the goal is clearly stated and does not conflict with other organizational goals, (3) teachers are provided with the resources to assist them in accomplishing the goal, and (4) teachers value the consequences of meeting the goal.

The use of performance-based incentives has grown steadily over the years as one of the policy tools utilized by state education agencies to stimulate student achievement. In this regard, policy makers have utilized a number of incentive structures, such as the publication of test scores, monetary awards, takeover or reconstitution of failing schools, retention and graduation standards, and student promotion (Elmore 2002). In 2001, at least twenty states had performance-based incentives for teachers linked to an increase in student achievement levels (Lashway 2001). Implementation of incentives has not, however, been without difficulties. A multiplicity of factors has stymied implementation efforts. These include political resistance, practical considerations, the amount of the monetary incentive (if the incentive structure is based on monetary compensation), the perceived fairness of the procedures that are used to determine if goals are attained, and whether goals are perceived to be realistic (Kelley et al. 2000; Lashway 2001).

Some states—for example, Kentucky and Maryland—tie their incentive systems to school level rather than individual teacher outcomes. Kentucky's accountability system grew out of the court decision in *Rose v. Council of Education* and the subsequent reform act that was enacted in 1990 (the Kentucky Education Reform Act). Maryland's incentive structure, in contrast, was influenced by the 1990 recommendations of the Sondheim Commission. In the Kentucky model, statistical analysis based on regression techniques is used to develop an accountability index in seven content areas. These are reading, math, science, social studies, arts/humanities, writing, and vocational/practical living; there are also measures of noncognitive growth, such as attendance, dropout rates, and retention. Two-year expectancy scores based on an annual improvement of 10 percent of the distance between the baseline and target (which requires all students to attain proficiency) are established for each school. Schools that meet and/or exceed their goals are rewarded based on the size of their faculty and the extent to which they exceed their goals. According to Kelley et al. (2000), the average size of the award during the first accountability cycle (1991–1994) was roughly $2,600 in Kentucky. In Maryland, school-based awards between 1996 and 1998 fell in a range of $14, 500 to $64,600 per school.

Maryland's accountability program uses a school performance index that represents a weighted average of the difference between a school's performance and state standards, to award schools for sustained and significant improvement in student achievement. The index is based on two assessment programs: the Maryland Assessment Program at the elementary level, and the Maryland High School Assessment Program. Schools are not permitted to use their performance recognition awards funds to compensate staff or to supplant or replace funds available from other sources.

More recently, the utilization of performance incentives has been recommended as one alternative method for circumventing the knotty problem of school finance. This has sparked debate in Texas, where the Republican governor, Rick Perry, has proposed the introduction of performance-based incentives that would link monetary award to student performance (Magers 2004). As we saw in Chapter 4, Texas has had a very contentious legal history with regard to school finance. Legislative differences among partisan groups within the General Assembly as well as groups representing different racial and class sectors of the state have made arriving at a consensus on the best way to create education adequacy difficult to attain. Governor Perry has expressed his opposition to providing additional funding for schools based on the *Edgewood* decisions. He has, however, signaled a willingness to support more funding if that funding is linked directly to performance (Magers 2004). The governor's proposal comes in the wake of a lawsuit filed by a group of school districts challenging the property tax cap of $1.50 per $100 valuation, and the continuing public and political debates around the so-called Robin Hood Plan (see Chapter 4). The governor's proposal has evoked strong criticism from different interest groups, including teacher organizations.

Is the use of incentive systems by state education departments an effective policy tool? The answer to this question appears to be ambiguous. Researchers have yet to determine that a causal relationship exists between incentives and student performance (Lashway 2001). Moreover, there is still some uncertainty as to whether incentive structures can be predictably expected to provide the same impact across multiple contexts (Elmore 2002). Incentives systems that are well designed do, however, seem to support school reform, although the exact manner in which incentives influence successful school reform is unclear. Some researchers argue that incentives act as motivators, and others contend that the use of these systems helps to redirect energies to specific outcomes (Clotfelter and Ladd 1996; Lashway 2001). In spite of the inconclusiveness of the effects of performance incentives on student improvement, educators and legislators still view incentives as an integral component of a viable accountability system.

Arguably, the use of performance incentives and performance contracting will continue to pose a number of difficulties for educators. For one, the success of incentive structures in inducing compliance behavior is contingent upon how clearly articulated the goals are, the ability to measure the accomplishment or progress toward these goals, and the minimization of distortions (Hannaway 1996). Distortions produced by reliance on incentives to stimulate behavior are likely to occur in two ways: first, by overemphasizing some goals to the expense of others; and second, by creating conditions in which teachers in order to meet the performance goals may focus on one group of pupils, in particular, those students who are in the middle range of the performance distribution. Thus, students at the lower and upper ends of the distribution are ignored (Hannaway 1996). This was found to be the case in the performance contracting experiments of the 1970s.

Linking rewards to student achievement may also be problematic because of the natural fluctuations and volatility of test scores. Changes in test score performance can occur for a variety of reasons, among them, sampling variations, differences in beginning level performance, and the size of a school. Given these sources of variations, basing incentives on single-year changes tends to be unreliable. A more reliable system of accountability in which incentives are an integral component needs to tie rewards to test-score changes that occur over multiple years.

Some have argued that the reliance upon external incentive structures by themselves may not be sufficient to transform schools and ensure an adequate education for all students (Elmore 2002). Rather, a combination of internal and external structures that draws upon the internal satisfaction from the act of schooling and learning and supported by external recognition is perhaps the most potent force for improving schools.

School-Based Management

Although school-based management is not seen as constituting an incentive structure, it is argued that when decentralization is used along with other incentive structures it can become a powerful tool to promote school improvement (Hanushek 1994; Hannaway 1996). Decentralization of decisionmaking allows for optimal decisionmaking at the local site and can result in pressures on local school actors to produce improvement. However, decentralization as a management strategy has inherent limitations, which makes it, when used as a single reform strategy, an insufficient method for producing improvement in student achievement. For example, effective decisionmaking is contingent upon the availability of sound information, it presumes that local actors are able to act upon this information in a way that will foster student achievement, and it assumes that the capacity and resources are readily available to support locally arrived-at decisions.

Research has shown that these assumptions are not always tenable (Walker 2002). A number of critical variables have been found to influence the effectiveness of decentralization. These include parental socioeconomic status, the role of the teachers' unions, and the relationship between schools and the central office, as well as the other pressing demands that are placed upon teachers and schools (Hannaway 1996; Walker 2002). Nonetheless, it is assumed that the use of incentive systems may help to attenuate some of the limitations that are associated with decentralization. For example, incentive structures that operate within a decentralized system of governance are seen to have the potential to effectively guide behavior toward desired goals (Hannaway 1996). By rewarding specific behaviors, incentives can help local school actors who are engaged in school-based decisions to focus and direct their attention to these behaviors, thereby tailoring their decisions to valued goals.

Incentive Systems that Operate outside Existing Schools

Proponents of school choice suggest that the introduction of choice serves as an incentive for school improvement. Choice is viewed as a more radical employment of performance incentives that leads to a dismantling of the monopolistic tendencies that tend to characterize public schooling (Hanushek 1996). Advocates for choice contend that the exercise of choice allows the market mechanisms to determine and reward schools that are effective (Hanushek 1996). For choice to be effective, certain preconditions must exist; for example, the availability of sound information about schools, the ability of parents and students to make informed choices, the flow of resources, and a range of available choices (Hanushek 1996, 104–106). Both federal and state policies have tended to reinforce the assumption that choice promotes educational equity and adequacy. For example, the federal government has provided extensive funding for choice programs, such as the Magnet Schools' Assistance Program, the Public Charter School Program, and the Voluntary Public School Choice Program.

Does choice lead to improvement in schools and student achievement? As was seen in the discussions on this topic in Chapter 1, the results are unclear as to the effectiveness of choice policies. The lack of conclusive data as to the effectiveness of the choice movement buttresses opponents' claims that the use of choice as a policy tool to promote educational growth may be unwarranted, particularly in light of the contention that choice leads to an erosion in confidence in the public school system and a siphoning off of much-needed resources from this system (Adelsheimer and Rix 1999).

Information and Technical Support

The discussion that was presented earlier in the chapter on the standards-based reform movement of the 1990s underscored the saliency of information and technical support in the form of capacity-building efforts in promoting successful school reform. Complex reform efforts require of state departments of education the deployment of a variety of policy tools that align with the ultimate goals of these reforms. Uncertainty during the early stages of a policy's implementation makes it necessary for the progenitors of the policy to provide implementers with information that can assist them with implementation. This is true even if the implementer is an agency, for example, state education departments' implementation of No Child Left Behind, or local school districts that are responding to state or federal policy initiatives. However, the timeliness of the information, its accuracy, and its clarity will be important in ensuring successful implementation. A national study of how state departments of education implemented the No Child Left Behind law underscored the difficulties that the states experienced in complying with certain sections of the act, because of a failure on the part of the U.S. Department of Education to provide states with timely and unambiguous information (Center on Education Policy 2003).

Studies of the implementation of adequacy policies reveal the important role that communication between state education departments and local districts and schools plays in ensuring successful implementation. For example, investigations into the implementation of the Abbott reforms in New Jersey, which grew out of the 1998 *Abbott v. Burke* court decision, revealed how a lack of information, and the untimeliness with which the state education department of education responded to districts' requests for clarification, hampered the implementation process (Walker and Gutmore 2000; Erlichson and Goertz 2001).

Schools not only require timely and accurate information when they are engaged in externally driven reform, but they also need technical assistance, as we saw previously, in order to assist them with the building of capacity. Some state departments of education that are involved in complex reforms linked with adequacy decisions have created infrastructures or have relied on external sources to provide schools with technical assistance. In New Jersey, the state education department created school review and improvement teams. During the early stages of implementation, these teams were responsible for working closely with local schools as they began making critical school-level decisions. When it began implementing its reforms, the Kentucky State Education Department established eight regional centers throughout the state that were responsible for providing technical support to schools.

A continuing challenge for state education departments is to create or utilize infrastructures that will be credible with teachers, parents, and other school district personnel, and which are able to provide these constituents with quality support. New Jersey's experience with the school improvement teams during the early years of its reform highlighted the implementation difficulties that occurred when teams are composed of individuals who lack an understanding of the purpose of the reform and who are unfamiliar with the educational contexts in which the reforms are being implemented (Walker and Gutmore 2000). Kentucky's experience in providing technical support to schools was decidedly more positive (Lusi 1997).

Administrative and Organizational Reform

Discussions on state educational agencies' abilities to effectively respond to complex policies for educational reform invariably focus on the organizational and administrative transformations that need to occur (Lusi 1997; Timar 1997; Massell 1998). These discussions are informed by the historical portraits that have been drawn over time of state education departments as highly segmented and balkanized structures. Departments of education themselves have tended to respond to these depictions by attempting to reorganize their organizational and administrative structures when confronted with new reform challenges. Various conceptual approaches have been forwarded to explain how departments of education reframe, or ought to reframe, their internal organization structuring when implementing state-led complex reforms.

Macro-level theories, for instance, focus on the processes used by state education departments to develop structures, instrumentalities, and other means for ensuring the effective execution of a policy (Walker 2004, 342). These theories suggest that departments of education will develop rational approaches to their internal organizational structures in order to support policy goals and agendas (Cibulka and Derlin 1998). The Kentucky Department of Education in 1991 underwent a major restructuring that aligned with the policy elements of its reform act. Departments and subunits were redesigned and renamed to reflect these elements, salary structures were renegotiated, and the regular state personnel mechanism for hiring state workers was by-passed in order to allow the department of education to attract quali-fied individuals from around the country, not just within the state (Lusi 1997). The New Jersey Department of Education has tended to create new units as part of its policy response to the decisions rendered by the State Supreme Court on educational adequacy. For example, in 1990 it created the Division of Urban Education as a vehicle for transforming the urban districts impacted by the passage of the Quality Education Act. In 1998, after the fifth *Abbot v. Burke* decision, it created two new units, the Office of Program Review and Improvement, and the Office of Fiscal Review and Improvement (Walker 2004). In 2002 it undertook a major reorganization in which it consolidated all of the departments that were engaged in the *Abbott* implementation process under one larger unit named the Division of Abbott Implementation. It renamed the Office of Program Review the Office of Program Planning and De-sign, and enlarged its functions. The department also created a new as-sistant commissioner's position titled Assistant Commissioner for Ab-bott Implementation.

Reframing education departments' organizational structures and functions, and attempts at cultivating new organizational behaviors, do not always necessarily result in an enhancement of efficiency either at the state, district, or school level with respect to implementation (Fire-stone, Goertz, and Natriello 1997). Studies have shown that depart-ments still tend to remain hierarchical in nature and that communica-tion between departments is problematic (Lusi 1997; Walker 2004). One of the pitfalls of relying primarily on organizational restructuring is the failure for newly created subunits to become institutionalized (Louis and Crowin 1984). In the case of New Jersey, for example, the Division of Urban Education was dissolved within a short time period.

Timar (1997) argues that though organizational capacity issues are important ones to raise, the history of state education departments reveals that they are not solely defined by their internal characteristics. Their roles are also determined and defined by the external political, so-cial, and cultural environments in which they exist (Timar 1997, 255). Consequently, in order to significantly change these departments, the sociopolitical forces that shape them will also need to be changed (Timar 1997).

Direct Government Supply

States as well as the federal government have a number of funding pol-icy levers that they can utilize to influence educational policy. Both states and the federal government are able, in addition to their direct control over education policy, to exert indirect control by providing conditional and discretionary grants that target specific policy areas. These grants are used to encourage schools to engage in policy areas and educational practices that are deemed at the governmental level to be important. As stated earlier in this chapter, the states' role in educational policy has significantly expanded over the past fifty years, and the 2001 No Child Left Behind legislation has had a similar effect on the federal role. With the growing involvement of both levels of government, the contribution of each to educational expenditures has increased relative to the local district share. Both the federal and state governments are consequently able to influence educational policy not only through the employment of mandates and incentives but through the direct supply of funds for targeted programs, practices, and populations. These discretionary funds allow districts and schools to undertake programs, engage in practices, and serve populations of students without having to bear the direct financial cost themselves. For example, since 1994, after-school programs have received a considerable amount of federal and state funding. Federal funding for one program—The 21st Century Community Learning Center Program—ballooned from $40 million in 1998 to $1 billion in 2002 (Kane 2004).

The state and federal governments can also shape education policies through performance monitoring. The federal government, for example, funds comprehensive studies that measure student progress. The most well known is the National Assessment of Educational Progress (NAEP), which tracks student performance. The federal government also provides funds for national evaluations and studies of major grant-awarded programs, including the Middle School Assistance Program, the 21st Century Learning Community Centers, and the Title 1 program. Results from these studies as well as other performance measures of educational progress help to shape priority areas in educational policy.

CONCLUSION

Adequacy decisions have placed state education departments in a cauldron in which reconciling conflicting policy demands, competing interests, and streams of diverse political pressures create additional administrative and institutional tensions. Departments are called upon to devise new funding formulae, create policies that are in compliance with court remedies, and develop guidelines and technical infrastructures that will assist local school districts with implementations. Not unlike the systemic reform movement, the challenge for state education departments and their modes of response has been framed primarily in terms of internal administrative and organizational reform. Historical glimpses into the evolution of these departments have shown that their abilities to successfully aid educational improvement, although in part contingent upon their internal modes of functioning, are also largely influenced by broader social and political forces. These forces have shaped the institutional relationship between education departments and local schools.

REFERENCES

Adelsheimer, E., and Rix, K. 1999. *What We Know about Vouchers: The Facts behind the Rhetoric.* San Francisco: Wested Policy Program.

Aguilar, A. 2004. "Illinois Education Board Finds Itself Embroiled in Politics." *STLtoday* (January 24):C1.

Apple, M. W. 1988. "What Reform Talk Does: Creating New Inequalities in Education." *Educational Administration Quarterly* 24, 3:257–271.

Association for Supervision and Curriculum Development. 1989. "Guidelines for Business Involvement in the Schools." *Educational Leadership* 47, 4:84–86.

Benderson, A. 1984. "Financing Excellence in Public Education." *ERIC Digest,* ED252916.

Block, S. 2002. "Comparing the Adequacy of New Jersey and Kentucky Court Mandates, Statutes, and Regulations to Remedy Unconstitutional Public Education." Doctoral Dissertation, Seton Hall University, NJ.

Brown, F., and A. R. Contreras. 1991. "Deregulation and Privatization of Education: A Flawed Concept." *Education and Urban Society* 23:144–157.

Center on Education Policy. 2003. *From the Capital to the Classroom: State and Federal Efforts to Implement the No Child Left Behind Act.* Washington, DC: Center on Education Policy.

Cibulka, J. G., and R. L. Derlin. 1998. "Reform and Systemic Initiatives in Colorado and Maryland." *Education and Urban Society* 30, 4:505–515.

Clotfelter, C. T., and H. F. Ladd. 1996. "Recognizing and Rewarding Success in Public Schools." In H. F. Ladd (ed.), *Holding Schools Accountable: Performance-based Reform in Education.* Washington DC: Brookings Institution.

Cohen, M. 1990. "Key Issues Confronting State Policymakers." In Richard F. Elmore (ed.), *Restructuring Schools: The Next Generation of Educational Reform.* San Francisco: Jossey-Bass.

Consortium for Policy Research in Education. 1992. "Ten Lessons about Regulation and Schooling." *CPRE Policy Briefs*. New Brunswick, NJ: Consortium for Policy Research in Education.

Dillon, S. C. 2004. President's Initiative to Shake Up Education Is Facing Protests in Many State Capitols. *New York Times* (March 8):A2, p. 12.

Elmore, R. F. 2002. *Bridging the Gap between Standards and Achievement*. Washington, DC: Albert Shanker Institute.

Erlichson, B., and M. Goertz. 2001. *Implementing Whole School Reform in New Jersey: Year 2*. New Brunswick, NJ: Rutgers University, Department of Public Policy and Center for Government Services.

Feiock, R. C., and C. Stream. 1998. "Explaining the Choice of Policy Instruments for State Environmental Protection: A Political Economy Approach." Paper presented at the Annual Meeting of the Western Political Science Association, Los Angeles.

Firestone, W. A., M. Goertz, and G. Natriello. 1997. *From Cashbox to Classroom: The Struggle for Fiscal Reform and Educational Change in New Jersey*. New York: Teachers College Press.

Firestone, W. A., S. Rosemblum, B. D. Bader, and D. Massell. 1991. *Education Reform from 1983 to 1990: State Action and District Response*. New Brunswick, NJ: Consortium for Policy Research in Education.

Folts, J. D. 1996. *History of the University of the State of New York and the State Education Department: 1784–1996*. New York: State Education Department.

Furhman, S., E. Huddle, and J. Armstrong. 1986. "Improving Schools: The State Role." *Phi Delta Kappan* 67, 8:594–596.

Goddu, R. 1972. "Dissemination Capacity Building in a State Department of Education." *ERIC Digest*, ED110460.

Hadderman, M. L. 1988. "State vs. Local Control of Schools." *ERIC Digest* 24:ED291164.

Hannaway, J. 1996. "Management Decentralization and Performance-based Incentives." In E. A. Hanushek and D. W. Jorgenson (eds.), *Improving America's Schools: The Role of Incentives*. Washington, DC: National Academy Press.

Hanushek, E. 1994. *Making Schools Work: Improving Performance and Controlling Costs*. Washington, DC: Brookings Institute.

———. 1996. "Outcomes, costs, and Incentives in Schools." In E. A. Hanushek and D. W. Jorgenson (eds.), *Improving America's Schools: The Role of Incentives*. Washington, DC: National Academy Press.

Hawley, W. D. 1995. "The False Premises and False Promises of the Movement to Privatize Public Education." *Teachers College Record* (Summer):96, 4:735–742.

Hertert, L. 1996. "Systemic Reform in the 1990s: A Local Perspective." *Educational Policy* 10, 3:379–392.

Institute for Educational Leadership. 2001. *Recognizing the State's Role in Public Education.* Washington, DC: Task Force on State Leadership.

Johnston, R. C. 1999. "Governors Vie with Chiefs on Policy, Politics." *Education Week* (May 12):1.

Jost, K. 1994. "Private Management of Public Schools." *Congressional Quarterly Researcher* 4:165–288.

Kaestle, C. 1983. *Pillars of the Republic: Common Schools and American Society.* New York: Hill and Wang.

Kane, T. J. 2004. *The Impact of After-school Programs: Interpreting the Results of Four Recent Evaluations.* New York: William T. Grant Foundation.

Kearns, D. T. 1988. "An Education Recovery Plan for America." *Phi Delta Kappan* 68, 9:565–570.

Kelley, C., A. Odden, A. Milanowski, and H. Heneman III. 2000. *The Motivational Effects of School-based Performance Awards.* Philadelphia: Consortium for Policy Research in Education, University of Pennsylvania.

Kerwin, C. M. 1999. *Rulemaking: How Government Agencies Write Law and Make Policy.* Washington, DC: Congressional Quarterly Press.

Lashway, L. 2001. "Incentives for Accountability." *ERIC Digest* 152.

Louis, K. S., and R. G. Crowin. 1984. "Organizational Decline: How State Agencies Adapt." *Education and Urban Society* 16, 2:165–188.

Lusi, S. F. 1997. *The Role of State Departments of Education in Complex School Reform.* New York: Teachers College Press.

Magers, P. 2004. "Texas Governor Calls for School Incentives." United Press International, January 26.

Marsh, P., and R. Gortner. 1963. *Federal Aid to Science Education Programs.* Syracuse, NY: Syracuse University Press.

Martineau, R. J. 1991. *Drafting Legislation and Rules in Plain English.* Eagen, MN: West Publishing Company.

Massell, D. 1998. *State Strategies for Building Local Capacity: Addressing the Needs of Standards-based Reform.* Philadelphia: Consortium for Policy Research, University of Pennsylvania.

Massell, D., M. Kirst, and M. Hoppe. 1997. *Persistence and Change: Standards-based Systemic Reform in Nine States.* Philadelphia: Consortium for Policy Research, University of Pennsylvania.

Murphy, J. 1990. "The Education Reform Movement of the 1980s: A Comprehensive Analysis." In J. Murphy (ed.), *The Educational Reform Movement of the 1980s: Perspective and Cases.* Berkeley, CA: McCutchan.

National Institute of Education. 1982. *Cutbacks, Consolidation, Deregulation: How They Affect Education Agencies in the Far West.* Washington, DC: National Institute of Education.

Odden, A., and B. Anderson. 1986. "State Initiatives Can Foster School Improvement." *Phi Delta Kappan* 67, 8:578–581.

Shipps, D. 1998. "Corporate Influence on Chicago School Reform." In C. Stone (ed.), *Changing Urban Education*. Lawrence: University of Kansas Press.

Timar, T. B. 1997. "The Institutional Role of State Education Departments: A Historical Perspective." *American Journal of Education* 105:231–260.

Tyack, D. 1974. *The One Best System: A History of American Urban Education*. Cambridge, MA: Harvard University Press.

Usdan, M. D. 2002. *The New State Politics of Education*. Alexandria, VA: National Association of State Boards of Education.

Walker, E. M. 2002. "The Politics of School-based Management: Understanding the Process of Devolving Authority in Urban School Districts." *Educational Policy Analysis Archives* 10, 33.

———. 2003. "Whole School Reform and Preschool Education: The Role of Preschool Education in Policy Decisions Regarding the Improvement of Disadvantaged School Systems." *Journal of Children and Poverty* 9, 1:71–88.

———. 2004. "The Impact of State Policies and Actions on Local Implementation Efforts: A Study of Whole School Reform in New Jersey." *Education Policy* 18, 2:338–363.

Walker, E. M., and D. Gutmore. 2000. *The Quest for Equity and Excellence in Education: A Study of Whole School Reform in New Jersey Special Needs Districts*. South Orange, NJ: Center for Urban Leadership, Renewal, and Research, Seton Hall University.

Chapter Six

✨ Impact on Schools

Many of the legal challenges to state school finance systems that were examined in this book were argued based on compelling evidence that irrefutably showed that students who lived in certain communities attended schools with substandard facilities, curriculum, and instructional materials. These schools' ambient learning environments (unlike schools attended by students from wealthier backgrounds) were not conducive to helping students develop the skills that would allow them to attain a quality education, become productive citizens, and meaningfully participate in a democratic society. Ultimately, adequacy decisions were about creating schools that are the sources of enriching educational opportunities for all students. Those who brought these cases before the courts, as well as those who continue to challenge existing systems, are hopeful that through judicial intervention schools can become better places. Although these cases have at their core concerns about fiscal equity, the decisions that have been crafted by several courts conclude that ensuring all students are afforded an *adequate education* implies more than achieving fiscal equity. *Adequacy* also means that students will be exposed to quality learning experiences, the schools in which these experiences occur will be transformed, students will be taught challenging academic content, and their social and emotional needs will be met. But most important of all, adequacy is ultimately about creating an educational system in which disparities in educational outcomes between any group of students is eviscerated. Given the vision inherent in the adequacy claims brought by school finance reform advocates, and the attempts by courts that affirmatively uphold these claims to contribute toward the realization of this vision, how have such decisions impacted schools? This chapter describes some of the major programmatic and organizational changes that have occurred over time in teaching, instructional practices, accountability, and governance in response to adequacy reform policies. These changes represent policy judgments about the resource levels and programmatic and organizational inputs that are necessary to achieve the performance standards that individual states have declared, and the courts have affirmed in some cases, as constituting evidence that an adequate education meeting the constitutional litmus test has been provided.

PRESCHOOL AND EARLY
CHILDHOOD EDUCATION

The compensatory and ameliorative benefits of preschool and early childhood education for at-risk students have been well established by the research community (Corey 2001). Studies on the immediate and sustaining effects of preschool attendance have shown that students who attend preschool are more likely to do better academically and are less likely to suffer from long-term problems such as welfare dependence, unemployment, poverty, and criminal behavior than students who have not had the benefit of a preschool education (Schweinhart et al. 1993; Corey 2001). Explanations on the positive effects of preschool education are based on theories of early childhood development. Although there is a lack of coherence among these theories, there are resonant themes in the literature that derive from two well-known theories of early child development: cognitive developmental models and maturational models. Cognitive developmental, or organismic, models have as a central postulate the notion that " the reciprocal interactions between the child and his/her environment influences development and learning" (Walker 2003, 76). Maturational models, in contrast, give importance to the acquisition of linguistic meaning and language that occurs as a result of the interaction patterns between the child, significant others, and the environment (Yawkey and Prewitt-Diaz 1990).

Educational adequacy policies have tended to place a strong emphasis on school readiness. Several states, among them Texas, Kentucky, Vermont, and New Jersey, have seen an expansion in preschool educational opportunities as a function of these policies. The 2003 preschool yearbook published by the National Institute for Early Education Research indicates that in Texas over 148,888 preschool-aged children out of a population of 325,211 are in state-funded preschool programs (Barnett et al. 2004). According to data furnished in the yearbook, New Jersey has 31,927 out of an eligible population of 116,942 enrolled in similar programs. Statewide enrollment data in other states include 15,892 preschoolers out of an eligible pool of 53,704 being served in Kentucky's state-funded programs; 1,081 out of a population of 7,209 in Vermont; 8,007 out of an estimated preschool population of 155,871 in Ohio; and 774 out of an eligible population of 59,905 in Alabama. New Jersey's preschool program, which was judicially mandated by the fifth *Abbott v. Burke* decision, has since 1999 almost doubled the number of students served (19,179 enrollees). Alabama, which had included in its Alabama First plan a preschool provision, serves the lowest number of eligible students among the states whose adequacy decisions were examined in Chapter 4. However, it should be noted that the House rejected the Alabama First plan in spite of the fact that it was twice approved in the Senate (see Chapter 4). Generally, implementation of quality preschool programs is not without challenges. Developing quality educational standards, ensuring that preschool teachers are properly prepared and certified, providing adequate funding for these programs, and having adequate physical facilities are just a few of the myriad problems that confront the creation of quality programs (Walker 2003).

Adequacy reform policies also emphasize the importance of a kindergarten experience for students. However, the force of the policy language on kindergarten requirements varies across states. New Jersey's Abbott reforms require all eligible students in the Abbott districts to be in a full-day kindergarten program; however, schools not covered by the *Abbott* decisions are permitted to offer half-day kindergarten. In all but nine states', districts offering of kindergarten is mandatory. These are Alaska, Colorado, Idaho, New Hampshire, New Jersey, New York, North Dakota, Pennsylvania, and Washington (Education Commission of the States 2004). Funding formulas for kindergarten programs differ as well. Only nine states fund statewide full-day kindergarten programs at a higher level than half-day programs (Alaska, Pennsylvania, Georgia, Illinois, Massachusetts, Nebraska, New Mexico, New York, and Wisconsin), and seven states fund some of their kindergarten programs or subpopulation of kindergarten students at the same level or higher than first grade (Alaska, Colorado, Georgia, Louisiana, Mississippi, South Carolina, and West Virginia).

PRIMARY EDUCATION

The organization of primary education in some schools has also been transformed as a consequence of adequacy policies. Kentucky's Education Reform Act contains a provision that calls for the creation of ungraded primary programs. Schools are required to establish multiage classrooms for students of age five to eight. Table 6.1 shows the program and organizational structure for the primary grades in Kentucky's schools during several school years, including 2002–2003. Inclusion of kindergartners in ungraded classrooms still remains an issue of some controversy in the state, and studies on the implementation of multi-grade grouping indicate that there is great variability among Kentucky's schools and classrooms (Adams 1997).

CLASS SIZE

Debate about the virtue of small class size has been swirling ever since the Tennessee STAR Project found a significant, positive, and sustaining effect of small class size on student achievement (Finn 1998). Proponents of small class size argue that reducing the size of classrooms allows teachers to cover in greater depth the subject matter, encourages student engagement, lessens the depersonalization that occurs in large classes, and reduces the number of disciplinary problems (Hertling et

Table 6.1

Overall Primary Program Structure/Organization in Kentucky's Schools, 1998 through the 2002/2003 School Year

Primary Program Structure	*1998– 1999*	*1999– 2000*	*2000– 2001*	*2001– 2002*	*2002– 2003*
Four-year age spans (5–8-year-olds grouped together)	2%	1%	1%	1%	2%
Three-year age spans (6–8-year-olds grouped together part-time inclusion of 5-year-olds)	3%	2%	2%	2%	3%
Dual age spans with full inclusion of 5-year-olds	18%	12%	12%	9%	12%
Dual age spans with separate primary classes for 5-year-olds	26%	21%	22%	20%	23%
Dual age spans with separate primary classes for 5-year-olds and exit-level students	—	6%	6%	7%	7%
Predominantly single-age groupings	24%	32%	42%	48%	47%
Looping practices (teachers keep the same students for more than one year)	—	38%	36%	3%	4%

Source: Kentucky State Department of Education.

al. 2000; Thompson and Cunningham 2001). Detractors suggest that evidence of the beneficial effects of smaller classes is less than compelling given the pecuniary and nonpecuniary cost associated with class-size reduction policies (Hanushek 1999). Conceptual and definitional differences, as well as the absence of a sound theoretical understanding of how class size affects student performance, have helped to contribute to the controversy. Moreover, measurement and study design issues have muddled the research findings on the impact of class size on student performance (Goldstein and Blatchford 1998).

In spite of the polemics surrounding the class-size debate, class-size reduction (CSR) policies have received support from both state and federal governments. In the 2001–2002 school year, federal funds for CSR policies totaled $1.6 billion (Schwartz 2003). The exact formulation of CSR policies varies among the states. California, New Jersey, Texas, and Wisconsin target specific grades, whereas the policies of others states—for example, Nevada, Iowa, and Illinois—are subject specific. States also differ in the strength of their class-size reduction policies. Utah, Texas, and South Carolina are three states that mandate smaller classes. In 1984, HB 72 mandated class size reduction to twenty-two students in grades K–4 in all schools in Texas (see Chapter 4). California, Iowa, and Illinois have voluntary CSR programs. California funds CSR programs on a per-pupil basis, and Iowa uses block grants to encourage districts to implement class-size reduction. In New Jersey, CSR is included as one element of a larger comprehensive school reform package that was approved by the state's supreme court in its 1998 *Abbott v. Burke* decision. The class-size limits imposed on schools in the Abbott districts are fifteen in preschool, twenty-one in grades K–3, twenty-three in grades 4–5, and twenty-five in grades 6–12.

COMPREHENSIVE SCHOOL REFORM

Starting in the fall of 1997 both Title 1 and Non-Title 1 schools were allowed to use federal funds to implement a school-design program that focused on comprehensive school reform. The Comprehensive School Reform Development Program (sometimes called the Obey-Porter Program after its congressional sponsors) had as its goal the creation of opportunities for schools to incorporate in their change efforts, programs, and supports that are high quality, well defined, well documented as to their impact on student performance and achievement, and highly replicable. These programs utilize school-level reform models that are premised on changing the whole rather than individual aspects of a school. Schools and districts typically purchase models or services from program developers who are affiliated with a university, non-profit organization, or corporation. Examples of some of these whole-school design models are the Modern Red School House (from the Modern Red Schoolhouse Institute, Nashville), Success for All/Roots and Wings (John Slavin, Johns Hopkins University), Coalition of Essential Schools (Ted Sizer), and the Comer School Development Program (James Comer, Yale University). Comprehensive School Reform models vary in their degree of prescription, the extent to which they focus upon academic as opposed to other areas of school change, and their cost.

Several states involved in implementing adequacy reforms as well as statewide school improvement efforts have relied upon these school-design models (for example, Delaware, Illinois, Kentucky, Maryland, Ohio, New Jersey, and Wisconsin). In New Jersey, the 1998 *Abbott v. Burke* decision identified several alternative models, with Success for All as the presumptive model for designing whole-school reform in the Abbott districts. Schools through a schoolwide vote that reflect the outcomes of a needs assessment are required to select from the available choices to include homegrown models, the model-design upon which their reform will be based. In 2001, the New Jersey Department of Education in order to encourage the selection of the preferred model provided schools that selected Success for All with a $70,000 implementation grant; other choices were awarded up to $45,000 in grants.

The research evidence indicates that there are several variables that impact the implementation and sustainability of these models over time. Factors such as the degree of support, training, and professional development that schools receive from the model developers; the congruence between the models and district and state accountability requirements; the fit between the model and schools' instructional and curricular programs; and the degree of teacher buy-in influence successful implementation and sustainability over time. In instances when these models are mandated, such as in the case of New Jersey, the degree and quality of state oversight become important in ensuring that implementation challenges that arise from the poor services provided by the model developers are resolved in a timely fashion. Since mandating whole-school reform, New Jersey's Department of Education has formulated policies that permit schools to abandon their whole-school reform models if schools can clearly demonstrate legitimate areas of dissatisfaction. This policy shift was engendered by the increasing levels of disgruntlement that schools vocalized about the quality of support that was provided by some model development teams.

DECENTRALIZATION

Adequacy reforms have embedded policies that attempt to redefine school governance structures within a framework of comprehensive change. The popularity of governance policies as a reform strategy is evidenced by the fact that in 1993, more than forty-four states had legislatively incorporated school decentralization in their reform agenda, and 56 percent of public schools nationwide had some form of participatory decisionmaking body (National Center for Education Statistics 1996; Walker 2002). To date, five states have mandated school-level participatory decisionmaking: Colorado, Florida, Kentucky, North Carolina, and Texas. In spite of its increasing popularity, the evidence has been inconsistent as to the effects of decentralization on student performance and classroom practices. The research has tended to suggest that the effects of decentralization are more pronounced in the areas of decisionmaking and teacher morale than in changed classroom practices or student performance (Summers and Johnson 1991; Wohlstetter and Mohrman 1996).

School decentralization assumes different forms from state to state and district to district. In addition, there is great discrepancy in the breadth and depth of policy functions that are relegated to school teams. In Kentucky, local school councils are responsible for, among other functions, the creation of the school budget, making curricular and instructional decisions, allocating staff positions, assigning staff time, and assigning students to programs and classes. School teams in New Jersey, in contrast, are given responsibilities over the school budget, curricular and instructional matters, and allocating positions, but they do not have power over staff assignment or student placement.

Although site-based management calls for broad participation among all stakeholders to include parents, the research has shown that site-based management tends to result in limited governance; that is, participation by some key constituencies is apt to be minimal (Hess 1999; Walker 2002). Teams or local councils tend to be dominated by school-level actors at the expense of parents and local community members. In addition to concerns about limited governance, the ability of teams to engage in legitimate decisionmaking is constrained by confusion about roles and responsibilities, the adequacy of training that is provided, resource shortages (including time), and the quality of support that they get from central office and state education department staff (Walker 2002).

ACCOUNTABILITY

Since the 1980s, adequacy reform policies have promoted the development of accountability systems in several states. These systems vary in stringency and complexity, and in their use of incentives mechanisms. Additionally, not all states—for instance, Texas—have fashioned a formal and coherent link between their school finance reforms and their accountability systems (Keller 2003). Nevertheless, most accountability systems are based on the adoption of curriculum standards in core content subjects, which are linked to performance standards that delineate what students ought to know and be able to do. In Chapter 4, these standards were discussed for the states whose legislative responses were reviewed. In this chapter a brief discussion of the accountability mechanisms that undergird states' academic standards are presented. It should be noted that at present, most state accountability systems are under review in order to ensure that they are in compliance with the accountability requirements of the No Child Left Behind legislation.

The most widely studied state system of school accountability is that of Kentucky. Kentucky's goals for all learners are based upon six goals that are linked with fifty-seven academic expectations. Kentucky's law requires accountability for student learning to be based on performance in writing, reading, mathematics, social studies, science, arts and humanities, practical living, and vocational studies. Incentives are tied to school-level performance in the core contents as well as student attendance, retention, drop-out rates, and other nonacademic measures of success (see Chapter 5). Similar to the assessments in other states, Kentucky's assessments use a variety of test items to measure proficiency. These include multiple-choice questions, writing prompts, and open-response questions (Heine 2002).

The accountability system is structured to take into account data on student performance on norm-referenced instruments, as well as information on achievement from portfolio assessments. For students in the performance arts, Kentucky's accountability system requires that they take a performance assessment examination. Schools are held accountable for progress based on a determination of the degree to which test score performance exceeds or fails to exceed growth targets. These targets are calculated from baseline data for the 1998–1999 and

1999–2000 school years. Growth is measured on a two-year cycle, and schools are categorized as meeting their goals, progressing toward their project growth targets, or in need of assistance. Schools in the first two categories are eligible for rewards, whereas schools in the assistance category are subject to various remedial activities depending on whether they are in level 1, level 2, or level 3. (Level 1 schools are in the top third of schools in the assistance category; level 2 are in the middle third, and level 3 are in the bottom one-third of schools that need assistance.) Annual report cards are issued for each school in the state. These cards provide a multitude of information about a school, including data on academic outcomes, attendance, retention, drop-out rate, school-to-work transition, and measures of the school's learning environment. In the 2000 accountability cycle, the Kentucky Department of Education provided monetary awards in excess of $22 million to approximately 711 schools. Approximately 148 schools were placed in the assistance category (Heine 2002).

Vermont's assessment program also has attracted widespread attention. Act 60, which was approved by Vermont's state board in July 2000, requires schools to meet a set of school quality standards that address a school's physical, social, and academic climate. Vermont's Comprehensive Assessment System measures student performance based on the state's framework of Standards and Learning Opportunities. A number of assessment programs make up the Comprehensive Assessment System. These are a statewide development assessment reading program in grade 2; the New Standards Reference exams in English/language arts and mathematics in grades 4, 8, and 10; VT-Pass, a science assessment in grades 5, 9, and 11; and school-based assessment, including the use of portfolios in additional subject areas and grade levels not included in the state assessments.

Some states are attempting to tie tenure reform for teachers and administrators to their school accountability policies. For instance, Alabama's governor has proposed legislation that would streamline the process of firing incompetent teachers. Under the governor's plan, which has gained the support of the Alabama Education Association (the state's largest teachers' union), dismissal of teachers would occur through a binding arbitration process rather than through the State Tenure Commission review process. It is envisioned that if the reforms were to be adopted by the legislature, the length of time that it takes to dismiss a teacher would be significantly reduced (*Mobile Register* 2004). In 2003, Alabama dismissed only a handful of educators (slightly more than fifteen) on the grounds of incompetence out of a total of 40,000 licensed teachers in the state (*Mobile Register* 2004).

SUPPLEMENTAL SERVICES

It has become axiomatic in the field of education that schooling involves more than the inculcation of cognitive skills and civic values. Decades of research have underscored the social, health, and affective needs of many students, and in particular students whose families live in impoverish communities. Clear links have been established between the cognitive domains of performance and the noncognitive needs of students. These findings have resulted in reform policies that have sought to address the noncognitive dimensions of the schooling experience. In states such as Kentucky and New Jersey, adequacy policies have included an extensive network of supplemental services. Both states encourage the adoption of supplemental programs that provide social services to students and families and enhanced learning and academic opportunities through the creation of instructionally based after-school programs. In New Jersey, schools are able to use supplemental funds to implement expanded nutrition programs. Data available from Kentucky indicate that in the 2001–2002 school year there were 774 social service centers serving 1,151 schools and 550,000 students and their families (Heine 2002). Kentucky also passed in 2002 Senate Bill 207, which requires vision screening examination for all students between the ages of three and six prior to their enrollment for the first time in school, preschool, or Head Start (Heine 2002, 11).

FACILITIES IMPROVEMENT

Research has established that school facilities influence academic performance (Crampton and Thompson 2004). Not surprisingly, therefore, adequacy reforms have sought to address issues related to the physical infrastructure of many schools. Approximately seventy-eight cases involving facilities issues have been heard by the courts, ten of these in the state of New Jersey alone (Crampton and Thompson 2004). These cases have been heard in all but seventeen states (the exceptions are Georgia, Hawaii, Idaho, Maine, Maryland, Massachusetts, Michigan, Minnesota, Montana, Nebraska, Nevada, New Hampshire, New Mexico, Oregon, Vermont, Virginia, and Wisconsin). In spite of some measure of improvement in the physical conditions of the nation's schools, the infrastructural needs of many schools are still unmet. Legislatures have devised various policy solutions to address this problem. For example, in 1997, the Texas state legislature authorized the Instructional Facilities

Allotment Program. This program provides assistance to school districts with their debt service payments and lease bond agreements. The program covers only those bonds and lease purchase proceeds that are used for the construction or renovation of an instructional facility. The state provides a maximum allotment that is based on the annual debt service payment or $250 per student in average daily attendance. Districts are required through levy to cover their local share. Between 1997 and 2001, approximately $350 million has been appropriated to the Instructional Facilities Allotment Program.

Ohio has seen a dramatic increase in appropriation for school facilities improvement. Ohio's school facilities improvement project falls under the auspices of the Ohio School Facilities Commission that was established in 1997 (see Chapter 4). Prior to the commission's establishment, Ohio's total expenditure on school construction between 1952 and 1997 was $508 billion. Since its creation, the commission has received over $3.3 billion in appropriation (Ohio School Facilities Commission 2003). Among the major facilities projects that are managed by the commission are the Classroom Facilities Assistance Program (CFAP) and the Exceptional Needs Program. Between 1998 and 2003 over $2.6 billion was allocated to the CFAP and approximately $358 million was appropriated for facilities improvement through the Exceptional Needs Program (Ohio School Facilities Commission 2003). Table 6.2 shows actual disbursements on school facilities projects between 1998 and 2002.

New Jersey's School Construction Program is one of the most ambitious in the country. However, progress toward improving the physical infrastructure of many New Jersey schools has been slow (Education Law Center 2004). The passage of the Educational Facilities Construction and Financing Act in 2000 during Republican governor Christine Whitman's administration had minimal impact on redressing the immediate school facilities needs of districts, because of organizational and personnel issues associated with the primary entity responsible for overseeing the school construction program (Education Law Center 2004). Consequently, between 2000 and 2002, in spite of district submittals of long-range facilities plans, very little progress was made on funding new construction, and "only 5 percent of the health and safety work was completed (Education Law Center 2004, 7). Since 2002, with the establishment of a separate corporate structure by Democratic governor Jim McGreevy—the School Construction Corporation (SCC)—progress with facilities improvement has dramatically improved. The SCC plans to build 50 new high-performance schools annually, at an annual cost of $1 billion. It has so far secured about $3.4 billion toward this goal.

Table 6.2
Disbursements of Funds by the Ohio School Facilities Commission, 1998–2002

Program	FY 98	FY 99	FY 00	FY 01	FY 02	Total Program
CFAP	$49,618,992.54	$134,140,769.49	$305,122,233.50	$553,475,039.43	$720,138,815.60	$1,762,495,850.56
Exceptional Needs	—	—	$7,827,628.52	$53,061,181.30	$81,363,337.23	$142,252,147.05
Emergency Repairs	$36,422,642.74	$57,160,233.71	$16,642,013.88	$4,010,882.92	$450,715.44	$114,686,488.69
Big 8	$21,480,323.89	$15,351,922.57	$20,405,854.16	$31,207,847.13	$11,296,103.43	$99,722,051.18
Disability Assistance	$74,579.73	$2,292,593.82	$2,563,080.18	$3,024,285.44	$1,006,226.38	$8,960,765.55
Total by Year	$107,596,538.90	$208,925,519.59	$352,560,810.24	$644,779,236.22	$81,255,198.08	$2,128,117,303.03

Source: Ohio School Facilities Commission, 2003, 11.

CONCLUSION

Although this chapter has described some of the major school-level changes that have ensued from the pursuit of educational adequacy, it has not treated in a systematic manner the level of implementation that is associated with each of these changes. How these changes are implemented in individual schools will have a profound impact on the outcomes for students. In addition, whereas some state policy initiatives have been well studied, others have not. Hence, the research and education community has yet to arrive at any definitive comprehensive understanding as to how adequacy reform policies have resulted in minimizing both the fiscal and educational disparities that exist between property-poor districts and more affluent school districts. Part of this dilemma has arisen from points that were previously raised in this book. For example, legislative responses to court decisions vary; the specificity of these decisions lacks uniformity from court to court; public support for these decisions is mixed; how adequacy is defined, financed, and measured differs among the states; and the research community is still in debate on how best to deduce or establish a link between educational inputs and outputs. These difficulties impede our abilities to make a broad generalization about the effectiveness of adequacy policies. There are other challenges that schools and policy makers face. As the fiscal burden for funding an adequate education becomes more onerous, questions regarding the effects of funding on programs assume heightened urgency. Budget shortfalls have forced policy makers to directly address this issue in states such as New Jersey and Texas.

Yet, in spite of these challenges and limitations, inquiries into the impact of adequacy decisions in ensuring fiscal parity and academic improvement must still be vigorously pursued. Data on some states suggest that these policies have positively contributed to improving performance and parity. For example, between 1989 and 1999, according to data published by the Kentucky Department of Education the gap in per-pupil expenditure of state and local funding between low-wealth and high-wealth districts was reduced by 36.9 percent; however, information furnished by the Prichard Committee for Academic Excellence indicates that in 2001 there was an increase in the gap (The Prichard Committee for Academic Excellence, 2004). Kentucky has also seen an improvement in high school graduation and college-going rates since the passage of the Kentucky Education Reform Act. As our cumulative knowledge about adequacy reform policies and their effects grows over time, educational policy makers, advocacy groups, parents and their communities, researchers, and those involved in the judicial system will be able to determine whether the courts have been able to secure for all students an education that meets the threshold of a constitutionally adequate education.

REFERENCES

Adams, J. 1997. "School Finance Policy and Students' Opportunities to Learn: Kentucky's Experience." *The Future of Children* 7, 3:79–95.

Barnett, W. S., K. Robin, J. Hustedt, and K. Schulman. 2004. *The State of Preschool: 2003 Preschool Yearbook.* New Brunswick, NJ: National Institute for Early Education Research, Rutgers University.

Corey, K. M. 2001. "Early Childhood Education: A Meta-analytical Affirmation of Short- and Long-term Benefits of Educational Opportunity." *School Psychology* 91, 4:9–30.

Crampton, F., and D. Thompson. 2004. "When the Legislative Process Fails: The Politics of Litigation in School Infrastructure Funding Equity." In K. DeMoss and K. Wong (eds.), *Money, Politics, and Law: Intersections and Conflicts in the Provision of Educational Opportunity.* New York: Eye on America.

Education Commission of the States. 2004. *How States Fund Full-day Kindergarten.* Denver, CO: Education Commission of the States.

Education Law Center. 2004. *Breaking Ground: Rebuilding New Jersey's Urban Schools—The Abbott School Construction Program.* Newark, NJ: Education Law Center.

Finn, J. D. 1998. *Class Size and Students at Risk: What Is Known? What Is Next?* Washington, DC: U.S. Department of Education, National Institute on the Education of At-Risk Students.

Goldstein, H., and P. Blatchford. 1998. "Class Size and Educational Achievement: A Review of Methodology with Particular Reference to Study Design." *British Educational Research Journal* 24:218–255.

Hanushek, E. A. 1999. "Some Findings from an Independent Investigation of the Tennessee STAR Experiment and from Other Investigations of Class Size Effects." *Educational Evaluation and Policy Analysis* 21, 2:143–164.

Heine, C. 2002. *Kentucky School Updates: A Parent/Citizen Guide.* Lexington, KY: Prichard Committee for Academic Excellence.

Hertling, E., C. Leonard, L. Lumsden, and S. C. Smith. 2000. "Class Size: Can School Districts Capitalize on the Benefits of Smaller Classes?"*ERIC Clearinghouse on Educational Management* (Spring):ED447584.

Hess, G. A. 1999. "Understanding Achievement and Other Changes under Chicago School Reform." *Educational Evaluation and Policy Analysis* 21, 1:67–83.

Keller, H. 2003. *School Finance in 2003: Keeping the System Afloat and Charting a Course for the Future.* Austin: Charles A. Dana Center, University of Texas.

Mobile (Alabama) *Register.* 2004. "Riley Pushes Tenure Reform." January 30, 1.

National Center for Education Statistics. 1996. *How Widespread Is Site-based Decision-making in the Public Schools?* Washington, DC: Government Printing Office.

Ohio School Facilities Commission. 2003. *Building Our Future: Annual Report FY02.* Columbus: Ohio School Facilities Commission.

Prichard Committee for Academic Excellence. 2004. *Kentucky School Updates: School Finance.* Lexington, KY: Prichard Committee for Academic Excellence.

Schwartz, W. 2003. "Class Size Reduction and Urban Students." *ERIC Digest* (ED472486)

Schweinhart, L. J., J. Barners, and D. P. Weikart. 1993. "Significant Benefits: The High Scope Perry Preschool Study through Age 27." Ypsilanti, MI: High/Scope Educational Research Foundation.

Summers, A. A. and A. W. Johnson. 1991. *A Review of the Evidence on the Effects of School-Based Management Plans.* Washington, DC: Panel on the Economics of Reform and Teaching.

Thompson, C. L., and E. K. Cunningham. 2001. *First in America Special Report: The Lessons of Class Size Reduction.* Chapel Hill: North Carolina Education Research Council.

Walker, E. M. 2002. "The Politics of School-based Management: Understanding the Process of Devolving Authority in Urban School Districts." *Educational Policy Analysis Archives* 10, 33.

———. 2003. "Whole School Reform and Preschool Education: The Role of Preschool Education in Policy Decisions Regarding the Improvement of Disadvantaged School Systems." *Journal of Children and Poverty* 9, 1:71–88.

Wohlstetter, P., and S. A. Mohrman. 1996. *Assessment of School-Based Management Volume I: Findings and Conclusions.* Studies of Education Reform. University of Southern California, Center of Educational Governance. Available from U.S. Government Printing Office.

Yawkey, T. D., and J. Prewitt-Diaz. 1990. "Early Childhood: Theories, Research Implications for Bilingual Students." Paper presented at the proceedings of the First Research Symposium on Limited English Proficient Student Issues. Washington, DC: Office of Bilingual Education and Minority Language Affairs.

Chapter Seven

✦ Organizations, Associations, and Governmental Agencies

Contributor, John W. Collins

The following are organizations, associations, and governmental agencies that provide information on education adequacy, policy, and school finance arguments.

A+ Education Foundation
P.O. Box 4433
Montgomery, AL 36103
Tel.: (334) 279-1886 or (800) 253-8865
Fax: (334) 279-1543
http://www.columbiagroup.org/a.htm

Established in 1993, the coalition is citizen-based, focusing on improving education in the state of Alabama. Resources are available to assist those in other states concerned with school reforms and adequacy issues.

The Albert Shanker Institute
555 New Jersey Avenue NW
Washington, DC 20001
Tel.: (202) 879-4001
Fax: (202) 879-4403
http://www.shankerinstitute.org

Established in 1998, the Albert Shanker Institute is named in honor of the late president of the American Federation of Teachers. The institute brings together influential leaders and thinkers from business, labor, government, and education. The institute is dedicated to three themes: children's education, unions as advocates for quality, and freedom of association. The institute commissions independent work by scholars in these areas in addition to organizing seminars, sponsoring publications, and funding selected projects.

American Education Finance Association (AEFA)
8365 Armadillo Trail
Evergreen, CO 80439
Tel.: (303) 674-0857
Fax: (303) 670-8986
http://www.aefa.cc/

Established in 1976, the AEFA serves administrators, policy specialists, and researchers through both forum and information exchanges throughout the United States, Canada, and other jurisdictions. Fiscal and economic components of education are emphasized with regard to school adequacy. Of particular note are the organization's yearbooks, available (back to 2000) from *Eye on Education,* online at http://www.eyeoneducation.com/.

Campaign for Fiscal Equity (CFE)
6 East 43rd Street
New York, NY 10017
Tel.: (212) 867-8455
Fax: (212) 867-8460
http://www.cfequity.org/
http://www.accessednetwork.org/

Since 1993, this not-for-profit corporation has served as a coalition of various school boards, parent groups, and advocates for the children of New York State. *CFE v. The State of New York* has led to a compilation of various research documents and cases studies regarding school finance in various states. The documents focus on the role of public involvement on school finance litigation.

Under the auspices of the CFE, the Advocacy Center for Children's Educational Success with Standards (ACCESS) Project was developed to provide national resources in the field. ACCESS provides resources for all advocates of school adequacy. Its state-by-state directory is particularly helpful for those needing specific information on a given state or region.

Cato Policy Analysis
1000 Massachusetts Avenue NW
Washington, DC 20001-5403
Tel.: (202) 842-0200
Fax: (202) 842-3490
http://www.cato.org

The Cato Institute was established in 1977 as a nonprofit organization interested in connecting policy research with the general public. Aspects that are emphasized include the role of government, intellectual public engagement, and constitutional precepts. The website has a set of comprehensive links for all major policy concerns, including school adequacy.

Center for Research on Evaluation, Standards, and Student Testing (CRESST)
UCLA CSE/CRESST
300 Charles E. Young Drive North
GSE & IS Building, 3rd Floor/Mailbox 951522
Los Angeles, CA 90095-1522
Tel.: (310) 206-1532
Fax: (310) 825-3883
http://cresst96.cse.ucla.edu/

The UCLA Center for the Study of Evaluation (CSE) and the national Center for Research on Evaluation, Standards, and Student Testing (CRESST) offers research and expertise developed under the guidance of UCLA's School of Education. Areas of study have included valid and reliable evaluation testing, school accountability, standards, and school reform. New initiatives encompass NCLB, technology use, and policy requirements for local, district, and state levels. CRESST has numerous K–12 constituencies and has embraced recent efforts to transcend elementary and secondary school settings.

The Civil Rights Project (CRP)
125 Mt. Auburn Street, 3rd Floor
Cambridge, MA 02138
Tel.: (617) 496-6367
Fax: (617) 495-5210
http://www.civilrightsproject.harvard.edu

Based in Harvard University, the Civil Rights Project (established in 1996) is multifaceted in dealing with inequality issues across the spectrum: affirmative action, criminal justice, electoral reform, higher education, K–12 education, metro and regional inequalities, race, ethnicity, and religion. Although school adequacy is most closely connected to its K–12 education work, all the links on the website are helpful in researching various societal connections.

Clearinghouse on Educational Policy and Management (CEPM) (formerly ERIC Clearinghouse on Educational Management)
College of Education, University of Oregon
5207 University of Oregon
Eugene, Oregon 97403-5207
Tel.: (541) 346-5044
Fax: (541) 346-2334
http://eric.uoregon.edu/

The Clearinghouse on Educational Policy and Management (CEPM) was established in December 2003 under the University of Oregon's College of Education. CEPM was previously a subset of the Education Resources Information Centers (ERIC) and many of the current contributors were active in the original clearinghouse. ERIC, which was funded by the United States Department of Education, is the world's largest database of journal and nonjournal articles on educational issues. CEPM is a major contributor in the production, distribution, and repository of various media covering the research and policy for school settings. Current trends and issues are quickly accessed through the website's home page. School adequacy topics are prolifically covered under school choice, school finance, school reform, and social and economic context links.

Consortium for Policy Research in Education (CPRE), University of Pennsylvania Graduate School of Education
3440 Market Street, Suite 560
Philadelphia, PA 19104-3325
Tel.: (215) 573-0700
Fax: (215) 573-7914
http://www.cpre.org

The Consortium for Policy Research in Education was established in 1985. Five major research institutions—Harvard University, Stanford University, the University of Michigan, the University of Pennsylvania, and the University of Wisconsin–Madison—provide the foundation for this organization. Their efforts are designed to improve elementary and secondary education through research. CPRE serves numerous constituents. Subject matter expertise is available through the website, allowing detailed and precise networking (via e-mail) for researchers and practitioners alike.

Council of Chief State School Officers (CCSSO)
One Massachusetts Avenue NW, Suite 700
Washington, DC 20001-1431

Tel.: (202) 336-7000
Fax: (202) 408-8072
http://www.ccsso.org

Established in 1984, CCSSO is an organization with national prominence, assisting chief administrators by providing resources to improve schools. Advocacy for student success is a major precept along with service and leadership. The website links to federal programs are specifically cited, with each major program having many helpful resources for school adequacy researchers, policy makers, and school leaders.

Education Commission of the States (ECS)
700 Broadway, #1200
Denver, CO 80203-3460
Tel.: (303) 299-3600
Fax: (303) 296-8332
http://www.ecs.org/

The ECS is a nonprofit organization established in 1965 to build partnerships among school leaders. These partnership are designed to formulate school policy based on sound practice and research. A pull-down menu for Education Issues on the website quickly allows researchers to pinpoint information from a wide variety of sources.

Education Law Association (ELA)
300 College Park
Dayton, OH 45469-0528
Tel.: (937) 229-3589
Fax: (937) 229-3845
http://www.educationlaw.org

One of the oldest such associations (established in 1954), the ELA is nonprofit and nonadvocacy-based. Education law information is provided to school leaders, teachers, students, and researchers in an unbiased forum. The ELA's online resources for education law (under *Links*) are especially noteworthy.

Education Law Center (ECL)
60 Park Place, Suite 300
Newark, NJ 07102
Tel.: (973) 624-1815
Fax: (973) 624-7339
http://www.edlawcenter.org/

The Education Law Center was founded in 1973 by a young law professor at Rutgers Law School. The center is a strong advocate on behalf of New Jersey's public school children having access to an equal and adequate education as guaranteed by state and federal law. The center is also devoted to ensuring that educational opportunity for low-income and students with disabilities is improved. The ECL has been the leading legal advocate in New Jersey's school finance and adequacy claims. All the original decisions in the *Robinson v. Cahill* and the *Abbott v. Burke* cases can be found on its website.

Education Policy Center (EPC)
College of Education, Michigan State University
201 Erickson Hall
East Lansing, MI 48824-1034
Tel.: (517) 355-4494
Fax: (517) 432-6202
http://www.epc.msu.edu/

Originally focusing on the education policy of Michigan when it was established in 2000, the EPC has since emerged as a national resource for improving the quality of schools and educational policy. A multitude of themes are tracked: assessment, accountability, charter schools, funding, migrant children, teacher quality, testing, and school choice. The *Education Policy* links on the website are annotated and well maintained.

Education Policy Institute (EPI)
PMB 294, 4401-A Connecticut Ave., NW
Washington, DC 20008-2322
Tel.: (202) 244-7535
Fax: (202) 244-7584
http://www.educationpolicy.org

Established in 1995 as a nonprofit organization, EPI provides resources to inform the public with alternatives with schooling in the United States. Clear connections exist with this organization and the National Education Association and the American Federation of Teachers (see annotations for these two selected nonprint resources in the next chapter). Research, policy analysis, and practice for both private and public schools are addressed. The *State Agencies* and *Links* on the website are worthy places of inquiry.

Indiana Education Policy Center (IEPC)
Indiana University

Suite 100, Smith Research Center
Bloomington, IN 47408-2698
Tel.: (812) 855-1240
Fax: (812) 855-0420
http://www.indiana.edu/~iepc

The IEPC was originally chartered (in 1990) to provide unbiased information and research on education issues for the state of Indiana. Like other organizations listed in this chapter, the center has evolved into a more global resource. Many issues are monitored, including teacher professional development, school finance, school reform, school safety, and special education within minorities.

National Academies Press (NAP)
500 Fifth Street NW
Lockbox 285
Washington, DC 20055
Tel.: (888) 624-8373 or (202) 334-3313
Fax: (202) 334-2451
http://www.nap.edu

The National Academies Press (NAP) was created by the National Academies, the last academy being established in 1970. The National Academies are the National Academy of Sciences, the National Academy of Engineering, the Institute of Medicine, and the National Research Council, each chartered by Congress. NAP publishes at least 200 publications each year, covering the fields supported by the different academies. Some of the research endeavors have included publications on school improvement.

National Association of State Boards of Education (NASBE)
277 South Washington Street, Suite 100
Alexandria, VA 22314
Tel.: (703) 684-4000
Fax: (703) 836-2313
http://www.nasbe.org/Educational_Issues/Finance.html

Established in 1958, NASBE is a nonprofit national association providing resources to state boards of education. Policy, research, and practice are the cornerstones of its work. The association advocates equality of access to education and citizen support for public education. Links under *Education Issues* from the website assist in information gathering efforts regarding school adequacy.

National Center for Educational Statistics (NCES)
1990 K Street NW
Washington, DC 20006
Tel.: (202) 502-7300
http://nces.ed.gov

The National Center for Education Statistics was established under the authority of the U.S. Department of Education, which was initially formed in 1867. NCES is the primary governmental agency responsible for collecting, synthesizing, analyzing, and reporting American education issues. Its scope includes all education levels in the United States and international comparisons with other nations. NCES is located within the Institute of Education Sciences of the U.S. Department of Education, along with many other research entities (contracted and governmental) that reach across the nation (for example, see WestEd). The NCES website *Electronic Catalog* is an outstanding focal point, complete with search filters that allow for professional inquiry on a wide variety of education topics.

National Center on Educational Outcomes (NCEO)
University of Minnesota
350 Elliott Hall
75 East River Road
Minneapolis, MN 55455
Tel.: (612) 626-1530
Fax: (612) 624-0879
http://education.umn.edu/NCEO

The National Center on Educational Outcomes was established in 1990 to provide national leadership in designing and building educational assessments and accountability systems that appropriately monitor educational results for all students, including students with disabilities and students with limited English proficiency.

The Ohio Coalition for Equity and Adequacy of School Funding
100 South Third Street
Columbus, Ohio 43215
Tel.: (614) 228-6540
Fax: (614) 228-6542
http://www.ohiocoalition.org/

The Ohio Coalition for Equity and Adequacy of School Funding originated in 1990 in response to challenges of school funding for the state of Ohio. The coalition's founding precept is to provide a high-quality education to all of Ohio's students. State-specific resources for school adequacy are replete throughout the website, especially from an Ohio state case-study perspective.

The Rural School and Community Trust
Washington Office:
1825 K Street NW, Suite 703
Washington, DC 20006
Tel.: (202) 955-7177
Fax: (202) 955-7179
http://www.ruraledu.org/issues/finance.htm

The Rural School and Community Trust's Rural Education Finance Center (REFC) was established in 1998. REFC is a nonprofit organization that accentuates the rural perspective on various schooling issues. Similar to other organizations, its themes include No Child Left Behind, school finance, small schools, place-based education, and education renewal (areas that have lost schools). The *School Finance* link on the website leads to a compendium of archives, newsletters, and research access to rural-specific websites and articles.

Texas Center for Educational Research (TCER)
P.O. Box 679002
Austin, TX 78767-9002
Tel.: (512) 467-3632 or (800) 580-8237
Fax: (512) 467-3618
http://www.tcer.org

The Texas Center for Educational Research (TCER) was chartered in 1995 as a nonprofit organization that emphasizes educational research for the Texas public school system. Its research agenda includes emerging issues, school finance, management and governance, teaching and learning, and economics of education. Although there is a Texas-based orientation in the center's work, many of its research undertakings could be used in other settings. A wide selection of publications in the above areas are available on the website.

WestEd Policy Program
2020 North Central Avenue, Suite 660
Phoenix, AZ 85004-4507
Tel.: (602) 322-7004
Fax: (602) 322-7007
http://www.wested.org/cs/pol/print/docs/pol/home.htm

The WestEd Policy Program is organized under the authority of WestEd, which was established in 1966. This is a policy resource that monitors a four-state region: Arizona, California, Nevada, and Utah. WestEd uses research to develop policy resources for school leaders. It deals with school improvement, funding, and best practices. The policy program receives support from the Institute of Education Sciences within the U.S. Department of Education. Its helpful website has a *Links* section that enhances the utility of the available publications and policy perspectives.

with No Child Left Behind (NCLB) legislation. This study was conducted one year after NCLB passage and forms part of an ongoing annual review of states' implementation efforts.

Clotfelter, C. T., and H. F. Ladd. **"Recognizing and Rewarding Success in Public Schools."** Pp. 23–63 in H. F. Ladd (ed.), *Holding Schools Accountable: Performance-based Reform in Education.* Washington, DC: Brookings Institution, 1996.

Clotfelter and Ladd discuss the debate regarding incentives as motivators for school personnel.

Consortium for Policy Research in Education. **"Ten Lessons about Regulation and Schooling."** *CPRE Policy Briefs.* New Brunswick, NJ: Rutgers University, 1992.

Offers a succinct discussion of the relationships between regulations and policy goals. This includes the difficulties that state education departments experience in determining the enforcement of state regulations in local school districts.

Council of Chief State School Officers. *Status Report: State Systemic Education Improvements.* Washington, DC: Council of Chief State School Officers, 1998.

Offers insights into the role of the states in leading systemic educational improvements during the 1990s.

Firestone, W. A., S. Rosemblum, B. D. Bader, and D. Massell. *Education Reform from 1983 to 1990: State Action and District Response.* New Brunswick, NJ: Consortium for Policy Research in Education, Rutgers University, 1991.

This policy document provides descriptions of the different waves of reform beginning in the 1980s. Of particular note is the contrasts made with the third wave of the reform movement to the previous two waves.

Hanushek, E. *Making Schools Work: Improving Performance and Controlling Costs.* Washington, DC: Brookings Institute, 1994.

A book based on the recommendations of the Panel on the Economics Educational Reform (PEER) on the use of incentive structures to promote educational efficiency.

Kelley, C., Odden, A., Milanowski, A., and H. Heneman III. *The Motivational Effects of School-based Performance Awards.* Philadelphia: Consortium for Policy Research in Education, University of Pennsylvania, 2000.

Explores the behavioral theories that underlie the potential impact of performance-based incentives on school-based actors' behavior.

Massell, D. *State Strategies for Building Local Capacity: Addressing the Needs of Standards-based Reform.* Philadelphia: Consortium for Policy Research, University of Pennsylvania, 1998.

This report is a comprehensive policy analysis of state education departments' organizational and administrative responses to the issue of capacity-building at both state and local levels.

Massell, D., M. Kirst, and M. Hoppe. *Persistence and Change: Standards-based Systemic Reform in Nine States.* Philadelphia: Consortium for Policy Research, University of Pennsylvania, 1997.

The authors describe the origin of the standards-based reform movement during the early and mid-1990s. Also, they analyze the unfolding of the movement in nine states.

National Institute of Education. *Cutbacks, Consolidation, Deregulation: How They Affect Education Agencies in the Far West.* Washington, DC: National Institute of Education, 1982.

Provides examples of how state education agencies responded to the decline in federal and state funding during the 1980s.

Orfield, G. M., and J. Yun. *Resegregation in American Schools.* Cambridge, MA: The Civil Rights Project, Harvard University, 1999.

Orfield and Yun track the progress of desegregation and analyze the extent to which school districts have been able to successfully desegregate. They then conclude that after decades of desegregation policies, what has emerged is a resegregation of American schools.

Reschovsky, A., and J. Imazeki. *Achieving Educational Adequacy through School Finance Reform.* CPRE Research Report Series Rr-045. Philadelphia: Consortium for Policy Research in Education, University of Pennsylvania, 2000.

The authors advocate a statistical model using data on per-pupil expenditures, student performance, and various characteristics of school districts to estimate cost functions for adequacy.

Trimble, S. **"Performance Trends and Use of Accommodations on a Statewide Assessment: Students with Disabilities in the KIRIS On-Demand Assessments from 1992–1993 through 1995–1996."** *National Center on Educational Outcomes Report* 3 (1998).

Trimble identifies the growing achievement gap between disabled and nondisabled students in most grade levels.

Usdan, M. D. *The New State Politics of Education.* Alexandria, VA: National Association of State Boards of Education, 2002.

In this seven-decade study, coverage is provided on the changes in state governance structures.

Walker, B. *Equity in Texas Public School Finance: Some Historical Perspective.* Austin: Texas Center for Educational Research, 1988.

Presents a historical perspective on public school finance reform in Texas.

BOOKS AND JOURNALS

Block, S. **"Comparing the Adequacy of New Jersey and Kentucky Court Mandates, Statutes, and Regulations to Remedy Unconstitutional Public Education."** Doctoral dissertation, Seton Hall University, NJ, 2002.

This dissertation compares the adequacy of New Jersey and Kentucky mandates, statutes, and regulations to remedy unconstitutional (at the state level) public education.

Cohen, M. **"Key Issues Confronting State Policymakers."** Pp. 251–288 in Richard F. Elmore, *Restructuring Schools: The Next Generation of Educational Reform.* San Francisco: Jossey-Bass, 1990.

Cohen deals with state leadership roles and the second and third waves of the reform movement.

Dunphy, D. **"Moving Mountains in the Granite State: Reforming School Finance and Designing Adequacy in New Hampshire."** *Studies in Judicial Remedies and Public Engagement* 2, 4 (2001):1–38.

Dunphy examines political mobilization over school finance reform in New Hampshire.

Kaestle, C. *Pillars of the Republic : Common Schools and American Society.* New York: Hill and Wang, 1983.

Kaestle's text outlines the history of American public education.

Lusi, S. F. *The Role of State Departments of Education in Complex School Reform.* New York: Teachers College Press, 1997.

This book is a comparative study on the roles of Kentucky and Vermont state departments of education during the standards-based reform era.

Martineau, R. J. *Drafting Legislation and Rules in Plain English.* Eagen, MN: Weat Publishing Company, 1991.

Martineau provides readers with guidelines for drafting legislation and writing regulations.

Murphy, J. **"The Education Reform Movement of the 1980s: A Comprehensive Analysis."** Pp. 3–55 in J. Murphy (ed.), *The Educational Reform Movement of the 1980s.* Perspective and cases. Berkeley, CA: McCutchan, 1990.

This book chapter covers the first wave of the educational reform movement, with a description of the top-down legislative mandates that were part of that first wave.

Tyack, D. *The One Best System: A History of American Urban Education.* Cambridge, MA: Harvard University Press, 1974.

Tyack's book is the seminal work on the history and evolution of urban education.

Walker, E. M. **"The Impact of State Policies and Actions on Local Implementation Efforts: A Study of Whole School Reform in New Jersey."** *Education Policy* 18, 2 (2004):338–363.

This study delineates the role of the New Jersey State Department of Education in influencing the implementation efforts of local schools in the state of New Jersey in response to the *Abbott v. Burke* court decisions.

WEBSITES

Administrators Net
http://www.administrators.net/

This is a network that provides numerous resources to educational administrators. The partner network is Teachers Net (see entry). Focus chat rooms and discussion boards are available to school administrators worldwide.

Alliance for Excellent Education
http://www.all4ed.org/

The Alliance for Excellent Education is a national advocacy, policy, and research organization that focuses on assisting approximately six million at-risk, low performing secondary students.

American Association of School Administrators (AASA)
http://www.aasa.org/

Since 1865, AASA has evolved into the premier professional organization for over 14,000 chief educational leaders across North America and numerous other countries. It assists school leaders with the improvement of school systems.

American Federation of Teachers (AFT)
http://www.aft.org/

AFT was established in 1916 by a small group of teachers in Winnetka, Illinois. Since this beginning, AFT has emerged as the predominant teachers organization for improving standards, work conditions, and overall school system quality.

Association of School Business Officials International (ASBO)
http://www.asbointl.org

ASBO International has become the major international organization for school business officials. Membership includes school business executives from across the nation and internationally. Their mission is to continually ameliorate the enterprise components of school systems.

Center for Policy Alternatives (CPA)
http://www.stateaction.org

The CPA has been supporting state legislators since 1975. This nonpartisan organization fosters reform networks, encourages value-based training, and provides various policy assistance.

Center on Education Policy (CEP)
http://www.ctredpol.org/

CEP was established in 1995 as an autonomous advocacy organization for public education. Nearly all of its funding is received from numerous philanthropic organizations that support education policy analysis.

National Association of Elementary School Principals (NAESP)
http://www.naesp.org

The NAESP provides advocacy for elementary and middle-level principals and other education leaders to improve their school systems.

National Association of Secondary School Principals (NASSP)
http://www.nassp.org

The NASSP provides advocacy for middle-level and high school and other education leaders to improve their school systems.

National Center for Policy Analysis (NCPA)
http://www.ncpa.org/iss/edu/

Established in 1983, the NCPA is a nonpartisan and nonprofit policy analysis organization seeking private-sector alternatives over governmental approaches.

National Center on Education Finance (NCEF)
http://www.ncsl.org/programs/educ/NCEF.htm

NCEF is a division of the National Conference of State Legislation that focuses on school finance policy for all fifty states.

National Education Association (NEA)
http://www.nea.org

NEA is one of the major educational organizations concerned with improving America's education from prekindergarten through university levels. Membership is approaching three million and includes affiliates in all fifty states.

⚡ Glossary

District power equalizing (DPE): one way in which states attempt to create fiscal or wealth neutrality. States employ state-aid formulas that attempt to equalize spending by raising in some cases the level at which poorer districts are funded. California was one of the first states to implement district power equalizing.

Educational adequacy: defined in many different ways. Some authors define adequacy in terms of the availability of a properly financed educational system that produces high minimum outcomes for all students. Courts and claimants look to the language of state's educational clauses to determine what constitutionally represents an adequate education. Adequacy claims focus not only on the inputs into the educational system but on the outputs as well.

Education clauses: figured prominently in adequacy court cases. All states with the exception of Mississippi have a provision in their constitutions that protects education and imposes an affirmative duty upon the legislature for the development of a system of free public education.

Equal protection clause of the Fourteenth Amendment: guarantees each individual equal protection of the law.

Fiscal neutrality: implies that no differences should exist between the education that students receive and the property wealth that supports that education.

Horizontal equity: holds that children who are similarly situated should be treated equally.

Judicial activism proponents: see the proper role of the courts as redressing constitutional wrongs by devising remedies that can affect the common good.

Judicial restraintists: view the proper function of the courts as interpreting the law and applying that interpretation to the case under consideration. These scholars believe that courts should neither make social policies nor encroach upon the powers of the executive and legislative branches of government.

Legal mobilization: defines the framing of an issue or a claim in terms of a constitutional right.

Majoritarian accountability: a central premise of the democratic system on which the American system is founded. Legislators and elected officials as well as policies and decisions that are made by them are subject to the scrutiny of the body polity that elects them.

Opportunity-to-learn standards: the criteria for assessing whether the quality and sufficiency of resources and conditions that exist at every level of the educational system permit all students to learn.

Policy instruments: the tools used by policy makers to promote policy goals. State education departments rely upon a variety of tools, for example, regulations, incentives, technical support, administrative reform, and financial support.

Political mobilization: represents those extra judicial activities that occur around an issue or claim.

Political question doctrine: holds that some issues are political in nature and their resolution lies with the political branches and not the judicial. This doctrine is closely linked with the notion of separation of power.

Separation of power doctrine: based on the principle of separate spheres of responsibility and unique power among the three branches of government: the executive, the legislative, and the judiciary.

Systemic reform movement: occurred during the 1990s and represented the adoption of a comprehensive approach by states to coherently restructure all aspects and levels of their educational systems.

Vertical equity: specifies that given the existence of differences among students, resources should be allocated differently to compensate for inequities in educational opportunities and outcomes that are associated with these differences.

•❖ Index

❧ About the Author

Elaine M. Walker, Ph.D., is an associate professor in the Department of Education Leadership, Management, and Policy at Seton Hall University, South Orange, New Jersey. She has researched and published several articles on reforms in New Jersey. These articles have appeared in *Education Policy Analysis Archives, Journal of Educational Policy, Journal of Children and Poverty,* and *Journal of Negro Education.*